MOLIÈRE: FOUR COMEDIES

ALSO BY RICHARD WILBUR

JEAN BAPTISTE POQUELIN DE MOLIÈRE

*Four
Comedies*

TRANSLATED INTO ENGLISH VERSE BY
RICHARD WILBUR

NEW YORK AND LONDON
HARCOURT BRACE JOVANOVICH, PUBLISHERS

CONTENTS

The School for Wives

COMEDY IN FIVE ACTS, 1662

Drawings by Enrico Arno

To the memory of
Louis Jouvet
1887–1951

INTRODUCTION

As Dorante says in the *Critique de l'École des femmes*, a comic monster need not lack all attractive qualities. Arnolphe, the hero of Molière's first great verse comedy, is a forty-two-year-old provincial bourgeois whom it is possible to like, up to a point, for his coarse heartiness and his generosity with money. He is, however, a madman, and his alienation is of a harmful and unlovable kind. What ails him is a deep general insecurity, which has somehow been focused into a specific terror of being cuckolded. In fear of that humiliation, he has put off marriage until what, for the seventeenth century, was a very ripe age; meanwhile, he has buttressed his frail vanity by gloating over such of his neighbors as have been deceived by their wives. He has, furthermore, become the guardian of a four-year-old child, Agnès, with a view to shaping her into his idea of a perfect bride, and for thirteen years has had her trained to be docile and ignorant. It is his theory, based upon much anxious observation, that a stupid wife will not shame her husband by infidelity. As the play begins, Arnolphe is about to marry Agnès and achieve a double satisfaction: he will quiet his long trepidation by marrying safely, and he will have the prideful pleasure of showing the world how to rig an infallible alliance. It goes without saying that poor, stultified Agnès is not his object but his victim.

Arnolphe, then, is one of Molière's coercers of life. Like Tartuffe, he proposes to manipulate the world for his own ends, and the play is one long joke about the futility of selfish calculation. Agnès is guileless; her young man, Horace, is a rash bumbler who informs his rival of all that he does and means to do; yet despite Arnolphe's mature canniness, and his twenty years' pondering and plotting, he loses out to a *jeune innocente* and a *jeune écervelé*. Why? There is much high talk in the play, especially from Arnolphe, of cruel

3

destiny, fate, and the stars, and this contributes, as J. D. Hubert has noted, to an effect of "burlesque tragedy"; it is not implacable fate, however, but ridiculous chance which repeatedly spoils Arnolphe's designs. And indeed, the plans of other characters, even when benign, meet constantly with the fortuitous: if Horace achieves his goal, it is certainly not because his blundering intrigues have mastered circumstance; and though Oronte and Enrique accomplish the premeditated union of their children, *le hasard* has already brought the pair together. The play seems to assert that any effort to impose expectations on life will meet with surprises, and that a narrow, rigid, and inhumane demand will not be honored by Nature.

The plot of *L'École des femmes* has often been criticized for its unlikelihood. Doubtless Molière was careless of the fact, since, as W. G. Moore has written, "The plot is not the main thing at all. . . . The high points of the play are not the turning points of the action; they are moments when the clash of youth and age, of spontaneity and automatism, takes shape in speech and scene." And yet it may not be too much to say that the absurdity of the plot is expressive, that it presents us with the world as Arnolphe is bound to experience it. To an obsessed man, the world will be full of exasperating irrelevancies: in this case, a dead kitten, a ribbon, the inopportune chatter of a notary. Similarly, a man who has for years left nothing to chance in the prosecution of a maniacal plan, and who encounters difficulties on the very eve of success, will experience the world as a chaos of disruptive accidents, a storm of casualty: in this case, an old friend's son will by chance gain the affections of Arnolphe's intended; in repeated chance meetings he will subject Arnolphe, whose new title he chances not to know, to tormenting confidences; Oronte and Enrique will chance to arrive in town on what was to have been Arnolphe's wedding day, and will reveal the true identity of the young woman whom Arnolphe once chanced to adopt. It is all too much, for Arnolphe and for us, and in

[*Introduction*]

the last-minute breathless summary of Enrique's story, delivered by Chrysalde and Oronte in alternating couplets, Molière both burlesques a species of comic dénouement and acknowledges the outrageousness of his own. At the same time, for this reader, the gay arbitrariness of the close celebrates a truth which is central to the comic vision—that life will not be controlled, but makes a fluent resistance to all crabbèd constraint. The most triumphant demonstration of life's (or Nature's) irrepressibility occurs within Arnolphe himself, when, after so many years of coldly exploiting Agnès for his pride's sake, he becomes vulnerably human by falling in love with her.

Spontaneity versus automatism, life's happy refusal to conform to cranky plans and theories: such terms describe the play for me. Some, however, may wish to be less general, and to discern here a thesis play about, say, education. This comedy is, indeed, permeated with the themes of instruction and learning. Arnolphe has Agnès minimally educated, so that she will have no attractive accomplishments; the nuns teach her to pray, spin, and sew (and somehow, though it is against her guardian's orders, she also learns to read). In Act III, Arnolphe himself becomes her teacher, or, rather, her priest, and with repeated threats of hell-fire informs her that the function of a wife is to live wholly for her husband, in absolute subjection. *The Maxims of Marriage*, which Agnès is then given to study, are likened by Arnolphe to the rules which a novice must learn on entering a convent; and very like they are, counseling as they do a cloistered and sacrificial life devoted to the worship of one's husband. Arnolphe's whole teaching is that the purpose of marriage is to preserve the husband's honor, which is like saying that the purpose of dancing is not to break a leg; and his whole education of Agnès is intended to incapacitate her for adultery by rendering her spiritless and uninteresting. There are moments, I think, when other characters burlesque Arnolphe as educator: the manservant Alain, informing Georgette in Act II, Scene 2

5

that "womankind is . . . the soup of man," caricatures his master's attitude toward women, as well as his patronizing pedagogical style; and the notary, torrentially instructing Arnolphe in contract law, resembles in his pedantic formulae the Arnolphe of the smug thesis, the airtight plan, and the *Maxims*. Much else in the play might be seen as extending the motif of instruction: Arnolphe rehearsing or drilling his servants; Chrysalde lecturing Arnolphe on the temperate view of cuckoldry; Arnolphe schooling himself in the causes of marital disaster, being guided by a Greek who counseled Augustus, or advising Oronte on the use of paternal power. But what is more surely pertinent, and stands in opposition to Arnolphe's kind of schooling, is the transformation of Horace and Agnès by that *grand maître*, Love. When we first meet him, Horace is a pretty-boy very full of himself and quite capable of seducing Agnès, but by the fifth act he has come to esteem and cherish her, and had "rather die than do her any wrong." Agnès, awakened by love to her own childish ignorance and dependence, proceeds like Juliet to develop gumption and resourcefulness, and discovers a wit which is the more devastating because of her continuing simplicity.

The play is full of "education"; granted. But it cannot convincingly be interpreted as a thesis play *about* education. What can Molière be said to advocate? Latin for women? The inclusion of love in the curriculum? Clearly Molière had a low opinion of Agnès' convent schooling, which was rather standard for the age; what really interests him, however, is not the deficiencies of such schooling but Arnolphe's ill-intended use of them. Similarly, Molière is concerned not with religion but with Arnolphe's selfish and Orgon-like abuse of it, his turning it into a bludgeon. Nor does he comment on parental authority in itself, but, rather, on Arnolphe's attempt to exploit it for his own ends. It will not do, in short, for the contemporary reader or director to inject this play with Student Unrest or Women's Liberation,

[*Introduction*]

or to descry in it a Generation Gap. That way lies melodrama.

Any director of this English version will have to solve for himself certain problems of interpretation and staging, but I shall say what I think. It is my own decided opinion that Chrysalde is *not* a cuckold, and that Arnolphe's second speech in Act I, Scene 1 is a bit of crude and objectionable ribbing. Chrysalde's discourses about cuckoldry should be regarded, I think, both as frequently dubious "reasoning" and as bear-baiting; a good actor would know where to modulate between them. Arnolphe's distaste for fuss and sophistication is likely to impress some as an endearing quality, but I do not see it so; rather, it is of a piece with the man's anxiety to prove himself superior to a society whose ridicule he fears, and like the "honesty" of the *Misanthrope*'s Alceste, it entails posturing and bad faith. Finally, there is the fact that much of the slapstick in the plot—the throwing of the brick, Horace's tumble from the ladder—occurs off stage, and that the on-stage proceedings consist in fair part of long speeches. I should be sorry to see any director right this apparent imbalance by introducing too much pie-throwing and bottom-pinching of his own invention. Once again, Dorante gives Molière's point of view: the long speeches, he says,"are themselves actions," involving incessant ironic *interplay* between speakers and hearers. To take the most obvious example, Horace's addresses to Arnolphe are rendered wonderfully "busy" by the fact that he does not know he is addressing M. de la Souche, that Arnolphe cannot enlighten him, and that Arnolphe must continually struggle to conceal his glee or anguish. To add any great amount of farcical "business" to such complex comedy would be to divert in an unfortunate sense.

This translation has aimed at a thought-for-thought fidelity, and has sought in its verse to avoid the metronomic, which is particularly fatal on the stage: I have sometimes been very limber indeed, as in the line "He's the most hideous Christian I ever did see." For a few words or phrases I am indebted to earlier English versions in blank verse or prose. I must also thank Jan Miel for helping me to improve these remarks; Robert Hollander, Stephen Porter, and William Jay Smith for reading and criticizing the translation; and John Berryman for encouraging me to undertake it.

CHARACTERS

ARNOLPHE, also known as MONSIEUR DE
    LA SOUCHE

AGNÈS, an innocent young girl, Arnolphe's
    ward

HORACE, Agnès' lover, Oronte's son

ALAIN, a peasant, Arnolphe's manservant

GEORGETTE, a peasant woman, servant to
    Arnolphe

CHRYSALDE, a friend of Arnolphe's

ENRIQUE, Chrysalde's brother-in-law,
    Agnès' father

ORONTE, Horace's father and Arnolphe's
    old friend

A NOTARY

The scene is a square in a provincial city.

First produced by the Phoenix Theatre,
New York, on February 16, 1971

SCENE ONE

CHRYSALDE, ARNOLPHE

CHRYSALDE

So, you're resolved to give this girl your hand?

ARNOLPHE

Tomorrow I shall marry her, as planned.

CHRYSALDE

We're quite alone here, and we can discuss
Your case with no one overhearing us:
Shall I speak openly, and as your friend?
This plan—for your sake—troubles me no end.
I must say that, from every point of view,
Taking a wife is a rash step for you.

ARNOLPHE

You think so? Might it be, friend, that you base
Your fears for me upon your own sad case?
Cuckolds would have us think that all who marry
Acquire a set of horns as corollary.

[*Act One · Scene One*]

CHRYSALDE

Fate gives men horns, and fate can't be withstood;
To fret about such matters does no good.
What makes me fear for you is the way you sneer
At every luckless husband of whom you hear.
You know that no poor cuckold, great or small,
Escapes your wit; you mock them one and all,
And take delight in making boisterous mention
Of all intrigues which come to your attention.

ARNOLPHE

Why not? What other town on earth is known
For. husbands so long-suffering as our own?
Can we not all too readily bring to mind
Ill-treated dupes of every shape and kind?
One husband's rich; his helpmeet shares the wealth
With paramours who cuckold him by stealth;
Another, with a scarcely kinder fate,
Sees other men heap gifts upon his mate—
Who frees his mind of jealous insecurity
By saying that they're tributes to her purity.
One cuckold impotently storms and rants;
Another mildly bows to circumstance,
And when some gallant calls to see his spouse,
Discreetly takes his hat and leaves the house.
One wife, confiding in her husband, mentions
A swain who bores her with his warm attentions;
The husband smugly pities the poor swain
For all his efforts—which are *not* in vain.
Another wife explains her wealthy state
By saying that she's held good cards of late;
Her husband thanks the Lord and gives Him praise,

14

Not guessing what bad game she truly plays.
Thus, all about us, there are themes for wit;
May I not, as an observer, jest a bit?
May I not laugh at—

CHRYSALDE

Yes; but remember, do,
That those you mock may someday mock at you.
Now, I hear gossip, I hear what people say
About the latest scandals of the day,
But whatsoever I'm told, I never hear it
With wicked glee and in a gloating spirit.
I keep my counsel; and though I may condemn
Loose wives, and husbands who put up with them,
And though I don't propose, you may be sure,
To endure the wrongs which some weak men endure,
Still, I am never heard to carp and crow,
For tables have been known to turn, you know,
And there's no man who can predict, in fact,
How in such circumstances he would act.
In consequence, should fate bestow on me
What all must fear, the horns of cuckoldry,
The world would treat me gently, I believe,
And be content with laughing up its sleeve.
There are, in fact, some kindly souls who might
Commiserate me in my sorry plight.
But you, dear fellow, with you it's not the same.
I say once more, you play a dangerous game.
Since with your jeering tongue you plague the lives
Of men who are unlucky in their wives,
And persecute them like a fiend from Hell,
Take care lest someday you be jeered as well.
If the least whisper about your wife were heard,

They'd mock you from the housetops, mark my word.
What's more—

ARNOLPHE

       Don't worry, friend; I'm not a fool.
I shan't expose myself to ridicule.
I know the tricks and ruses, shrewd and sly,
Which wives employ, and cheat their husbands by;
I know that women can be deep and clever;
But I've arranged to be secure forever:
So simple is the girl I'm going to wed
That I've no fear of horns upon my head.

CHRYSALDE

Simple! You mean to bind yourself for life—

ARNOLPHE

A man's not simple to take a simple wife.
Your wife, no doubt, is a wise, virtuous woman,
But brightness, as a rule, is a bad omen,
And I know men who've undergone much pain
Because they married girls with too much brain.
I want no intellectual, if you please,
Who'll talk of nothing but her Tuesday teas,
Who'll frame lush sentiments in prose and verse
And fill the house with wits, and fops, and worse,
While I, as her dull husband, stand about
Like a poor saint whose candles have gone out.
No, keep your smart ones; I've no taste for such.
Women who versify know far too much.
I want a wife whose thought is not sublime,

[*Act One · Scene One*]

Who has no notion what it is to rhyme,
And who, indeed, if she were asked in some
Insipid parlor game, "What rhymes with drum?"
Would answer in all innocence, "A fife."
In short, I want an unaccomplished wife,
And there are four things only she must know:
To say her prayers, love me, spin, and sew.

CHRYSALDE

Stupidity's your cup of tea, I gather.

ARNOLPHE

I'd choose an ugly, stupid woman rather
Than a great beauty who was over-wise.

CHRYSALDE

But wit and beauty—

ARNOLPHE

Virtue is what I prize.

CHRYSALDE

But how can you expect an idiot
To know what's virtuous and what is not?
Not only would it be a lifelong bore
To have a senseless wife, but what is more,
I hardly think you could depend upon her
To guard her husband's forehead from dishonor.
If a bright woman breaks her wedding vow,

She knows what she is doing, anyhow;
A simpleton, however, can commit
Adultery without suspecting it.

ARNOLPHE

To that fine argument I can but say
What Pantagruel says in Rabelais:
Preach and harangue from now till Whitsuntide
Against my preference for a stupid bride;
You'll be amazed to find, when you have ceased,
That I've not been persuaded in the least.

CHRYSALDE

So be it.

ARNOLPHE

       Each man has his own design
For wedded bliss, and I shall follow mine.
I'm rich, and so can take a wife who'll be
Dependent, in the least respect, on me—
A sweet, submissive girl who cannot claim
To have brought me riches or an ancient name.
The gentle, meek expression which she wore
Endeared Agnès to me when she was four;
Her mother being poor, I felt an urge
To make the little thing my ward and charge,
And the good peasant woman was most pleased
To grant my wish, and have her burden eased.
In a small convent, far from the haunts of man,
The girl was reared according to my plan:
I told the nuns what means must be employed
To keep her growing mind a perfect void,

[*Act One · Scene One*]

And, God be praised, they had entire success.
As a grown girl, her simple-mindedness
Is such that I thank Heaven for granting me
A bride who suits my wishes to a T.
She's out of the convent now, and since my gate
Stands open to society, early and late,
I keep her here, in another house I own,
Where no one calls, and she can be alone:
And, to protect her artless purity,
I've hired two servants as naïve as she.
I've told you all this so that you'll understand
With what great care my marriage has been planned;
And now, to clinch my story, I invite
You, my dear friend, to dine with her tonight;
I want you to examine her, and decide
Whether or not my choice is justified.

CHRYSALDE

Delighted.

ARNOLPHE

   You'll gain, I think, a lively sense
Of her sweet person and her innocence.

CHRYSALDE

As to her innocence, what you've related
Leaves little doubt—

ARNOLPHE

     My friend, 't was understated.
Her utter naïveté keeps me in stitches.

[*Act One* · *Scene One*]

I laugh so that I almost burst my breeches.
You won't believe this, but the other day
She came and asked me in a puzzled way,
And with a manner touchingly sincere,
If children are begotten through the ear.

CHRYSALDE

I'm happy indeed, Monsieur Arnolphe—

ARNOLPHE

                              For shame!
Why must you always use my former name?

CHRYSALDE

I'm used to it, I suppose. What's more, I find
That *de la Souche* forever slips my mind.
What in the devil has persuaded you
To debaptize yourself at forty-two
And take a lordly title which you base
On an old tree stump at your country place?

ARNOLPHE

The name La Souche goes with the property
And sounds much better than Arnolphe to me.

CHRYSALDE

But why forsake the name your fathers bore
For one that's fantasy and nothing more?
Yet lately that's become the thing to do.

[*Act One · Scene One*]

I am reminded—no offense to you—
Of a peasant named Gros-Pierre, who owned a small
Parcel of land, an acre or so in all;
He dug a muddy ditch around the same
And took Monsieur de l'Isle for his new name.

ARNOLPHE

I can dispense with stories of that kind.
My name is de la Souche, if you don't mind.
I like that title, and it's mine by right;
To address me otherwise is impolite.

CHRYSALDE

Your new name is employed by few, at best;
Much of your mail, I've noticed, comes addressed—

ARNOLPHE

I don't mind that, from such as haven't been told;
But you—

CHRYSALDE

Enough. Enough. No need to scold.
I hereby promise that, at our next meeting,
"Good day, Monsieur de la Souche" shall be my greeting.

ARNOLPHE

Farewell. I'm going to knock now on my door
And let them know that I'm in town once more.

[*Act One* · *Scene One*]

CHRYSALDE, *aside, as he moves off*

The man's quite mad. A lunatic, in fact.

ARNOLPHE, *alone*

On certain subjects he's a trifle cracked.
It's curious to see with what devotion
A man will cling to some quite pointless notion.
Ho, there!

SCENE TWO

ALAIN, GEORGETTE, ARNOLPHE

ALAIN, *within*

Who's knocking?

ARNOLPHE

Ho! (*Aside:*) They'll greet me, after
My ten days' trip, with smiles and happy laughter.

ALAIN

Who's there?

ARNOLPHE

It's I.

ALAIN

Georgette!

GEORGETTE

What?

[*Act One · Scene Two*]

ALAIN

Open below!

GEORGETTE

Do it yourself!

ALAIN

You do it!

GEORGETTE

I won't go!

ALAIN

I won't go either!

ARNOLPHE

Gracious servants, these,
To leave me standing here. Ho! If you please!

GEORGETTE

Who's there?

ARNOLPHE

Your master.

[*Act One · Scene Two*]

GEORGETTE

Alain!

ALAIN

What?

GEORGETTE

Go lift the latch!

It's him.

ALAIN

You do it.

GEORGETTE

I'm getting the fire to catch.

ALAIN

I'm keeping the cat from eating the canary.

ARNOLPHE

Whoever doesn't admit me, and in a hurry,
Will get no food for four long days, and more.
Aha!

GEORGETTE

I'll get it; what are you coming for?

[*Act One · Scene Two*]

ALAIN

Why you, not me? That's a sneaky trick to play!

GEORGETTE

Get out of the way.

ALAIN

No, *you* get out of the way.

GEORGETTE

I want to open that door.

ALAIN

I want to, too.

GEORGETTE

You won't.

ALAIN

And you won't either.

GEORGETTE

Neither will you.

ARNOLPHE, *to himself*

My patience with these two amazes me.

26

[*Act One · Scene Two*]

ALAIN

I've opened the door, Sir.

GEORGETTE

No, I did it! See?
'T was I.

ALAIN

If only the master, here, weren't present,
I'd—

ARNOLPHE, *receiving a blow from Alain,*
meant for Georgette

Blast you!

ALAIN

Sorry, Sir.

ARNOLPHE

You clumsy peasant!

ALAIN

It's her fault too, Sir.

ARNOLPHE

Both of you, stop this row.
I want to question you; no nonsense, now.
Alain, is everything going smoothly here?

[*Act One · Scene Two*]

ALAIN

Well, Sir, we're—
> (*Arnolphe removes Alain's hat; Alain*
> *obliviously puts it back on.*)
> > Well, Sir—
> > > (*Hat business again.*)
> > > > Well, thank God, Sir, we're—
> > > > (*Arnolphe removes Alain's hat a third time,*
> > > > *and throws it to the ground.*)

ARNOLPHE

Where did you learn, you lout, to wear a hat
While talking to your master? Answer me that.

ALAIN

You're right, I'm wrong.

ARNOLPHE

> > > Now, have Agnès come down.
> (*To Georgette:*)
Was she unhappy while I was out of town?

GEORGETTE

Unhappy? No.

ARNOLPHE

> No?

[*Act One · Scene Two*]

Yes.

ARNOLPHE

For what reason, then?

GEORGETTE

Well, she kept thinking you'd be back again,
So that whatever passed on the avenue—
Horse, mule, or ass—she thought it must be you.

SCENE THREE

AGNÈS, ALAIN, GEORGETTE, ARNOLPHE

ARNOLPHE

Her needlework in hand! That's a good sign.
Well, well, Agnès, I'm back and feeling fine.
Are you glad to see me?

AGNÈS

Oh, yes, Sir; thank the Lord.

ARNOLPHE

I'm glad to see you too, my little ward.
I take it everything has been all right?

AGNÈS

Except for the fleas, which bothered me last night.

ARNOLPHE

Well, there'll be someone soon to drive them away.

AGNÈS

I shall be glad of that.

[*Act One · Scene Three*]

Yes, I dare say.
What are you making?

AGNÈS

A headpiece, Sir, for me;
Your nightshirts are all finished, as you'll see.

ARNOLPHE

Excellent. Well, upstairs with you, my dear:
I'll soon come back and see you, never fear;
There's serious talk in which we must engage.
    (*Exeunt all but Arnolphe.*)
O learned ladies, heroines of the age,
Gushers of sentiment, I say that you,
For all your verse, and prose, and billets-doux,
Your novels, and your bright accomplishments,
Can't match this good and modest ignorance.

SCENE FOUR

HORACE, ARNOLPHE

ARNOLPHE

What does her lack of money matter to me?
What matters— Oh! What's this? No! Can it be?
I'm dreaming. Yes, it's he, my dear friend's boy.
Well!

HORACE

Sir!

ARNOLPHE

Horace!

HORACE

Arnolphe!

ARNOLPHE

Ah, what a joy!
How long have you been in town?

[*Act One · Scene Four*]

HORACE

Nine days.

ARNOLPHE

Ah, so.

HORACE

I called at your house, in vain, a week ago.

ARNOLPHE

I'd left for the country.

HORACE

Yes, you were three days gone.

ARNOLPHE

How quickly children grow! How time rolls on!
I am amazed that you're so big and tall.
I can remember when you were—
                    (*He makes a gesture of measuring from the floor.*)
                                        that small.

HORACE

Yes, time goes by.

ARNOLPHE

                    But come now, tell me of
Oronte, your father, whom I esteem and love:

33

How's my old friend? Still spry and full of zest?
In all that's his, I take an interest.
Alas, it's four years since I talked with him,
And we've not written in the interim.

HORACE

Seigneur Arnolphe, he's spry enough for two;
He gave me this little note to give to you,
But now he writes me that he's coming here
Himself, for reasons not entirely clear.
Some fellow-townsman of yours, whom you may know,
Went to America fourteen years ago;
He's come back rich. Do you know of whom I speak?

ARNOLPHE

No. Did the letter give his name?

HORACE

Enrique.

ARNOLPHE

No . . . no . . .

HORACE

My father writes as if I ought
To recognize that name, but I do not.
He adds that he and Enrique will soon set out
On some great errand that he's vague about.

34

[*Act One · Scene Four*]

ARNOLPHE

I long to see your father, that sterling man.
I'll welcome him as royally as I can.
      (*He reads the note from Oronte.*)
A friendly letter needn't flatter and fuss.
All this politeness is superfluous,
And even without his asking, I'd have desired
To lend you any money you required.

HORACE

I'll take you at your word, Sir. Can you advance
Fifty *pistoles* or so, by any chance?

ARNOLPHE

I'm grateful that you let me be of use,
And what you ask, I happily can produce.
Just keep the purse.

HORACE

Here—

ARNOLPHE

                    Forget the I.O.U.
Now, how does our town impress you? Tell me, do.

HORACE

It's rich in people, sublime in architecture,
And full of fine amusements, I conjecture.

[*Act One · Scene Four*]

ARNOLPHE

There's pleasure here for every taste; and those
The world calls gallants, ladies' men, or beaux
Find here the sport on which their hearts are set,
Since every woman in town's a born coquette.
Our ladies, dark or fair, are pliant creatures;
Their husbands, likewise, have permissive natures;
Oh, it's a capital game; it's often made
Me double up with mirth to see it played.
But you've already broken some hearts, I'd guess;
Have you no gallant conquest to confess?
Cuckolds are made by such as you, young man,
And looks like yours buy more than money can.

HORACE

Well, since you ask, I'll lay my secrets bare.
I *have* been having a covert love affair—
Which, out of friendship, I shall now unveil.

ARNOLPHE

Good, good; 't will be another rakish tale
Which I can put into my repertory.

HORACE

Sir, I must beg you: don't divulge my story.

ARNOLPHE

Of course not.

[*Act One · Scene Four*]

HORACE

As you know, Sir, in these matters,
One word let slip can leave one's hopes in tatters.
To put the business plainly, then, my heart's
Been lost to a lady dwelling in these parts.
My overtures, I'm very pleased to state,
Have found her ready to reciprocate,
And not to boast, or slur her reputation,
I think I'm in a hopeful situation.

ARNOLPHE, *laughing*

Who is she?

HORACE

A girl whose beauty is past telling,
And yonder red-walled mansion is her dwelling.
She's utterly naïve, because a blind
Fool has sequestered her from humankind,
And yet, despite the ignorance in which
He keeps her, she has charms that can bewitch;
She's most engaging, and conveys a sense
Of sweetness against which there's no defense.
But you, perhaps, have seen this star of love
Whose many graces I'm enamoured of.
Her name's Agnès.

ARNOLPHE, *aside*

Oh, death!

[*Act One · Scene Four*]

HORACE

                The man, I hear,
Is called La Zousse, La Source, or something queer;
I didn't pay much attention to the name.
He's rich, I gather, but his wits are lame,
And he's accounted a ridiculous fellow.
D'you know him?

ARNOLPHE, *aside*

Ugh, what a bitter pill to swallow!

HORACE

I said, do you know him?

ARNOLPHE

                Yes, I do, in a way.

HORACE

He's a dolt, isn't he?

ARNOLPHE

        Oh!

HORACE

                What? What did you say?
He is, I take it. And a jealous idiot, too?
An ass? I see that all they said was true.

38

[*Act One* · *Scene Four*]

Well, to repeat, I love Agnès, a girl
Who is, to say the least, an orient pearl,
And it would be a sin for such a treasure
To be subjected to that old fool's pleasure.
Henceforth, my thoughts and efforts shall combine
To break his jealous hold and make her mine;
This purse, which I made bold to borrow, will lend
Me great assistance toward that worthy end.
As you well know, whatever means one tries,
Money's the key to every enterprise,
And this sweet metal, which all men hanker for,
Promotes our conquests, whether in love or war.
You look disturbed, Sir; can it be that you
Do not approve of what I mean to do?

ARNOLPHE

No; I was thinking—

HORACE

                I'm boring you. Farewell, then.
I'll soon drop by, to express my thanks again.

ARNOLPHE, *to himself*

How could this happen—

HORACE, *returning*

              Again, Sir, I entreat
You not to tell my secret; be discreet.
     (*He leaves.*)

39

[*Act One · Scene Four*]

ARNOLPHE, *to himself*

I'm thunderstruck.

HORACE, *returning*

Above all, don't inform
My father; he might raise a dreadful storm.
  (*He leaves.*)

ARNOLPHE (*He expects Horace to return again;
that not occurring, he talks to himself.*)

Oh! . . . What I've suffered during this conversation!
No soul has ever endured such agitation.
With what imprudence, and how hastily
He came and told the whole affair . . . to me!
He didn't know I'd taken a new title;
Still, what a rash and blundering recital!
I should, however, have kept myself in hand,
So as to learn what strategy he's planned,
And prompt his indiscretion, and discover
To what extent he has become her lover.
Come, I'll catch up with him; he can't be far;
I'll learn from him precisely how things are.
Alas, I'm trembling; I fear some further blow;
One can discover more than one wants to know.

SCENE ONE

ARNOLPHE

ARNOLPHE

It's just as well, no doubt, that I should fail
To catch him—that I somehow lost his trail:
For I could not have managed to dissemble
The turbulence of soul which makes me tremble;
He'd have perceived my present near-despair,
Of which it's best that he be unaware.
But I'm not one to be resigned and meek
And turn this little fop the other cheek.
I'll stop him; and the first thing I must do
Is find out just how far they've gone, those two.
This matter involves my honor, which I prize;
The girl's my wife already, in my eyes;
If she's been tarnished, I am covered with shame,
And all she's done reflects on my good name.
Oh, why did I take that trip? Oh, dear, oh, dear.
    (*He knocks at his door.*)

SCENE TWO

ALAIN, GEORGETTE, ARNOLPHE

ALAIN

Ah! *This* time, Sir—

ARNOLPHE

      Hush! Both of you come here:
This way, this way. Come, hurry! Do as you're told!

GEORGETTE

You frighten me; you make my blood run cold.

ARNOLPHE

So! In my absence, you have disobeyed me!
The two of you, in concert, have betrayed me!

GEORGETTE, *falling on her knees*

Don't eat me, Sir; don't eat me alive, I beg.

ALAIN, *aside*

I'd swear some mad dog's nipped him in the leg.

44

[*Act Two · Scene Two*]

ARNOLPHE, *aside*

Oof! I'm too tense to speak. I'd like to shed
These blasted clothes. I'm burning up with dread.
        (*To Alain and Georgette:*)
You cursèd scoundrels, while I was gone you let
A man into this house—
       (*To Alain, who has made a move to flee:*)
                   No, not just yet!
Tell me at once— (*To Georgette:*) Don't move! I want
   you two
To tell me— Whff! I mean to learn from you—
       (*Alain and Georgette rise and try to escape.*)
If anyone moves, I'll squash him like a louse.
Now tell me, how did that man get into my house?
Well, speak! Come, hurry. Quickly! Time is fleeting!
Let's hear it! Speak!

ALAIN *and* GEORGETTE, *falling on their knees*

Oh! Oh!

GEORGETTE

My heart's stopped beating.

ALAIN

I'm dying.

ARNOLPHE, *aside*

I'm sweating, and I need some air.
I must calm down: I'll walk around the square.

When I saw him in his cradle, I didn't know
What he'd grow up and do to me. O woe!
Perhaps—yes, I'd do better to receive
The truth from her own lips, I now believe.
I'll mute my rage as well as I know how;
Patience, my wounded heart! Beat softly, now!
     (*To Alain and Georgette:*)
Get up, and go inside, and call Agnès.
Wait. (*Aside:*) That way her surprise would be the less.
They'd warn her of my anger, I don't doubt.
I'd best go in myself and bring her out.
     (*To Alain and Georgette:*)
Wait here.

SCENE THREE

ALAIN, GEORGETTE

GEORGETTE

God help us, but his rage is terrible!
The way he glared at me—it was unbearable.
He's the most hideous Christian I ever did see.

ALAIN

He's vexed about that man, as I said he'd be.

GEORGETTE

But why does he order us, with barks and roars,
Never to let the mistress go outdoors?
Why does he want us to conceal her here
From all the world, and let no man come near?

ALAIN

It's jealousy that makes him treat her so.

GEORGETTE

But how did he get like that, I'd like to know?

47

[*Act Two · Scene Three*]

ALAIN

It comes of being jealous, I assume.

GEORGETTE

But why is he jealous? Why must he rage and fume?

ALAIN

Well, jealousy—listen carefully, Georgette—
Is a thing—a thing—which makes a man upset,
And makes him close his doors to everyone.
I'm going to give you a comparison,
So that you'll clearly understand the word.
Suppose you were eating soup, and it occurred
That someone tried to take what you were eating:
Wouldn't you feel like giving him a beating?

GEORGETTE

Yes, I see that.

ALAIN

          Then grasp this, if you can.
Womankind is, in fact, the soup of man,
And when a man perceives that others wish
To dip their dirty fingers into his dish,
His temper flares, and bursts into a flame.

GEORGETTE

Yes. But not everybody feels the same.
Some husbands seem to be delighted when
Their wives consort with fancy gentlemen.

48

[*Act Two · Scene Three*]

ALAIN

Not every husband is the greedy kind
That wants to have it all.

GEORGETTE

If I'm not blind,
He's coming back.

ALAIN

It's he; your eyes are keen.

GEORGETTE

He's scowling.

ALAIN

That's because he's feeling mean.

SCENE FOUR

ARNOLPHE, *aside*

A certain Greek presumed once to advise
The great Augustus, and his words were wise:
When you are vexed, he said, do not forget,
Before you act, to say the alphabet,
So as to cool your temper, and prevent
Rash moves which later on you might repent.
In dealing with Agnès, I have applied
That counsel, and I've bidden her come outside,
Under the pretext of a morning stroll,
So that I can relieve my jangled soul
By seeking dulcetly to draw her out
And learn the truth, and put an end to doubt.
(*Calling:*) Come out, Agnès. (*To Alain and Georgette:*)
  Go in.

SCENE FIVE

ARNOLPHE

The weather's mild.

AGNÈS

Oh, yes.

ARNOLPHE

Most pleasant.

AGNÈS

Indeed!

ARNOLPHE

What news, my child?

AGNÈS

The kitten died.

[*Act Two* · *Scene Five*]

ARNOLPHE

Too bad, but what of that?
All men are mortal, my dear, and so's a cat.
While I was gone, no doubt it rained and poured?

AGNÈS

No.

ARNOLPHE

You were bored, perhaps?

AGNÈS

I'm never bored.

ARNOLPHE

During my ten days' absence, what did you do?

AGNÈS

Six nightshirts, I believe; six nightcaps, too.

ARNOLPHE, *after a pause*

My dear Agnès, this world's a curious thing.
What wicked talk one hears, what gossiping!
While I was gone, or so the neighbors claim,
There was a certain strange young man who came
To call upon you here, and was received.
But such a slander's not to be believed,
And I would wager that their so-called news—

[*Act Two · Scene Five*]

AGNÈS

Heavens! Don't wager; you'd be sure to lose.

ARNOLPHE

What! Is it true, then, that a man—

AGNÈS

                              Oh, yes.
In fact, he all but lived at this address.

ARNOLPHE, *aside*

That frank reply would seem to demonstrate
That she's still free of guile, at any rate.
    (*Aloud:*)
But I gave orders, Agnès, as I recall,
That you were to see no one, no one at all.

AGNÈS

I disobeyed you, but when I tell you why,
You'll say that you'd have done the same as I.

ARNOLPHE

Perhaps; well, tell me how this thing occurred.

AGNÈS

It's the most amazing story you ever heard.
I was sewing, out on the balcony, in the breeze,

When I noticed someone strolling under the trees.
It was a fine young man, who caught my eye
And made me a deep bow as he went by.
I, not to be convicted of a lack
Of manners, very quickly nodded back.
At once, the young man bowed to me again.
I bowed to him a second time, and then
It wasn't very long until he made
A third deep bow, which I of course repaid.
He left, but kept returning, and as he passed,
He'd bow, each time, more gracefully than the last,
While I, observing as he came and went,
Gave each new bow a fresh acknowledgment.
Indeed, had night not fallen, I declare
I think that I might still be sitting there,
And bowing back each time he bowed to me,
For fear he'd think me less polite than he.

ARNOLPHE

Go on.

AGNÈS

     Then an old woman came, next day,
And found me standing in the entryway.
She said to me, "May Heaven bless you, dear,
And keep you beautiful for many a year.
God, who bestowed on you such grace and charm,
Did not intend those gifts to do men harm,
And you should know that there's a heart which bears
A wound which you've inflicted unawares."

[*Act Two · Scene Five*]

ARNOLPHE, *aside*

Old witch! Old tool of Satan! Damn her hide!

AGNÈS

"You say I've wounded somebody?" I cried.
"Indeed you have," she said. "The victim's he
Whom yesterday you saw from the balcony."
"But how could such a thing occur?" I said;
"Can I have dropped some object on his head?"
"No," she replied, "your bright eyes dealt the blow;
Their glances are the cause of all his woe."
"Good heavens, Madam," said I in great surprise,
"Is there some dread contagion in my eyes?"
"Ah, yes, my child," said she. "Your eyes dispense,
Unwittingly, a fatal influence:
The poor young man has dwindled to a shade;
And if you cruelly deny him aid,
I greatly fear," the kind old woman went on,
"That two days more will see him dead and gone."
"Heavens," I answered, "that would be sad indeed.
But what can I do for him? What help does he need?"
"My child," said she, "he only asks of you
The privilege of a little interview;
It is your eyes alone which now can save him,
And cure him of the malady they gave him."
"If that's the case," I said, "I can't refuse;
I'll gladly see him, whenever he may choose."

ARNOLPHE, *aside*

O "kind old woman"! O vicious sorceress!
May Hell reward you for your cleverness!

[*Act Two · Scene Five*]

AGNÈS

And so I saw him, which brought about his cure.
You'll grant I did the proper thing, I'm sure.
How could I have the conscience to deny
The succor he required, and let him die—
I, who so pity anyone in pain,
And cannot bear to see a chicken slain?

ARNOLPHE, *aside*

It's clear that she has meant no wrong, and I
Must blame that foolish trip I took, whereby
I left her unprotected from the lies
That rascally seducers can devise.
Oh, what if that young wretch, with one bold stroke,
Has compromised her? That would be no joke.

AGNÈS

What's wrong? You seem a trifle irritated.
Was there some harm in what I just related?

ARNOLPHE

No, but go on. I want to hear it all.
What happened when the young man came to call?

AGNÈS

Oh, if you'd seen how happy he was, how gay,
And how his sickness vanished right away,
And the jewel-case he gave me—not to forget
The coins he gave to Alain and to Georgette,
You would have loved him also, and you too—

56

[*Act Two · Scene Five*]

ARNOLPHE

And when you were alone, what did he do?

AGNÈS

He swore he loved me with a matchless passion,
And said to me, in the most charming fashion,
Things which I found incomparably sweet,
And never tire of hearing him repeat,
So much do they delight my ear, and start
I know not what commotion in my heart.

ARNOLPHE, *aside*

O strange interrogation, where each reply
Makes the interrogator wish to die!
     (*To Agnès:*)
Besides these compliments, these sweet addresses,
Were there not also kisses, and caresses?

AGNÈS

Oh, yes! He took my hands, and kissed and kissed
Them both, as if he never would desist.

ARNOLPHE

And did he not take—something else as well?
    (*He notes that she is taken aback.*)
Agh!

AGNÈS

    Well, he—

[*Act Two · Scene Five*]

ARNOLPHE

Yes?

AGNÈS

Took—

ARNOLPHE

What?

AGNÈS

I dare not tell.
I fear that you'll be furious with me.

ARNOLPHE

No.

AGNÈS

Yes.

ARNOLPHE

No, no.

AGNÈS

Then promise not to be.

ARNOLPHE

I promise.

[*Act Two* · *Scene Five*]

AGNÈS

He took my—oh, you'll have a fit.

ARNOLPHE

No.

AGNÈS

Yes.

ARNOLPHE

No, no. The devil! Out with it!
What did he take from you?

AGNÈS

He took—

ARNOLPHE, *aside*

God save me!

AGNÈS

He took the pretty ribbon that you gave me.
Indeed, he begged so that I couldn't resist.

ARNOLPHE, *taking a deep breath*

Forget the ribbon. Tell me: once he'd kissed
Your hands, what else did he do, as you recall?

59

[*Act Two · Scene Five*]

AGNÈS

Does one do other things?

ARNOLPHE

No, not at all;
But didn't he ask some further medicine
For the sad state of health that he was in?

AGNÈS

Why, no. But had he asked, you may be sure
I'd have done anything to speed his cure.

ARNOLPHE, *aside*

I've got off cheap this once, thanks be to God;
If I slip again, let all men call me clod.
    (*To Agnès:*)
Agnès, my dear, your innocence is vast;
I shan't reproach you; what is past is past.
But all that trifler wants to do—don't doubt it—
Is to deceive you, and then boast about it.

AGNÈS

Oh, no. He's often assured me otherwise.

ARNOLPHE

Ah, you don't know how that sort cheats and lies.
But do grasp this: to accept a jewel-case,
And let some coxcomb praise your pretty face,

And be complaisant when he takes a notion
To kiss your hands and fill you with "commotion"
Is a great sin, for which your soul could die.

AGNÈS

A sin, you say! But please, Sir, tell me why.

ARNOLPHE

Why? Why? Because, as all authority states,
It's just such deeds that Heaven abominates.

AGNÈS

Abominates! But why should Heaven feel so?
It's all so charming and so sweet, you know!
I never knew about this sort of thing
Till now, or guessed what raptures it could bring.

ARNOLPHE

Yes, all these promises of love undying,
These sighs, these kisses, are most gratifying,
But they must be enjoyed in the proper way;
One must be married first, that is to say.

AGNÈS

And once you're married, there's no evil in it?

ARNOLPHE

That's right.

[*Act Two · Scene Five*]

AGNÈS

Oh, let me marry, then, this minute!

ARNOLPHE

If that's what you desire, I feel the same;
It was to plan your marriage that I came.

AGNÈS

What! Truly?

ARNOLPHE

Yes.

AGNÈS

How happy I shall be!

ARNOLPHE

Yes, wedded life will please you, I foresee.

AGNÈS

You really intend that we two—

ARNOLPHE

Yes, I do.

[*Act Two · Scene Five*]

AGNÈS

Oh, how I'll kiss you if that dream comes true!

ARNOLPHE

And I'll return your kisses, every one.

AGNÈS

I'm never sure when people are making fun.
Are you quite serious?

ARNOLPHE

Yes, I'm serious. Quite.

AGNÈS

We're to be married?

ARNOLPHE

Yes.

AGNÈS

But when?

ARNOLPHE

Tonight.

63

[*Act Two · Scene Five*]

AGNÈS, *laughing*

Tonight?

ARNOLPHE

Tonight. It seems you're moved to laughter.

AGNÈS

Yes.

ARNOLPHE

Well, to see you happy is what I'm after.

AGNÈS

Oh, Sir, I owe you more than I can express!
With him, my life will be pure happiness!

ARNOLPHE

With whom?

AGNÈS

With . . . him.

ARNOLPHE

With *him!* Well, think again.
You're rather hasty in your choice of men.
It's quite another husband I have in mind;

64

And as for "him," as you call him, be so kind,
Regardless of his pitiable disease,
As never again to see him, if you please.
When next he calls, girl, put him in his place
By slamming the door directly in his face;
Then, if he knocks, go up and drop a brick
From the second-floor window. That should do the trick.
Do you understand, Agnès? I shall be hidden
Nearby, to see that you do as you are bidden.

AGNÈS

Oh, dear, he's so good-looking, so—

ARNOLPHE

Be still!

AGNÈS

I just won't have the heart—

ARNOLPHE

Enough; you will.
Now go upstairs.

AGNÈS

How can you—

ARNOLPHE

Do as I say.
I'm master here; I've spoken; go, obey.

Act 3

SCENE ONE

ARNOLPHE

Yes, I'm most pleased; it couldn't have gone better.
By following my instructions to the letter,
You've put that young philanderer to flight:
See how wise generalship can set things right.
Your innocence had been abused, Agnès;
Unwittingly, you'd got into a mess,
And, lacking my good counsel, you were well
Embarked upon a course which leads to Hell.
Those beaux are all alike, believe you me:
They've ribbons, plumes, and ruffles at the knee,
Fine wigs, and polished talk, and brilliant teeth,
But they're all scales and talons underneath—
Indeed, they're devils of the vilest sort,
Who prey on women's honor for their sport.
However, owing to my watchful care,
You have emerged intact from this affair.
The firm and righteous way in which you threw
That brick at him, and dashed his hopes of you,
Persuades me that there's no cause to delay
The wedding which I promised you today.
But first, it would be well for me to make
A few remarks for your improvement's sake.
    (*To Alain, who brings a chair:*)

I'll sit here, where it's cool.
    (*To Georgette:*) Remember, now—

GEORGETTE

Oh, Sir, we won't forget again, I vow.
That young man won't get round us any more.

ALAIN

I'll give up drink if he gets through that door.
Anyway, he's an idiot; we bit
Two coins he gave us, and they were counterfeit.

ARNOLPHE

Well, go and buy the food for supper, and then
One of you, as you're coming home again,
Can fetch the local notary from the square.
Tell him that there's a contract to prepare.

SCENE TWO

ARNOLPHE, AGNÈS

ARNOLPHE, *seated*

Agnès, stop knitting and hear what I have to say.
Lift up your head a bit, and turn this way.
        (*Putting his finger to his forehead:*)
Look at me *there* while I talk to you, right *there*,
And listen to my every word with care.
My dear, I'm going to wed you, and you should bless
Your vast good fortune and your happiness.
Reflect upon your former low estate,
And judge, then, if my goodness is not great
In raising you, a humble peasant lass,
To be a matron of the middle class,
To share the bed and the connubial bliss
Of one who's shunned the married state till this,
Withholding from a charming score or two
The honor which he now bestows on you.
Be ever mindful, Agnès, that you would be,
Without this union, a nonentity;
And let that thought incline your heart to merit
The name which I shall lend you, and to bear it
With such propriety that I shall never
Regret my choice for any cause whatever.
Marriage, Agnès, is no light matter; the role
Of wife requires austerity of soul,

And I do not exalt you to that station
To lead a life of heedless dissipation.
Yours is the weaker sex, please realize;
It is the beard in which all power lies,
And though there are two portions of mankind,
Those portions are not equal, you will find:
One half commands, the other must obey;
The second serves the first in every way;
And that obedience which the soldier owes
His general, or the loyal servant shows
His master, or the good child pays his sire,
Or the stern abbot looks for in the friar,
Is nothing to the pure docility,
The deep submission and humility
Which a good wife must ever exhibit toward
The man who is her master, chief, and lord.
Should he regard her with a serious air,
She must avert her eyes, and never dare
To lift them to his face again, unless
His look should change to one of tenderness.
Such things aren't understood by women today,
But don't let bad example lead you astray.
Don't emulate those flirts whose indiscretions
Are told all over town at gossip-sessions,
Or yield to Satan's trickery by allowing
Young fops to please you with their smiles and bowing.
Remember that, in marrying, I confide
To you, Agnès, my honor and my pride;
That honor is a tender, fragile thing
With which there can be no light dallying;
And that all misbehaving wives shall dwell
In ever-boiling cauldrons down in Hell.
These are no idle lessons which I impart,
And you'll do well to get them all by heart.

Your soul, if you observe them, and abjure
Flirtation, will be lily-white and pure;
But deviate from honor, and your soul
Will forthwith grow as vile and black as coal;
All will abhor you as a thing of evil,
Till one day you'll be taken by the Devil,
And Hell's eternal fire is where he'll send you—
From which sad fate may Heaven's grace defend you.
Make me a curtsey. Now then, just as a novice,
Entering the convent, learns by heart her office,
So, entering wedlock, you should do the same.
                    (*He rises.*)
I have, in my pocket, a book of no small fame
From which you'll learn the office of a wife.
'T was written by some man of pious life.
Study his teaching faithfully, and heed it.
Here, take the book; let's hear how well you read it.

AGNÈS, *reading*

The Maxims of Marriage
or
The Duties of a Married Woman,
Together with Her Daily Exercises.

First Maxim:
A woman who in church has said
She'll love and honor and obey
Should get it firmly in her head,
Despite the fashions of the day,
That he who took her for his own
Has taken her for his bed alone.

ARNOLPHE

I shall explain that; doubtless you're perplexed.
But, for the present, let us hear what's next.

AGNÈS, *continuing*

Second Maxim:
   She needs no fine attire
   More than he may desire
   Who is her lord and master.
To dress for any taste but his is vain;
   If others find her plain,
      'T is no disaster.

Third Maxim:
   Let her not daub her face
   With paint and patch and powder-base
And creams which promise beauty on the label.
   It is not for their husbands' sake
   But vanity's, that women undertake
      The labors of the dressing table.

Fourth Maxim:
Let her be veiled whenever she leaves the house,
So that her features are obscure and dim.
If she desires to please her spouse,
She must please no one else but him.

Fifth Maxim:
   Except for friends who call
To see her husband, let her not admit
      Anyone at all.

74

[*Act Three · Scene Two*]

A visitor whose end
Is to amuse the wife with gallant wit
    Is *not* the husband's friend.

Sixth Maxim:

To men who would confer kind gifts upon her,
She must reply with self-respecting nays.
Not to refuse would be to court dishonor.
Nothing is given for nothing nowadays.

Seventh Maxim:

She has no need, whatever she may think,
Of writing table, paper, pen, or ink.
In a proper house, the husband is the one
To do whatever writing's to be done.

Eighth Maxim:

    At those licentious things
    Called social gatherings,
Wives are corrupted by the worldly crowd.
Since, at such functions, amorous plots are laid
    And married men betrayed,
    They should not be allowed.

Ninth Maxim:

Let the wise wife, who cares for her good name,
Decline to play at any gambling game.
In such seductive pastimes wives can lose
Far more than coins, or bills, or I.O.U.'s.

Tenth Maxim:

    It is not good for wives
    To go on gay excursions,
    Picnics, or country drives.

75

In all such light diversions,
No matter who's the host,
The husbands pay the most.

Eleventh Maxim—

ARNOLPHE

Good. Read the rest to yourself. I'll clarify
Whatever may confuse you, by and by.
I've just recalled some business I'd forgot;
'T will only take a moment, like as not.
Go in, and treat that precious book with care.
If the notary comes, tell him to have a chair.

SCENE THREE

What could be safer than to marry her?
She'll do and be whatever I prefer.
She's like a lump of wax, and I can mold her
Into what shape I like, as she grows older.
True, she was almost lured away from me,
Whilst I was gone, through her simplicity;
But if one's wife must have some imperfection,
It's best that she should err in that direction.
Such faults as hers are easy to remove:
A simple wife is eager to improve,
And if she has been led astray, a slight
Admonitory talk will set her right.
But a clever wife's another kettle of fish:
One's at the mercy of her every wish;
What she desires, she'll have at any cost,
And reasoning with her is labor lost.
Her wicked wit makes virtues of her crimes,
Makes mock of principle, and oftentimes
Contrives, in furtherance of some wicked plan,
Intrigues which can defeat the shrewdest man.
Against her there is no defense, for she's
Unbeatable at plots and strategies,
And once she has resolved to amputate
Her husband's honor, he must bow to fate.

There's many a decent man could tell that story.
But that young fool will have no chance to glory
In my disgrace: he has too loose a tongue,
And that's a fault of Frenchmen, old or young.
When they are lucky in a love affair,
To keep the secret's more than they can bear;
A foolish vanity torments them, till
They'd rather hang, by Heaven, than be still.
What but the spells of Satan could incline
Women to favor men so asinine?
But here he comes; my feelings must not show
As I extract from him his tale of woe.

SCENE FOUR

HORACE

I've just been at your house, and I begin
To fear I'm fated never to find you in.
But I'll persist, and one day have the joy—

ARNOLPHE

Ah, come, no idle compliments, my boy.
All this fine talk, so flowery and so polished,
Is something I'd be glad to see abolished.
It's a vile custom: most men waste two-thirds
Of every day exchanging empty words.
Let's put our hats on, now, and be at ease.
Well, how's your love life going? Do tell me, please.
I was a bit distrait when last we met,
But what you told me I did not forget:
Your bold beginnings left me much impressed,
And now I'm all agog to hear the rest.

HORACE

Since I unlocked my heart to you, alas,
My hopes have come to an unhappy pass.

[*Act Three · Scene Four*]

ARNOLPHE

Oh, dear! How so?

HORACE

       Just now—alas—I learned
That my beloved's guardian has returned.

ARNOLPHE

That's bad.

HORACE

      What's more, he's well aware that we've
Been meeting secretly, without his leave.

ARNOLPHE

But how could he so quickly find that out?

HORACE

I don't know, but he has, beyond a doubt.
I went at my usual hour, more or less,
To pay my homage to her loveliness,
And found the servants changed in attitude.
They barred my way; their words and looks were rude.
"Be off!" they told me, and with no good grace
They slammed the door directly in my face.

ARNOLPHE

Right in your face!

[*Act Three · Scene Four*]

HORACE

Yes.

ARNOLPHE

Dreadful. Tell me more.

HORACE

I tried to reason with them through the door,
But whatsoever I said to them, they cried,
"The master says you're not to come inside."

ARNOLPHE

They wouldn't open it?

HORACE

No. And then Agnès,
On orders from her guardian, as one could guess,
Came to her window, said that she was sick
Of my attentions, and threw down a brick.

ARNOLPHE

A brick, you say!

HORACE

A brick; and it wasn't small.
Not what one hopes for when one pays a call.

[*Act Three* · *Scene Four*]

ARNOLPHE

Confound it! That's no mild rebuff, my lad.
I fear your situation's pretty bad.

HORACE

Yes, that old fool's return has spoiled my game.

ARNOLPHE

You have my deepest sympathy; it's a shame.

HORACE

He's wrecked my plans.

ARNOLPHE

            Oh, come; you've lost some
                ground,
But some means of recouping will be found.

HORACE

With a little inside help, I might by chance
Outwit this jealous fellow's vigilance.

ARNOLPHE

That should be easy. The lady, as you say,
Loves you.

[*Act Three · Scene Four*]

HORACE

Indeed, yes.

ARNOLPHE

Then you'll find a way.

HORACE

I hope so.

ARNOLPHE

You must not be put to flight
By that ungracious brick.

HORACE

Of course you're right.
I knew at once that that old fool was back
And secretly directing the attack.
But what amazed me (you'll be amazed as well)
Was something else she did, of which I'll tell—
A daring trick one wouldn't expect to see
Played by a girl of such simplicity.
Love is indeed a wondrous master, Sir,
Whose teaching makes us what we never were,
And under whose miraculous tuition
One suddenly can change one's disposition.
It overturns our settled inclinations,
Causing the most astounding transformations:
The miser's made a spendthrift overnight,
The coward valiant, and the boor polite;

83

Love spurs the sluggard on to high endeavor,
And moves the artless maiden to be clever.
Well, such a miracle has changed Agnès.
She cried, just now, with seeming bitterness,
"Go! I refuse to see you, and don't ask why;
To all your questions, here is my reply!"—
And having made that statement, down she threw
The brick I've mentioned, and a letter, too.
Note how her words apply to brick *and* letter:
Isn't that fine? Could any ruse be better?
Aren't you amazed? Do you see what great effect
True love can have upon the intellect?
Can you deny its power to inspire
The gentlest heart with fortitude and fire?
How do you like that trick with the letter, eh?
A most astute young woman, wouldn't you say?
As for my jealous rival, isn't the role
He's played in this affair extremely droll?
Well?

ARNOLPHE

Yes, quite droll.

HORACE

       Well, laugh, if that's the case!
(*Arnolphe gives a forced laugh.*)
My, what a fool! He fortifies his place
Against me, using bricks for cannon balls,
As if he feared that I might storm the walls;
What's more, in his anxiety he rallies
His two domestics to repulse my sallies;
And then he's hoodwinked by the girl he meant

To keep forever meek and innocent!
I must confess that, though this silly man's
Return to town has balked my amorous plans,
The whole thing's been so comical that I find
That I'm convulsed whenever it comes to mind.
You haven't laughed as much as I thought you would.

ARNOLPHE, *with a forced laugh*

I beg your pardon; I've done the best I could.

HORACE

But let me show you the letter she wrote, my friend.
What her heart feels, her artless hand has penned
In the most touching terms, the sweetest way,
With pure affection, purest naïveté;
Nature herself, I think, would so express
Love's first awakening and its sweet distress.

ARNOLPHE, *aside*

Behold what scribbling leads to! It was quite
Against my wishes that she learned to write.

HORACE, *reading*

I am moved to write to you, but I am much at a loss as to how to begin. I have thoughts which I should like you to know of; but I don't know how to go about telling them to you, and I mistrust my own words. I begin to perceive that I have always been kept in a state of ignorance, and so I am fearful of writing something I shouldn't, or of saying more than I ought. In truth, I

85

don't know what you have done to me, but I know that I am mortally vexed by the harsh things I am made to do to you, that it will be the most painful thing in the world to give you up, and that I would be happy indeed to be yours. Perhaps it is rash of me to say that; but in any case I cannot help saying it, and I wish that I could have my desire without doing anything wrong. I am constantly told that all young men are deceivers, that they mustn't be listened to, and that all you have said to me is mere trickery; I assure you, however, that I have not yet been able to think that of you, and your words so touch me that I cannot believe them false. Please tell me frankly what you intend; for truly, since my own intentions are blameless, it would be very wicked of you to deceive me, and I think that I should die of despair.

ARNOLPHE, *aside*

The bitch!

HORACE

What's wrong?

ARNOLPHE

Oh, nothing: I was sneezing.

HORACE

Was ever a style so amiable, so pleasing?
Despite the tyranny she's had to bear,
Isn't her nature sweet beyond compare?
And is it not a crime of the basest kind

For anyone to stifle such a mind,
To starve so fine a spirit, and to enshroud
In ignorance a soul so well-endowed?
Love has begun to waken her, however,
And if some kind star favors my endeavor
I'll free her from that utter beast, that black
Villain, that wretch, that brute, that maniac—

ARNOLPHE

Good-bye.

HORACE

What, going?

ARNOLPHE

I've just recalled that I'm
Due somewhere else in a few minutes' time.

HORACE

Wait! Can you think of someone who might possess
An entrée to that house, and to Agnès?
I hate to trouble you, but do please lend
Whatever help you can, as friend to friend.
The servants, as I said, both man and maid,
Have turned against my cause, and can't be swayed.
Just now, despite my every blandishment,
They eyed me coldly, and would not relent.
I had, for a time, the aid of an old woman
Whose talent for intrigue was superhuman;
She served me, at the start, with much success,

87

But died four days ago, to my distress.
Don't you know someone who could help me out?

ARNOLPHE

I don't; but you'll find someone, I don't doubt.

HORACE

Farewell, then, Sir. You'll be discreet, I know.

SCENE FIVE

ARNOLPHE

ARNOLPHE

In that boy's presence, what hell I undergo,
Trying to hide my anguish from his eye!
To think that an innocent girl should prove so sly!
Either she's fooled me, and never *was* naïve,
Or Satan's just now taught her to deceive.
That cursèd letter! I wish that I were dead.
Plainly that callow wretch has turned her head,
Captured her mind and heart, eclipsed me there,
And doomed me to distraction and despair.
The loss of her entails a double hell:
My honor suffers, and my love as well.
It drives me mad to see myself displaced,
And all my careful planning gone to waste.
To be revenged on her, I need but wait
And let her giddy passion meet its fate;
The upshot can't be anything but bad.
But oh, to lose the thing one loves is sad.
Good Lord! To rear her with such calculation,
And then fall victim to infatuation!
She has no funds, no family, yet she can dare
Abuse my lavish kindness and my care;
And what, for Heaven's sake, is my reaction?
In spite of all, I love her to distraction!
Have you no shame, fool? Don't you resent her crimes?

Oh, I could slap my face a thousand times!
I'll go inside for a bit, but only to see
How she will face me after her treachery.
Kind Heaven, let no dishonor stain my brow;
Or if it is decreed that I must bow
To that misfortune, lend me at least, I pray,
Such patient strength as some poor men display.

Act 4

SCENE ONE

ARNOLPHE, *entering from the house, alone*

I can't hold still a minute, I declare.
My anxious thoughts keep darting here and there,
Planning defenses, seeking to prevent
That rascal from achieving his intent.
How calm the traitress looked when I went in!
Despite her crimes, she shows no sense of sin,
And though she's all but sent me to my grave,
How like a little saint she dares behave!
The more she sat there, cool and unperturbed,
The less I thought my fury could be curbed;
Yet, strange to say, my heart's increasing ire
Seemed only to redouble my desire.
I was embittered, desperate, irate,
And yet her beauty had never seemed so great.
Never did her bright eyes so penetrate me,
So rouse my spirit, so infatuate me;
Oh, it would break the heart within my breast
Should fate subject me to this cruel jest.
What! Have I supervised her education
With loving care and long consideration,
Sheltered her since she was a tiny creature,
Cherished sweet expectations for her future,
For thirteen years molded her character
And based my hopes of happiness on her,

Only to see some young fool steal the prize
Of her affection, under my very eyes,
And just when she and I were all but wed?
Ah, no, young friend! Ah, no, young chucklehead!
I mean to stop you; I swear that you shall not
Succeed, however well you scheme and plot,
And that you'll have no cause to laugh at me.

SCENE TWO

NOTARY

Ah, here you are, Sir! I am the notary.
So, there's a contract which you'd have me draw?

ARNOLPHE, *unaware of the notary*

How shall I do it?

NOTARY

According to the law.

ARNOLPHE, *still oblivious*

I must be prudent, and think what course is best.

NOTARY

I shall do nothing against your interest.

ARNOLPHE, *oblivious*

One must anticipate the unexpected.

[*Act Four · Scene Two*]

NOTARY

In my hands, you'll be thoroughly protected.
But do remember, lest you be betrayed,
To sign no contract till the dowry's paid.

ARNOLPHE, *oblivious*

I must act covertly; if this thing gets out,
The gossips will have much to blab about.

NOTARY

If you're so anxious not to make a stir,
The contract can be drawn in secret, Sir.

ARNOLPHE, *oblivious*

But how shall she be dealt with? Can I condone—

NOTARY

The dowry is proportional to her own.

ARNOLPHE, *oblivious*

It's hard to be strict with one whom you adore.

NOTARY

In that case, you may wish to give her more.

ARNOLPHE, *oblivious*

How should I treat the girl? I must decide.

[*Act Four · Scene Two*]

NOTARY

As a general rule, the husband gives the bride
A dowry that's one-third the size of hers;
But he may increase the sum, if he prefers.

ARNOLPHE, *oblivious*

If—

NOTARY, *Arnolphe now noticing him*

As for property, and its division
In case of death, the husband makes provision
As he thinks best.

ARNOLPHE

Eh?

NOTARY

He can make certain of
His bride's security, and show his love,
By jointure, or a settlement whereby
The gift is canceled should the lady die,
Reverting to her heirs, if so agreed;
Or go by common law; or have a deed
Of gift appended to the instrument,
Either by his sole wish, or by consent.
Why shrug your shoulders? Am I talking rot?
Do I know contracts, Sir, or do I not?
Who could instruct me? Who would be so bold?
Do I not know that spouses jointly hold

Goods, chattels, lands, and money in their two names,
Unless one party should renounce all claims?
Do I not know that a third of the bride's resources
Enters the joint estate—

ARNOLPHE

All that, of course, is
True. But who asked for all this pedantry?

NOTARY

You did! And now you sniff and shrug at me,
And treat my competence with ridicule.

ARNOLPHE

The devil take this ugly-featured fool!
Good day, good day. An end to all this chatter.

NOTARY

Did you not ask my aid in a legal matter?

ARNOLPHE

Yes, yes, but now the matter's been deferred.
When your advice is needed, I'll send word.
Meanwhile, stop blathering, you blatherskite!

NOTARY

He's mad, I judge; and I think my judgment's right.

SCENE THREE

THE NOTARY, ALAIN, GEORGETTE, ARNOLPHE

NOTARY, *to Alain and Georgette*

Your master sent you to fetch me, isn't that so?

ALAIN

Yes.

NOTARY

How you feel about him I don't know,
But I regard him as a senseless boor.
Tell him I said so.

GEORGETTE

We will, you may be sure.

SCENE FOUR

ALAIN

Sir—

ARNOLPHE

   Ah, come here, my good friends, tried and true:
You've amply proved that I may count on you.

ALAIN

The notary—

ARNOLPHE

      Tell me later, will you not?
My honor's threatened by a vicious plot;
Think, children, what distress you'd feel, what shame,
If some dishonor touched your master's name!
You wouldn't dare to leave the house, for fear
That all the town would point at you, and sneer.
Since we're together, then, in this affair,
You must be ever watchful, and take care
That no approach that gallant may adopt—

[*Act Four · Scene Four*]

GEORGETTE

We've learned our lesson, Sir; he shall be stopped.

ARNOLPHE

Beware his fine words and his flatteries.

ALAIN

Of course.

GEORGETTE

We can resist such talk with ease.

ARNOLPHE, *to Alain*

What if he said, "Alain, for mercy's sake,
Do me a kindness"—what answer would you make?

ALAIN

I'd say, "You fool!"

ARNOLPHE

Good, good. (*To Georgette:*)
"Georgette, my dear,
I'm sure you're just as sweet as you appear."

GEORGETTE

"Fathead!"

ARNOLPHE

Good, good. (*To Alain:*) "Come, let me in.
You know
That my intent is pure as the driven snow."

ALAIN

"Sir, you're a knave!"

ARNOLPHE

Well said. (*To Georgette:*) "Unless you take
Pity on my poor heart, it's sure to break."

GEORGETTE

"You are an impudent ass!"

ARNOLPHE

Well said, Georgette.
"I'm not the sort of person to forget
A favor, or begrudge the *quid pro quo*,
As these few coins, Alain, will serve to show.
And you, Georgette, take this and buy a dress.
       (*Both hold out their hands and take the money.*)
That's but a specimen of my largesse.
And all I ask is that you grant to me
An hour of your young mistress' company."

GEORGETTE, *giving him a shove*

"You're crazy!"

[*Act Four · Scene Four*]

ARNOLPHE

Good!

ALAIN, *shoving Arnolphe*

"Move on!"

ARNOLPHE

Good!

GEORGETTE, *shoving Arnolphe*

"Out of my
sight!"

ARNOLPHE

Good, good—but that's enough.

GEORGETTE

Did I do it right?

ALAIN

Is that how we're to treat him?

ARNOLPHE

You were fine;
Except for the money, which you should decline.

GEORGETTE

We didn't think, Sir. That was wrong indeed.

ALAIN

Would you like to do it over again?

ARNOLPHE

                    No need;
Go back inside.

ALAIN

        Sir, if you say the word, we—

ARNOLPHE

No, that will do; go in at once; you heard me.
Just keep the money; I shall be with you shortly.
Be on your guard, and ready to support me.

SCENE FIVE

ARNOLPHE

The cobbler at the corner is sharp of eye;
I think that I'll enlist him as a spy.
As for Agnès, I'll keep her under guard,
And all dishonest women shall be barred—
Hairdressers, glovers, handkerchief-makers, those
Who come to the door with ribbons, pins, and bows,
And often, as a sideline to such wares,
Are go-betweens in secret love affairs.
I know the world, and the tricks that people use;
That boy will have to invent some brand-new ruse
If he's to get a message in to her.

SCENE SIX

HORACE

What luck to find you in this quarter, Sir!
I've just had a narrow escape, believe you me!
Just after I left you, whom did I chance to see
Upon her shady balcony, but the fair
Agnès, who had come out to take the air!
She managed, having signaled me to wait,
To steal downstairs and open the garden gate.
We went to her room, and were no sooner there
Than we heard her jealous guardian on the stair;
In which great peril I was thrust by her
Into a wardrobe where her dresses were.
He entered. I couldn't see him, but I heard
Him striding back and forth without a word,
Heaving deep sighs of woe again and again,
Pounding upon the tables now and then,
Kicking a little dog, who yipped in fright,
And throwing her possessions left and right.
What's more, to give his fury full release,
He knocked two vases off her mantelpiece.
Clearly the old goat had some vague, dismaying
Sense of the tricks his captive had been playing.
At last, when all his anger had been spent
On objects which were dumb and innocent,
The frantic man, without a word, went striding

Out of the room, and I came out of hiding.
Quite naturally, we didn't dare extend
Our rendezvous, because our jealous friend
Was still about; tonight, however, I
Shall visit her, quite late, and on the sly.
Our plan is this: I'll cough, three times, outside;
At that, the window will be opened wide;
Then, with a ladder and the assistance of
Agnès, I'll climb into our bower of love.
Since you're my only friend, I tell you this—
For telling, as you know, augments one's bliss.
However vast the joy, one must confide
In someone else before one's satisfied.
You share, I know, my happy expectations.
But now, farewell; I must make preparations.

SCENE SEVEN

ARNOLPHE

ARNOLPHE

The evil star that's hounding me to death
Gives me no time in which to catch my breath!
Must I, again and again, be forced to see
My measures foiled through their complicity?
Shall I, at my ripe age, be duped, forsooth,
By a green girl and by a harebrained youth?
For twenty years I've sagely contemplated
The woeful lives of men unwisely mated,
And analyzed with care the slips whereby
The best-planned marriages have gone awry;
Thus schooled by others' failures, I felt that I'd
Be able, when I chose to take a bride,
To ward off all mischance, and be protected
From griefs to which so many are subjected.
I took, to that end, all the shrewd and wise
Precautions which experience could devise;
Yet, as if fate had made the stern decision
That no man living should escape derision,
I find, for all my pondering of this
Great matter, all my keen analysis,
The twenty years and more which I have spent
In planning to escape the embarrassment
So many husbands suffer from today,
That I'm as badly victimized as they.

[*Act Four · Scene Seven*]

But no, damned fate, I challenge your decree!
The lovely prize is in my custody,
And though her heart's been filched by that young pest,
I guarantee that he'll not get the rest,
And that this evening's gallant rendezvous
Won't go as smoothly as they'd like it to.
There's one good thing about my present fix—
That I'm forewarned of all my rival's tricks,
And that this oaf who's aiming to undo me
Confesses all his bad intentions to me.

SCENE EIGHT

CHRYSALDE, ARNOLPHE

CHRYSALDE

Well, shall we dine, and then go out for a stroll?

ARNOLPHE

No, no, the dinner's off.

CHRYSALDE

Well, well, how droll!

ARNOLPHE

Forgive me: there's a crisis I must face.

CHRYSALDE

Your wedding plans have changed? Is that the case?

ARNOLPHE

I have no need of your solicitude.

[*Act Four · Scene Eight*]

CHRYSALDE

Tell me your troubles, now, and don't be rude.
I'd guess, friend, that your marriage scheme has met
With difficulties, and that you're upset.
To judge by your expression, I'd almost swear it.

ARNOLPHE

Whatever happens, I shall have the merit
Of not resembling some in this community,
Who let young gallants cheat them with impunity.

CHRYSALDE

It's odd that you, with your good intellect,
Are so obsessive in this one respect,
Measure all happiness thereby, and base
On it alone men's honor or disgrace.
Greed, envy, vice, and cowardice are not
Important sins to you; the one grave blot
You find on any scutcheon seems to be
The crime of having suffered cuckoldry.
Now, come: shall a man be robbed of his good name
Through an ill chance for which he's not to blame?
Shall a good husband lacerate his soul
With guilt for matters not in his control?
When a man marries, why must we scorn or praise him
According to whether or not his wife betrays him?
And if she does so, why must her husband see
The fact as an immense catastrophe?
Do realize that, to a man of sense,
There's nothing crushing in such accidents;
That, since no man can dodge the blows of fate,

One's sense of failure should not be too great,
And that there's no harm done, whatever they say,
If one but takes things in the proper way.
In difficulties of this sort, it seems,
As always, wiser to avoid extremes.
One shouldn't ape those husbands who permit
Such scandal, and who take a pride in it,
Dropping the names of their wives' latest gallants,
Praising their persons, bragging of their talents,
Professing warm regard for them, attending
The parties that they give, and so offending
Society, which properly resents
Displays of laxity and impudence.
Needless to say, such conduct will not do;
And yet the other extreme's improper too.
If men do wrong to flatter their wives' gallants,
It's no less bad when, lacking tact and balance,
They vent their grievances with savage fury,
Calling the whole world to be judge and jury,
And won't be satisfied till they acquaint
All ears whatever with their loud complaint.
Between these two extremes, my friend, there lies
A middle way that's favored by the wise,
And which, if followed, will preserve one's face
However much one's wife may court disgrace.
In short, then, cuckoldry need not be dreaded
Like some dire monster, fierce and many-headed;
It can be lived with, if one has the wit
To take it calmly, and make the best of it.

ARNOLPHE

For that fine speech, the great fraternity
Of cuckolds owes you thanks, your Excellency;

And all men, if they heard your wisdom, would
Make joyous haste to join the brotherhood.

CHRYSALDE

No, that I shouldn't approve. But since it's fate
Whereby we're joined to one or another mate,
One should take marriage as one takes picquette,
In which, if one has made a losing bet,
One takes the setback calmly, and takes pains
To do the best one can with what remains.

ARNOLPHE

In other words, eat hearty and sleep tight,
And tell yourself that everything's all right.

CHRYSALDE

Laugh on, my friend; but I can, in all sobriety,
Name fifty things which cause me more anxiety,
And would, if they occurred, appall me more
Than this misfortune which you so abhor.
Had I to choose between adversities,
I'd rather be a cuckold, if you please,
Than marry one of those good wives who find
Continual reason to upbraid mankind,
Those virtuous shrews, those fiendish paragons,
As violently chaste as Amazons,
Who, having had the goodness not to horn us,
Accord themselves the right to nag and scorn us,
And make us pay for their fidelity
By being as vexatious as can be.
Do learn, friend, that when all is said and done,

Cuckoldry's what you make of it; that one
Might welcome it in certain situations,
And that, like all things, it has compensations.

ARNOLPHE

Well, if you want it, may you get your wish;
But, as for me, it's not at all my dish.
Before I'd let my brow be decked with horn—

CHRYSALDE

Tut, tut! Don't swear, or you may be forsworn.
If fate has willed it, your resolves will fail,
And all your oaths will be of no avail.

ARNOLPHE

I! I a cuckold?

CHRYSALDE

Don't let it fret you so.
It happens to the best of men, you know.
Cuckolds exist with whom, if I may be frank,
You can't compare for person, wealth, or rank.

ARNOLPHE

I have no wish to be compared with such.
Enough, now, of your mockery; it's too much.
You try my patience.

[*Act Four · Scene Eight*]

CHRYSALDE

        So, you're annoyed with me?
Ah, well. Good-bye. But bear in mind that he
Who thumps his chest and swears upon his soul
That he will never play the cuckold's role
Is studying for the part, and may well get it.

ARNOLPHE

That won't occur, I swear; I shall not let it.
I shall remove that threat this very minute.
        (*He knocks at his own gate.*)

SCENE NINE

ALAIN, GEORGETTE, ARNOLPHE

ARNOLPHE

My friends, the battle's joined, and we must win it.
Your love for me, by which I'm touched and moved,
Must now, in this emergency, be proved,
And if your deeds repay my confidence,
You may expect a handsome recompense.
This very night—don't tell a soul, my friends—
A certain rascal whom you know intends
To scale the wall and see Agnès; but we
Shall lay a little trap for him, we three.
You'll both be armed with clubs, and when the young
Villain has almost reached the topmost rung
(I meanwhile shall have flung the shutters wide),
You shall lean out and so lambaste his hide,
So bruise his ribs by your combined attack,
That he will never dream of coming back.
Don't speak my name while this is happening, mind you,
Or let him know that I am there behind you.
Have you the pluck to serve me in this action?

ALAIN

If blows are called for, we can give satisfaction.
I'll show you that this good right arm's not lame.

[*Act Four · Scene Nine*]

GEORGETTE

Mine looks less strong than his, but all the same
Our foe will know that he's been beaten by it.

ARNOLPHE

Go in, then; and, whatever you do, keep quiet.
                    (*Alone:*)
Tonight, I'll give a lesson to mankind.
If all endangered husbands took a mind
To greet their wives' intrusive gallants thus,
Cuckolds, I think, would be less numerous.

Act 5

SCENE ONE

ALAIN, GEORGETTE, ARNOLPHE

ARNOLPHE

You brutes! What made you be so heavy-handed?

ALAIN

But, Sir, we only did as you commanded.

ARNOLPHE

Don't put the blame on me; your guilt is plain.
I wished him beaten; I didn't wish him slain.
And furthermore, if you'll recall, I said
To hit him on the ribs, not on the head.
It's a ghastly situation in which I'm placed;
How is this young man's murder to be faced?
Go in, now, and be silent as the grave
About that innocent command I gave.
                    (*Alone:*)
It's nearly daybreak. I must take thought, and see
How best to cope with this dire tragedy.
God help me! What will the boy's father say
When this appalling story comes his way?

SCENE TWO

HORACE, ARNOLPHE

HORACE

Who's this, I wonder. I'd best approach with care.

ARNOLPHE

How could I have foreseen . . . I say, who's there?

HORACE

Seigneur Arnolphe?

ARNOLPHE

Yes—

HORACE

It's Horace, once more.
My, you're up early! I was heading for
Your house, to ask a favor.

ARNOLPHE

Oh, God, I'm dizzy.
Is he a vision? Is he a ghost? What is he?

[Act Five · Scene Two]

HORACE

Sir, I'm in trouble once again, I fear.
It's providential that you should appear
Just at the moment when your help was needed.
My plans, I'm happy to tell you, have succeeded
Beyond all expectations, and despite
An incident which might have spoiled them quite.
I don't know how it happened, but someone knew
About our contemplated rendezvous;
For, just as I'd almost reached her window sill,
I saw some frightful figures, armed to kill,
Lean out above me, waving their clubs around.
I lost my footing, tumbled to the ground,
And thus, though rather scratched and bruised, was spared
The thumping welcome which they had prepared.
Those brutes (of whom Old Jealous, I suppose,
Was one) ascribed my tumble to their blows,
And since I lay there, motionless, in the dirt
For several minutes, being stunned and hurt,
They judged that they had killed me, and they all
Took fright at that, and so began to brawl.
I lay in silence, hearing their angry cries:
They blamed each other for my sad demise,
Then tiptoed out, in darkness and in dread,
To feel my body, and see if I were dead.
As you can well imagine, I played the part
Of a limp, broken corpse with all my heart.
Quite overcome with terror, they withdrew,
And I was thinking of withdrawing, too,
When young Agnès came hurrying, out of breath
And much dismayed by my supposèd death:
She had been able, of course, to overhear
All that my foes had babbled in their fear,

123

And while they were distracted and unnerved
She'd slipped from the house, entirely unobserved.
Ah, how she wept with happiness when she found
That I was, after all, both safe and sound!
Well, to be brief: electing to be guided
By her own heart, the charming girl decided
Not to return to her guardian, but to flee,
Entrusting her security to me.
What must his tyranny be, if it can force
So shy a girl to take so bold a course!
And think what peril she might thus incur,
If I were capable of wronging her.
Ah, but my love's too pure for that, too strong;
I'd rather die than do her any wrong;
So admirable is she that all I crave
Is to be with her even to the grave.
I know my father: this will much displease him,
But we shall manage somehow to appease him.
In any case, she's won my heart, and I
Could not desert her, even if I chose to try.
The favor I ask of you is rather large:
It's that you take my darling in your charge,
And keep her, if you will, for several days
In your own house, concealed from the world's gaze.
I ask your help in this because I'm bent
On throwing all pursuers off the scent;
Also because, if she were seen with me,
There might be talk of impropriety.
To you, my loyal friend, I've dared to impart,
Without reserve, the secrets of my heart,
And likewise it's to you I now confide
My dearest treasure and my future bride.

[Act Five · Scene Two]

ARNOLPHE

I'm at your service; on that you may depend.

HORACE

You'll grant the favor that I ask, dear friend?

ARNOLPHE

Of course; most willingly. I'm glad indeed
That I can help you in your hour of need.
Thank Heaven that you asked me! There's no request
To which I could accede with greater zest.

HORACE

How kind you are! What gratitude I feel!
I feared you might refuse my rash appeal;
But you're a man of the world, urbane and wise,
Who looks upon young love with tolerant eyes.
My man is guarding her, just down the street.

ARNOLPHE

It's almost daylight. Where had we better meet?
Someone might see me, if you brought her here,
And should you bring her to my house, I fear
'T would start the servants talking. We must look
For some more shadowy and secluded nook.
That garden's handy; I shall await her there.

125

[*Act Five · Scene Two*]

HORACE

You're right, Sir. We must act with the utmost care.
I'll go, and quickly bring Agnès to you,
Then seek my lodgings without more ado.

ARNOLPHE, *alone*

Ah, Fortune! This good turn will compensate
For all the tricks you've played on me of late.
(*He hides his face in his cloak.*)

SCENE THREE

AGNÈS, HORACE, ARNOLPHE

HORACE

Just come with me; there's no cause for alarm.
I'm taking you where you'll be safe from harm.
To stay together would be suicide:
Go in, and let this gentleman be your guide.
> (*Arnolphe, whom she does not recognize,
> takes her hand.*)

AGNÈS

Why are you leaving me?

HORACE

Dear Agnès, I must.

AGNÈS

You'll very soon be coming back, I trust?

HORACE

I shall; my yearning heart will see to that.

[*Act Five · Scene Three*]

AGNÈS

Without you, life is miserable and flat.

HORACE

When I'm away from you, I pine and grieve.

AGNÈS

Alas! If that were so, you wouldn't leave.

HORACE

You know how strong my love is, and how true.

AGNÈS

Ah, no, you don't love me as I love you.
    (*Arnolphe tugs at her hand.*)
Why does he pull my hand?

HORACE

         'T would ruin us,
My dear, if we were seen together thus,
And therefore this true friend, who's filled with worry
About our welfare, urges you to hurry.

AGNÈS

But why must I go with him—a perfect stranger?

[*Act Five · Scene Three*]

HORACE

Don't fret. In his hands you'll be out of danger.

AGNÈS

I'd rather be in *your* hands; that was why—
      (*To Arnolphe, who tugs her hand again:*)
Wait, wait.

HORACE

It's daybreak. I must go. Good-bye.

AGNÈS

When shall I see you?

HORACE

Very soon, I swear.

AGNÈS

Till that sweet moment, I'll be in despair.

HORACE, *leaving, to himself*

My happiness is assured; my fears may cease;
Praise be to Heaven, I now can sleep in peace.

SCENE FOUR

ARNOLPHE, *hiding his face in his cloak, and
disguising his voice*

Come, this is not where you're to stay, my child;
It's elsewhere that you shall be domiciled.
You're going to a safe, sequestered place.
    (*Revealing himself, and using his normal voice:*)
Do you know me?

AGNÈS, *recognizing him*

    Aagh!

ARNOLPHE

              You wicked girl! My face
Would seem, just now, to give you rather a fright.
Oh, clearly I'm a most unwelcome sight:
I interfere with your romantic plan.
    (*Agnès turns and looks in vain for Horace.*)
No use to look for help from that young man;
He couldn't hear you now; he's gone too far.
Well, well! For one so young, how sly you are!
You ask—most innocently, it would appear—
If children are begotten through the ear,
Yet you know all too well, I now discover,

[*Act Five · Scene Four*]

How to keep trysts—at midnight—with a lover!
What honeyed words you spoke to him just now!
Who taught you such beguilements? Tell me how,
Within so short a time, you've learned so much!
You used to be afraid of ghosts and such:
Has your gallant taught you not to fear the night?
You ingrate! To deceive me so, despite
The loving care with which you have been blessed!
Oh, I have warmed a serpent at my breast
Until, reviving, it unkindly bit
The very hand that was caressing it!

AGNÈS

Why are you cross with me?

ARNOLPHE

Oh! So I'm unfair?

AGNÈS

I've done no wrong of which I am aware.

ARNOLPHE

Was it right, then, to run off with that young beau?

AGNÈS

He wants me for his wife; he's told me so.
I've only done as you advised; you said
That, so as not to sin, one ought to wed.

[*Act Five · Scene Four*]

ARNOLPHE

Yes, but I made it perfectly clear that I'd
Resolved, myself, to take you as my bride.

AGNÈS

Yes; but if I may give my point of view,
He'd suit me, as a husband, better than you.
In all your talk of marriage, you depict
A state that's gloomy, burdensome, and strict;
But, ah! when *he* describes the married state,
It sounds so sweet that I can hardly wait.

ARNOLPHE

Ah! So you love him, faithless girl!

AGNÈS

Why, yes.

ARNOLPHE

Have you the gall to tell me that, Agnès?

AGNÈS

If it's the truth, what's wrong with telling it?

ARNOLPHE

How dared you fall in love with him, you chit?

[*Act Five · Scene Four*]

AGNÈS

It was no fault of mine; he made me do it.
I was in love with him before I knew it.

ARNOLPHE

You should have overcome your amorous feeling.

AGNÈS

It's hard to overcome what's so appealing.

ARNOLPHE

Didn't you know that I would be put out?

AGNÈS

Why, no. What have you to complain about?

ARNOLPHE

Nothing, of course! I'm wild with happiness!
You don't, I take it, love me.

AGNÈS

Love you?

ARNOLPHE

Yes.

[*Act Five · Scene Four*]

AGNÈS

Alas, I don't.

ARNOLPHE

You *don't?*

AGNÈS

Would you have me lie?

ARNOLPHE

Why don't you love me, hussy? Tell me why!

AGNÈS

Good heavens, it's not I whom you should blame.
He made me love him; why didn't you do the same?
I didn't hinder you, as I recall.

ARNOLPHE

I tried to make you love me; I gave my all;
Yet all my pains and strivings were in vain.

AGNÈS

He has more aptitude than you, that's plain;
To win my heart, he scarcely had to try.

[*Act Five · Scene Four*]

ARNOLPHE, *aside*

This peasant girl can frame a neat reply!
What lady wit could answer with more art?
Either she's bright, or in what concerns the heart
A foolish girl can best the wisest man.
    (*To Agnès:*)
Well, then, Miss Back-Talk, answer this if you can:
Did I raise you, all these years, at such expense,
For another's benefit? Does that make sense?

AGNÈS

No. But he'll gladly pay you for your trouble.

ARNOLPHE, *aside*

Such flippancy! It makes my rage redouble.
    (*To Agnès:*)
You minx! How could he possibly discharge
Your obligations to me? They're too large.

AGNÈS

Frankly, they don't seem very large to me.

ARNOLPHE

Did I not nurture you from infancy?

AGNÈS

Yes, that you did. I'm deeply obligated.
How wondrously you've had me educated!

Do you fancy that I'm blind to what you've done,
And cannot see that I'm a simpleton?
Oh, it humiliates me; I revolt
Against the shame of being such a dolt.

ARNOLPHE

Do you think you'll gain the knowledge that you need
Through that young dandy's tutelage?

AGNÈS

                   Yes, indeed.
It's thanks to him I know what little I do;
I owe far more to him than I do to you.

ARNOLPHE

What holds me back, I ask myself, from treating
So insolent a girl to a sound beating?
Your coldness irks me to the point of tears,
And it would ease my soul to box your ears.

AGNÈS

Alas, then, beat me, if you so desire.

ARNOLPHE, *aside*

Those words and that sweet look dissolve my ire,
Restoring to my heart such tender feeling
As makes me quite forget her double-dealing.
How strange love is! How strange that men, from such
Perfidious beings, will endure so much!

136

[*Act Five · Scene Four*]

Women, as all men know, are fraily wrought:
They're foolish and illogical in thought,
Their souls are weak, their characters are bad,
There's nothing quite so silly, quite so mad,
So faithless; yet, despite these sorry features,
What won't we do to please the wretched creatures?
    (*To Agnès:*)
Come, traitress, let us be at peace once more.
I'll pardon you, and love you as before.
Repay my magnanimity, and learn
From my great love to love me in return.

AGNÈS

Truly, if I were able to, I would.
I'd gladly love you if I only could.

ARNOLPHE

You can, my little beauty, if you'll but try.
    (*He sighs.*)
Just listen to that deep and yearning sigh!
Look at my haggard face! See how it suffers!
Reject that puppy, and the love he offers:
He must have cast a spell on you; with me,
You'll be far happier, I guarantee.
I know that clothes and jewels are your passion;
Don't worry: you shall always be in fashion.
I'll pet you night and day; you shall be showered
With kisses; you'll be hugged, caressed, devoured.
And you shall have your wish in every way.
I'll say no more; what further could I say?
    (*Aside:*)
Lord, what extremes desire will drive us to!

[*Act Five · Scene Four*]

(*To Agnès:*)

In short, no love could match my love for you.
Tell me, ungrateful girl, what proof do you need?
Shall I weep? Or beat myself until I bleed?
What if I tore my hair out—would that sway you?
Shall I kill myself? Command, and I'll obey you.
I'm ready, cruel one, for you to prove me.

AGNÈS

Somehow, your lengthy speeches fail to move me.
Horace, in two words, could be more engaging.

ARNOLPHE

Enough of this! Your impudence is enraging.
I have my plans for you, you stubborn dunce,
And I shall pack you out of town at once.
You've spurned my love, and baited me as well—
Which you'll repent of in a convent cell.

SCENE FIVE

ALAIN, ARNOLPHE, AGNÈS

ALAIN

It's very strange, but Agnès has vanished, Sir.
I think that corpse has run away with her.

ARNOLPHE

She's here. Go shut her in my room, securely.
That's not where he'd come looking for her, surely,
And she'll be there but half an hour, at most.
Meanwhile I'll get a carriage, in which we'll post
To a safe retreat. Go now, and lock up tight,
And see that you don't let her out of sight.
          (*Alone:*)
Perhaps a change of scene and circumstance
Will wean her from this infantile romance.

SCENE SIX

HORACE, ARNOLPHE

HORACE

Seigneur Arnolphe, I'm overwhelmed with grief,
And Heaven's cruelty is beyond belief;
It seems now that a brutal stroke of fate
May force my love and me to separate.
My father, just this minute, chanced to appear,
Alighting from his coach not far from here,
And what has brought him into town this morning
Is a dire errand of which I'd had no warning:
He's made a match for me, and, ready or not,
I am to marry someone on the spot.
Imagine my despair! What blacker curse
Could fall on me, what setback could be worse?
I told you, yesterday, of Enrique. It's he
Who's brought about my present misery;
He's come with Father, to lead me to the slaughter,
And I am doomed to wed his only daughter.
When they told me that, it almost made me swoon;
And, since my father spoke of coming soon
To see you, I excused myself, in fright,
And hastened to forewarn you of my plight.
Take care, Sir, I entreat you, not to let him
Know of Agnès and me; 't would much upset him.
And try, since he so trusts your judgment, to
Dissuade him from the match he has in view.

[*Act Five · Scene Six*]

ARNOLPHE

I shall.

HORACE

That failing, you could be of aid
By urging that the wedding be delayed.

ARNOLPHE

Trust me.

HORACE

On you, my dearest hopes repose.

ARNOLPHE

Fine, fine.

HORACE

You're a father to me, Heaven knows.
Tell him that young men— Ah! He's coming! I spy him.
Here are some arguments with which to ply him.
 (*They withdraw to a corner of the stage, and
 confer in whispers.*)

SCENE SEVEN

ENRIQUE, ORONTE, CHRYSALDE, HORACE, ARNOLPHE

ENRIQUE, *to Chrysalde*

No need for introductions, Sir. I knew
Your name as soon as I set eyes on you.
You have the very features of your late
Sister, who was my well-belovèd mate;
Oh, how I wish that cruel Destiny
Had let me bring my helpmeet back with me,
After such years of hardship as we bore,
To see her home and family once more.
But fate has ruled that we shall not again
Enjoy her charming presence; let us, then,
Find solace in what joys we may design
For the sole offspring of her love and mine.
You are concerned in this; let us confer,
And see if you approve my plans for her.
Oronte's young son, I think, is a splendid choice;
But in this matter you've an equal voice.

CHRYSALDE

I've better judgment, Brother, than to question
So eminently worthy a suggestion.

[*Act Five · Scene Seven*]

ARNOLPHE, *to Horace*

Yes, yes, don't worry; I'll represent you well.

HORACE

Once more, don't tell him—

ARNOLPHE

I promise not to tell.
(*Arnolphe leaves Horace, and crosses to
embrace Oronte.*)

ORONTE

Ah, my old friend: what a warm, hearty greeting!

ARNOLPHE

Oronte, dear fellow, what a welcome meeting!

ORONTE

I've come to town—

ARNOLPHE

You needn't say a word;
I know what brings you.

ORONTE

You've already heard?

143

ARNOLPHE

Yes.

ORONTE

Good.

ARNOLPHE

      Your son regards this match with dread;
His heart rebels at being forced to wed,
And I've been asked, in fact, to plead his case.
Well, do you know what I'd do, in your place?
I'd exercise a father's rightful sway
And tie the wedding knot without delay.
What the young need, my friend, is discipline;
We only do them harm by giving in.

HORACE, *aside*

Traitor!

CHRYSALDE

      If the prospect fills him with revulsion,
Then surely we should not employ compulsion.
My brother-in-law, I trust, would say the same.

ARNOLPHE

Shall a man be governed by his son? For shame!
Would you have a father be so meek and mild
As not to exact obedience from his child?

[*Act Five · Scene Seven*]

At his wise age, 't would be grotesque indeed
To see him led by one whom he should lead.
No, no; my dear old friend is honor-bound;
He's given his word, and he must not give ground.
Let him be firm, as a father should, and force
His son to take the necessary course.

ORONTE

Well said: we shall proceed with this alliance,
And I shall answer for my son's compliance.

CHRYSALDE, *to Arnolphe*

It much surprises me to hear you press
For this betrothal with such eagerness.
What is your motive? I can't make you out.

ARNOLPHE

Don't worry, friend; I know what I'm about.

ORONTE

Indeed, Arnolphe—

CHRYSALDE

             He finds that name unpleasant.
Monsieur de la Souche is what he's called at present.

ARNOLPHE

No matter.

145

[*Act Five · Scene Seven*]

HORACE

What do I hear?

ARNOLPHE, *turning toward Horace*

Well, now you know,
And now you see why I have spoken so.

HORACE

Oh, what confusion—

SCENE EIGHT

GEORGETTE, ENRIQUE, ORONTE, CHRYSALDE,
HORACE, ARNOLPHE

GEORGETTE

     Sir, please come. Unless
You do, I fear we can't restrain Agnès.
The girl is frantic to escape, I swear,
And might jump out of the window in despair.

ARNOLPHE

Bring her to me: I'll take her away from here
Posthaste, this very minute.
  (*To Horace:*)
      Be of good cheer.
Too much good luck could spoil you; and, as they say
In the proverb, every dog must have his day.

HORACE

What man, O Heaven, was ever betrayed like this,
Or hurled into so hopeless an abyss?

ARNOLPHE, *to Oronte*

Pray don't delay the nuptials—which, dear friend,
I shall be most delighted to attend.

ORONTE

I shan't delay.

SCENE NINE

AGNÈS, ALAIN, GEORGETTE, ORONTE, ENRIQUE,
ARNOLPHE, HORACE, CHRYSALDE

ARNOLPHE

Come, come, my pretty child,
You who are so intractable and wild.
Here is your gallant: perhaps he should receive
A little curtsey from you, as you leave.
(*To Horace:*)
Farewell: your sweet hopes seem to have turned to gall;
But love, my boy, can't always conquer all.

AGNÈS

Horace! Will you let him take me away from you?

HORACE

I'm dazed with grief, and don't know what to do.

ARNOLPHE

Come, chatterbox.

AGNÈS

No. Here I shall remain.

[*Act Five · Scene Nine*]

ORONTE

Now, what's the mystery? Will you please explain?
All this is very odd; we're baffled by it.

ARNOLPHE

When I've more time, I'll gladly clarify it.
Till then, good-bye.

ORONTE

                Where is it you mean to go?
And why won't you tell us what we ask to know?

ARNOLPHE

I've told you that, despite your stubborn son,
You ought to hold the wedding.

ORONTE

                    It shall be done.
But weren't you told that his intended spouse
Is the young woman who's living in your house—
The long-lost child of that dear Angélique
Who secretly was married to Enrique?
What, then, did your behavior mean just now?

CHRYSALDE

His words amazed me, too, I must allow.

[*Act Five · Scene Nine*]

ARNOLPHE

What? What?

CHRYSALDE

My sister married secretly;
Her daughter's birth was kept from the family.

ORONTE

The child was placed with an old country dame,
Who reared her under a fictitious name.

CHRYSALDE

My sister's husband, beset by circumstance,
Was soon obliged to take his leave of France,

ORONTE

And undergo great trials and miseries
In a strange, savage land beyond the seas,

CHRYSALDE

Where, through his labors, he regained abroad
What here he'd lost through men's deceit and fraud.

ORONTE

Returning home, he sought at once to find
The nurse to whom his child had been consigned,

[*Act Five · Scene Nine*]

CHRYSALDE

And the good creature told him, as was true,
That she'd transferred her little charge to you,

ORONTE

Because of your benevolent disposition,
And the dire poverty of her condition.

CHRYSALDE

What's more, Enrique, transported with delight,
Has brought the woman here to set things right.

ORONTE

She'll join us in a moment, and then we'll see
A public end to all this mystery.

CHRYSALDE, *to Arnolphe*

I know that you're in a painful state of mind;
Yet what the Fates have done is not unkind.
Since your chief treasure is a hornless head,
The safest course, for you, is not to wed.

ARNOLPHE, *leaving in a speechless passion*

Oof!

ORONTE

Why is he rushing off without a word?

HORACE

Father, a great coincidence has occurred.
What in your wisdom you projected, chance
Has wondrously accomplished in advance.
The fact is, Sir, that I am bound already,
By the sweet ties of love, to this fair lady;
It's she whom you have come to seek, and she
For whose sake I opposed your plans for me.

ENRIQUE

I recognized her from the very first,
With such deep joy, I thought my heart would burst.
Dear daughter, let me take you in my embrace.
                    (*He does so.*)

CHRYSALDE

I have the same urge, Brother, but this place
Will hardly do for private joys like these.
Let us go in, resolve all mysteries,
Commend our friend Arnolphe, and for the rest
Thank Heaven, which orders all things for the best.

The Misanthrope

COMEDY IN FIVE ACTS, 1666

Drawings by Enrico Arno

To Harry Levin

INTRODUCTION

The idea that comedy is a ritual in which society's laughter corrects individual extravagance is particularly inapplicable to *The Misanthrope*. In this play, society itself is indicted, and though Alceste's criticisms are indiscriminate, they are not unjustified. It is true that falseness and intrigue are everywhere on view; the conventions enforce a routine dishonesty, justice is subverted by influence, love is overwhelmed by calculation, and these things are accepted, even by the best, as "natural." The cold vanity of Oronte, Acaste, and Clitandre, the malignant hypocrisy of Arsinoé, the insincerity of Célimène, are to be taken as exemplary of the age, and Philinte's philosophic tolerance will not quite do in response to such a condition of things. The honest Éliante is the one we are most to trust, and this is partly because she sees that Alceste's intransigence *A quelque chose en soy de noble & d'héroïque.*

But *The Misanthrope* is not only a critique of society; it is also a study of impurity of motive in a critic of society. If Alceste has a rage for the genuine, and he truly has, it is unfortunately compromised and exploited by his vast, unconscious egotism. He is a jealous friend (*Je veux qu'on me distingue*), and it is Philinte's polite effusiveness toward another which prompts his attack on promiscuous civility. He is a jealous lover, and his "frankness" about Oronte's sonnet owes something to the fact that Oronte is his rival, and that the sonnet is addressed to Célimène. Like many humorless and indignant people, he is hard on everybody but himself, and does not perceive it when he fails his own ideal. In one aspect, Alceste seems a moral giant misplaced in a trivial society, having (in George Eliot's phrase) "a certain spiritual grandeur ill-matched with the meanness of opportunity"; in another aspect, he seems an unconscious fraud who magnifies the petty faults of others in order to dramatize himself in his own eyes.

He is, of course, both at once: but the two impressions predominate by turns. A victim, like all around him, of the moral enervation of the times, he cannot consistently be the Man of Honor—simple, magnanimous, passionate, decisive, true. It is his distinction that he is aware of that ideal, and that he can fitfully embody it; his comic flaw consists in a Quixotic confusion of himself with the ideal, a willingness to distort the world for his own self-deceptive and histrionic purposes. Paradoxically, then, the advocate of true feeling and honest intercourse is the one character most artificial, most out-of-touch, most in danger of that nonentity and solitude which all, in the chattery, hollow world of this play, are fleeing. He must play-act continually in order to believe in his own existence, and he welcomes the fact or show of injustice as a dramatic cue. At the close of the play, when Alceste has refused to appeal his lawsuit and has spurned the hand of Célimène, one cannot escape the suspicion that his indignation is in great part instrumental, a desperate means of counterfeiting an identity.

Martin Turnell (whose book *The Classical Moment* contains a fine analysis of *The Misanthrope*) observes that those speeches of Alceste which ring most false are, as it were, parodies of "Cornelian *tirade*." To duplicate this parody-tragic effect in English it was clearly necessary to keep the play in verse, where it would be possible to control the tone more sharply, and to recall our own tragic tradition. There were other reasons, too, for approximating Molière's form. The constant of rhythm and rhyme was needed, in the translation as in the original, for bridging great gaps between high comedy and farce, lofty diction and ordinary talk, deep character and shallow. Again, while prose might

preserve the thematic structure of the play, other "musical"
elements would be lost, in particular the frequently intricate
arrangements of balancing half-lines, lines, couplets, quatrains, and sestets. There is no question that words, when
dancing within such patterns, are not their prosaic selves,
but have a wholly different mood and meaning.

Consider, finally, two peculiarities of the dialogue of the
play: redundancy and logic. When Molière has a character
repeat essentially the same thing in three successive couplets,
it will sometimes have a very clear dramatic point; but it
will always have the intention of stabilizing the idea against
the movement of the verse, and of giving a specifically rhe-
torical pleasure. In a prose rendering, these latter effects are
lost, and the passage tends to seem merely prolix. As for
logic, it is a convention of *The Misanthrope* that its main
characters can express themselves logically, and in the most
complex grammar; Molière's dramatic verse, which is almost
wholly free of metaphor, derives much of its richness from
argumentative virtuosity. Here is a bit of logic from
Arsinoé:

> *Madame, l'Amitié doit sur tout éclater*
> *Aux choses qui le plus nous peuvent importer:*
> *Et comme il n'en est point de plus grande importance*
> *Que celles de l'Honneur et de la Bienséance,*
> *Je viens par un avis qui touche vostre honneur*
> *Témoigner l'amitié que pour vous a mon Coeur.*

In prose it might come out like this: "Madam, friendship
should most display itself when truly vital matters are in
question: and since there are no things more vital than
decency and honor, I have come to prove my heartfelt
friendship by giving you some advice which concerns your
reputation." Even if that were better rendered, it would
still be plain that Molière's logic loses all its baroque exuber-
ance in prose; it sounds lawyerish; without rhyme and verse

to phrase and emphasize the steps of its progression, the logic becomes obscure like Congreve's, not crystalline and followable as it was meant to be.

For all these reasons, rhymed verse seemed to me obligatory. The choice did not preclude accuracy, and what follows is, I believe, a line-for-line verse translation quite as faithful as any which have been done in prose. I hasten to say that I am boasting only of patience; a translation may, alas, be faithful on all counts, and still lack quality.

One word about diction. This is a play in which French aristocrats of 1666 converse about their special concerns, and employ the moral and philosophical terms peculiar to their thought. Not all my words, therefore, are strictly modern; I had for example to use "spleen" and "phlegm"; but I think that I have avoided the zounds sort of thing, and that at best the diction mediates between then and now, suggesting no one period. There are occasional vulgarities, but for these there is precedent in the original, Molière's people being aristocrats and therefore not genteel.

If this English version is played or read aloud, the names should be pronounced in a fashion *roughly* French, without nasal and uvular agonies. Damon should be *dah-MOAN*, and for rhythmic convenience Arsinoé should be *ar-SIN-oh-eh*.

My translation was begun in late 1952 in New Mexico, during a fellowship from the Guggenheim Foundation, and finished this year in Rome under grants from the American Academy of Arts & Letters and the Chapelbrook Foundation. To these organizations, and to certain individuals who have befriended the project, I am very grateful.

CHARACTERS

ALCESTE, in love with Célimène
PHILINTE, Alceste's friend
ORONTE, in love with Célimène
CÉLIMÈNE, Alceste's beloved
ELIANTE, Célimène's cousin
ARSINOÉ, a friend of Célimène's
ACASTE ⎫
CLITANDRE ⎬ marquesses
BASQUE, Célimène's servant
A GUARD of the Marshalsea
DUBOIS, Alceste's valet

The scene throughout is in Célimène's house at Paris.

First produced by The Poets' Theatre, *Cambridge, on October 25th, 1955*

Act 1

SCENE ONE

PHILINTE, ALCESTE

PHILINTE

Now, what's got into you?

ALCESTE, *seated*

Kindly leave me alone.

PHILINTE

Come, come, what is it? This lugubrious tone . . .

ALCESTE

Leave me, I said; you spoil my solitude.

PHILINTE

Oh, listen to me, now, and don't be rude.

ALCESTE

I choose to be rude, Sir, and to be hard of hearing.

163

PHILINTE

These ugly moods of yours are not endearing;
Friends though we are, I really must insist . . .

ALCESTE, *abruptly rising*

Friends? Friends, you say? Well, cross me off your list.
I've been your friend till now, as you well know;
But after what I saw a moment ago
I tell you flatly that our ways must part.
I wish no place in a dishonest heart.

PHILINTE

Why, what have I done, Alceste? Is this quite just?

ALCESTE

My God, you ought to die of self-disgust.
I call your conduct inexcusable, Sir,
And every man of honor will concur.
I see you almost hug a man to death,
Exclaim for joy until you're out of breath,
And supplement these loving demonstrations
With endless offers, vows, and protestations;
Then when I ask you "Who was that?", I find
That you can barely bring his name to mind!
Once the man's back is turned, you cease to love him,
And speak with absolute indifference of him!
By God, I say it's base and scandalous
To falsify the heart's affections thus;

[*Act One · Scene One*]

If I caught myself behaving in such a way,
I'd hang myself for shame, without delay.

PHILINTE

It hardly seems a hanging matter to me;
I hope that you will take it graciously
If I extend myself a slight reprieve,
And live a little longer, by your leave.

ALCESTE

How dare you joke about a crime so grave?

PHILINTE

What crime? How else are people to behave?

ALCESTE

I'd have them be sincere, and never part
With any word that isn't from the heart.

PHILINTE

When someone greets us with a show of pleasure,
It's but polite to give him equal measure,
Return his love the best that we know how,
And trade him offer for offer, vow for vow.

ALCESTE

No, no, this formula you'd have me follow,
However fashionable, is false and hollow,

And I despise the frenzied operations
Of all these barterers of protestations,
These lavishers of meaningless embraces,
These utterers of obliging commonplaces,
Who court and flatter everyone on earth
And praise the fool no less than the man of worth.
Should you rejoice that someone fondles you,
Offers his love and service, swears to be true,
And fills your ears with praises of your name,
When to the first damned fop he'll say the same?
No, no: no self-respecting heart would dream
Of prizing so promiscuous an esteem;
However high the praise, there's nothing worse
Than sharing honors with the universe.
Esteem is founded on comparison:
To honor all men is to honor none.
Since you embrace this indiscriminate vice,
Your friendship comes at far too cheap a price;
I spurn the easy tribute of a heart
Which will not set the worthy man apart:
I choose, Sir, to be chosen; and in fine,
The friend of mankind is no friend of mine.

PHILINTE

But in polite society, custom decrees
That we show certain outward courtesies. . . .

ALCESTE

Ah, no! we should condemn with all our force
Such false and artificial intercourse.
Let men behave like men; let them display

[*Act One · Scene One*]

Their inmost hearts in everything they say;
Let the heart speak, and let our sentiments
Not mask themselves in silly compliments.

PHILINTE

In certain cases it would be uncouth
And most absurd to speak the naked truth;
With all respect for your exalted notions,
It's often best to veil one's true emotions.
Wouldn't the social fabric come undone
If we were wholly frank with everyone?
Suppose you met with someone you couldn't bear;
Would you inform him of it then and there?

ALCESTE

Yes.

PHILINTE

Then you'd tell old Emilie it's pathetic
The way she daubs her features with cosmetic
And plays the gay coquette at sixty-four?

ALCESTE

I would.

PHILINTE

And you'd call Dorilas a bore,
And tell him every ear at court is lame
From hearing him brag about his noble name?

ALCESTE

Precisely.

PHILINTE

Ah, you're joking.

ALCESTE

Au contraire:
In this regard there's none I'd choose to spare.
All are corrupt; there's nothing to be seen
In court or town but aggravates my spleen.
I fall into deep gloom and melancholy
When I survey the scene of human folly,
Finding on every hand base flattery,
Injustice, fraud, self-interest, treachery. . . .
Ah, it's too much; mankind has grown so base,
I mean to break with the whole human race.

PHILINTE

This philosophic rage is a bit extreme;
You've no idea how comical you seem;
Indeed, we're like those brothers in the play
Called *School for Husbands*, one of whom was
   prey . . .

ALCESTE

Enough, now! None of your stupid similes.

168

[*Act One · Scene One*]

PHILINTE

Then let's have no more tirades, if you please.
The world won't change, whatever you say or do;
And since plain speaking means so much to you,
I'll tell you plainly that by being frank
You've earned the reputation of a crank,
And that you're thought ridiculous when you rage
And rant against the manners of the age.

ALCESTE

So much the better; just what I wish to hear.
No news could be more grateful to my ear.
All men are so detestable in my eyes,
I should be sorry if they thought me wise.

PHILINTE

Your hatred's very sweeping, is it not?

ALCESTE

Quite right: I hate the whole degraded lot.

PHILINTE

Must all poor human creatures be embraced,
Without distinction, by your vast distaste?
Even in these bad times, there are surely a few . . .

ALCESTE

No, I include all men in one dim view:
Some men I hate for being rogues; the others
I hate because they treat the rogues like brothers,
And, lacking a virtuous scorn for what is vile,
Receive the villain with a complaisant smile.
Notice how tolerant people choose to be
Toward that bold rascal who's at law with me.
His social polish can't conceal his nature;
One sees at once that he's a treacherous creature;
No one could possibly be taken in
By those soft speeches and that sugary grin.
The whole world knows the shady means by which
The low-brow's grown so powerful and rich,
And risen to a rank so bright and high
That virtue can but blush, and merit sigh.
Whenever his name comes up in conversation,
None will defend his wretched reputation;
Call him knave, liar, scoundrel, and all the rest,
Each head will nod, and no one will protest.
And yet his smirk is seen in every house,
He's greeted everywhere with smiles and bows,
And when there's any honor that can be got
By pulling strings, he'll get it, like as not.
My God! It chills my heart to see the ways
Men come to terms with evil nowadays;
Sometimes, I swear, I'm moved to flee and find
Some desert land unfouled by humankind.

[*Act One · Scene One*]

PHILINTE

Come, let's forget the follies of the times
And pardon mankind for its petty crimes;
Let's have an end of rantings and of railings,
And show some leniency toward human failings.
This world requires a pliant rectitude;
Too stern a virtue makes one stiff and rude;
Good sense views all extremes with detestation,
And bids us to be noble in moderation.
The rigid virtues of the ancient days
Are not for us; they jar with all our ways
And ask of us too lofty a perfection.
Wise men accept their times without objection,
And there's no greater folly, if you ask me,
Than trying to reform society.
Like you, I see each day a hundred and one
Unhandsome deeds that might be better done,
But still, for all the faults that meet my view,
I'm never known to storm and rave like you.
I take men as they are, or let them be,
And teach my soul to bear their frailty;
And whether in court or town, whatever the scene,
My phlegm's as philosophic as your spleen.

ALCESTE

This phlegm which you so eloquently commend,
Does nothing ever rile it up, my friend?
Suppose some man you trust should treacherously
Conspire to rob you of your property,
And do his best to wreck your reputation?
Wouldn't you feel a certain indignation?

[*Act One · Scene One*]

PHILINTE

Why, no. These faults of which you so complain
Are part of human nature, I maintain,
And it's no more a matter for disgust
That men are knavish, selfish and unjust,
Than that the vulture dines upon the dead,
And wolves are furious, and apes ill-bred.

ALCESTE

Shall I see myself betrayed, robbed, torn to bits,
And not . . . Oh, let's be still and rest our wits.
Enough of reasoning, now. I've had my fill.

PHILINTE

Indeed, you would do well, Sir, to be still.
Rage less at your opponent, and give some thought
To how you'll win this lawsuit that he's brought.

ALCESTE

I assure you I'll do nothing of the sort.

PHILINTE

Then who will plead your case before the court?

ALCESTE

Reason and right and justice will plead for me.

[*Act One · Scene One*]

PHILINTE

Oh, Lord. What judges do you plan to see?

ALCESTE

Why, none. The justice of my cause is clear.

PHILINTE

Of course, man; but there's politics to fear. . . .

ALCESTE

No, I refuse to lift a hand. That's flat.
I'm either right, or wrong.

PHILINTE

        Don't count on that.

ALCESTE

No, I'll do nothing.

PHILINTE

        Your enemy's influence
Is great, you know . . .

ALCESTE

        That makes no difference.

[*Act One · Scene One*]

PHILINTE

It will; you'll see.

ALCESTE

    Must honor bow to guile?
If so, I shall be proud to lose the trial.

PHILINTE

Oh, really . . .

ALCESTE

    I'll discover by this case
Whether or not men are sufficiently base
And impudent and villainous and perverse
To do me wrong before the universe.

PHILINTE

What a man!

ALCESTE

    Oh, I could wish, whatever the cost,
Just for the beauty of it, that my trial were lost.

PHILINTE

If people heard you talking so, Alceste,
They'd split their sides. Your name would be a jest.

174

[*Act One · Scene One*]

ALCESTE

So much the worse for jesters.

PHILINTE

                              May I enquire
Whether this rectitude you so admire,
And these hard virtues you're enamored of
Are qualities of the lady whom you love?
It much surprises me that you, who seem
To view mankind with furious disesteem,
Have yet found something to enchant your eyes
Amidst a species which you so despise.
And what is more amazing, I'm afraid,
Is the most curious choice your heart has made.
The honest Eliante is fond of you,
Arsinoé, the prude, admires you too;
And yet your spirit's been perversely led
To choose the flighty Célimène instead,
Whose brittle malice and coquettish ways
So typify the manners of our days.
How is it that the traits you most abhor
Are bearable in this lady you adore?
Are you so blind with love that you can't find them?
Or do you contrive, in her case, not to mind them?

ALCESTE

My love for that young widow's not the kind
That can't perceive defects; no, I'm not blind.
I see her faults, despite my ardent love,

[*Act One · Scene One*]

And all I see I fervently reprove.
And yet I'm weak; for all her falsity,
That woman knows the art of pleasing me,
And though I never cease complaining of her,
I swear I cannot manage not to love her.
Her charm outweighs her faults; I can but aim
To cleanse her spirit in my love's pure flame.

PHILINTE

That's no small task; I wish you all success.
You think then that she loves you?

ALCESTE

       Heavens, yes!
I wouldn't love her did she not love me.

PHILINTE

Well, if her taste for you is plain to see,
Why do these rivals cause you such despair?

ALCESTE

True love, Sir, is possessive, and cannot bear
To share with all the world. I'm here today
To tell her she must send that mob away.

PHILINTE

If I were you, and had your choice to make,
Eliante, her cousin, would be the one I'd take;

176

[*Act One · Scene One*]

That honest heart, which cares for you alone,
Would harmonize far better with your own.

ALCESTE

True, true: each day my reason tells me so;
But reason doesn't rule in love, you know. ⌇ *love*

PHILINTE

I fear some bitter sorrow is in store;
This love . . .

SCENE TWO

ORONTE, *to Alceste*

The servants told me at the door
That Eliante and Célimène were out,
But when I heard, dear Sir, that you were about,
I came to say, without exaggeration,
That I hold you in the vastest admiration,
And that it's always been my dearest desire
To be the friend of one I so admire.
I hope to see my love of merit requited,
And you and me in friendship's bond united.
I'm sure you won't refuse—if I may be frank—
A friend of my devotedness—and rank.
> (*During this speech of Oronte's, Alceste is ab-*
> *stracted, and seems unaware that he is being*
> *spoken to. He only breaks off his reverie when*
> *Oronte says:*)
It was for you, if you please, that my words were in-
tended.

ALCESTE

For me, Sir?

ORONTE

Yes, for you. You're not offended?

ALCESTE

By no means. But this much surprises me. . . .
The honor comes most unexpectedly. . . .

ORONTE

My high regard should not astonish you;
The whole world feels the same. It is your due.

ALCESTE

Sir . . .

ORONTE

Why, in all the State there isn't one
Can match your merits; they shine, Sir, like the sun.

ALCESTE

Sir . . .

ORONTE

You are higher in my estimation
Than all that's most illustrious in the nation.

[*Act One · Scene Two*]

ALCESTE

Sir . . .

ORONTE

If I lie, may heaven strike me dead!
To show you that I mean what I have said,
Permit me, Sir, to embrace you most sincerely,
And swear that I will prize our friendship dearly.
Give me your hand. And now, Sir, if you choose,
We'll make our vows.

ALCESTE

Sir . . .

ORONTE

What! You refuse?

ALCESTE

Sir, it's a very great honor you extend:
But friendship is a sacred thing, my friend;
It would be profanation to bestow
The name of friend on one you hardly know.
All parts are better played when well-rehearsed;
Let's put off friendship, and get acquainted first.
We may discover it would be unwise
To try to make our natures harmonize.

[*Act One · Scene Two*]

ORONTE

By heaven! You're sagacious to the core;
This speech has made me admire you even more.
Let time, then, bring us closer day by day;
Meanwhile, I shall be yours in every way.
If, for example, there should be anything
You wish at court, I'll mention it to the King.
I have his ear, of course; it's quite well known
That I am much in favor with the throne.
In short, I am your servant. And now, dear friend,
Since you have such fine judgment, I intend
To please you, if I can, with a small sonnet
I wrote not long ago. Please comment on it,
And tell me whether I ought to publish it.

ALCESTE

You must excuse me, Sir; I'm hardly fit
To judge such matters.

ORONTE

Why not?

ALCESTE

                    I am, I fear,
Inclined to be unfashionably sincere.

ORONTE

Just what I ask; I'd take no satisfaction
In anything but your sincere reaction.
I beg you not to dream of being kind.

ALCESTE

Since you desire it, Sir, I'll speak my mind.

ORONTE

Sonnet. It's a sonnet. . . . *Hope* . . . The poem's ad-
dressed
To a lady who wakened hopes within my breast.
Hope . . . this is not the pompous sort of thing,
Just modest little verses, with a tender ring.

ALCESTE

Well, we shall see.

ORONTE

                    Hope . . . I'm anxious to hear
Whether the style seems properly smooth and clear,
And whether the choice of words is good or bad.

ALCESTE

We'll see, we'll see.

ORONTE

Perhaps I ought to add
That it took me only a quarter-hour to write it.

ALCESTE

The time's irrelevant, Sir: kindly recite it.

ORONTE, *reading*

Hope comforts us awhile, t'is true,
Lulling our cares with careless laughter,
And yet such joy is full of rue,
My Phyllis, if nothing follows after.

PHILINTE

I'm charmed by this already; the style's delightful.

ALCESTE, *sotto voce, to Philinte*

How can you say that? Why, the thing is frightful.

ORONTE

Your fair face smiled on me awhile,
But was it kindness so to enchant me?
'Twould have been fairer not to smile,
If hope was all you meant to grant me.

[Act One · Scene Two]

PHILINTE

What a clever thought! How handsomely you phrase it!

ALCESTE, *sotto voce, to Philinte*

You know the thing is trash. How dare you praise it?

ORONTE

If it's to be my passion's fate
Thus everlastingly to wait,
Then death will come to set me free:
For death is fairer than the fair;
Phyllis, to hope is to despair
When one must hope eternally.

PHILINTE

The close is exquisite—full of feeling and grace.

ALCESTE, *sotto voce, aside*

Oh, blast the close; you'd better close your face
Before you send your lying soul to hell.

PHILINTE

I can't remember a poem I've liked so well.

[*Act One · Scene Two*]

ALCESTE, *sotto voce, aside*

Good Lord!

ORONTE, *to Philinte*

I fear you're flattering me a bit.

PHILINTE

Oh, no!

ALCESTE, *sotto voce, aside*

What else d'you call it, you hypocrite?

ORONTE, *to Alceste*

But you, Sir, keep your promise now: don't shrink
From telling me sincerely what you think.

ALCESTE

Sir, these are delicate matters; we all desire
To be told that we've the true poetic fire.
But once, to one whose name I shall not mention,
I said, regarding some verse of his invention,
That gentlemen should rigorously control
That itch to write which often afflicts the soul;
That one should curb the heady inclination
To publicize one's little avocation;
And that in showing off one's works of art
One often plays a very clownish part.

[*Act One · Scene Two*]

ORONTE

Are you suggesting in a devious way
That I ought not . . .

ALCESTE

                        Oh, that I do not say.
Further, I told him that no fault is worse
Than that of writing frigid, lifeless verse,
And that the merest whisper of such a shame
Suffices to destroy a man's good name.

ORONTE

D'you mean to say my sonnet's dull and trite?

ALCESTE

I don't say that. But I went on to cite
Numerous cases of once-respected men
Who came to grief by taking up the pen.

ORONTE

And am I like them? Do I write so poorly?

ALCESTE

I don't say that. But I told this person, "Surely
You're under no necessity to compose;
Why you should wish to publish, heaven knows.

186

[*Act One · Scene Two*]

There's no excuse for printing tedious rot
Unless one writes for bread, as you do not.
Resist temptation, then, I beg of you;
Conceal your pastimes from the public view;
And don't give up, on any provocation,
Your present high and courtly reputation,
To purchase at a greedy printer's shop
The name of silly author and scribbling fop."
These were the points I tried to make him see.

ORONTE

I sense that they are also aimed at me;
But now—about my sonnet—I'd like to be told . . .

ALCESTE

Frankly, that sonnet should be pigeonholed.
You've chosen the worst models to imitate.
The style's unnatural. Let me illustrate:

For example, *Your fair face smiled on me awhile,*
Followed by, *'Twould have been fairer not to smile!*
Or this: *such joy is full of rue;*
Or this: *For death is fairer than the fair;*
Or, *Phyllis, to hope is to despair*
    When one must hope eternally!

This artificial style, that's all the fashion,
Has neither taste, nor honesty, nor passion;
It's nothing but a sort of wordy play,
And nature never spoke in such a way.
What, in this shallow age, is not debased?
Our fathers, though less refined, had better taste;

187

I'd barter all that men admire today
For one old love-song I shall try to say:

> *If the King had given me for my own*
> *Paris, his citadel,*
> *And I for that must leave alone*
> *Her whom I love so well,*
> *I'd say then to the Crown,*
> *Take back your·glittering town;*
> *My darling is more fair, I swear,*
> *My darling is more fair.*

The rhyme's not rich, the style is rough and old,
But don't you see that it's the purest gold
Beside the tinsel nonsense now preferred,
And that there's passion in its every word?

> *If the King had given me for my own*
> *Paris, his citadel,*
> *And I for that must leave alone*
> *Her whom I love so well,*
> *I'd say then to the Crown,*
> *Take back your glittering town;*
> *My darling is more fair, I swear,*
> *My darling is more fair.*

There speaks a loving heart. (*To Philinte*) You're laugh-
    ing, eh?
Laugh on, my precious wit. Whatever you say,
I hold that song's worth all the bibelots
That people hail today with ah's and oh's.

ORONTE

And I maintain my sonnet's very good.

ALCESTE

It's not at all surprising that you should.
You have your reasons; permit me to have mine
For thinking that you cannot write a line.

ORONTE

Others have praised my sonnet to the skies.

ALCESTE

I lack their art of telling pleasant lies.

ORONTE

You seem to think you've got no end of wit.

ALCESTE

To praise your verse, I'd need still more of it.

ORONTE

I'm not in need of your approval, Sir.

ALCESTE

That's good; you couldn't have it if you were.

[*Act One* · *Scene Two*]

ORONTE

Come now, I'll lend you the subject of my sonnet;
I'd like to see you try to improve upon it.

ALCESTE

I might, by chance, write something just as shoddy;
But then I wouldn't show it to everybody.

ORONTE

You're most opinionated and conceited.

ALCESTE

Go find your flatterers, and be better treated.

ORONTE

Look here, my little fellow, pray watch your tone.

ALCESTE

My great big fellow, you'd better watch your own.

PHILINTE, *stepping between them*

Oh, please, please, gentlemen! This will never do.

[*Act One · Scene Two*]

ORONTE

The fault is mine, and I leave the field to you.
I am your servant, Sir, in every way.

ALCESTE

And I, Sir, am your most abject valet.

SCENE THREE

PHILINTE

Well, as you see, sincerity in excess
Can get you into a very pretty mess;
Oronte was hungry for appreciation. . . .

ALCESTE

Don't speak to me.

PHILINTE

What?

ALCESTE

No more conversation.

PHILINTE

Really, now . . .

192

[*Act One · Scene Three*]

ALCESTE

Leave me alone.

PHILINTE

If I . . .

ALCESTE

Out of my sight!

PHILINTE

But what . . .

ALCESTE

I won't listen.

PHILINTE

But . . .

ALCESTE

Silence!

PHILINTE

Now, is it polite . . .

ALCESTE

By heaven, I've had enough. Don't follow me.

PHILINTE

Ah, you're just joking. I'll keep you company.

Act 2

SCENE ONE

ALCESTE, CÉLIMÈNE

ALCESTE

Shall I speak plainly, Madam? I confess
Your conduct gives me infinite distress,
And my resentment's grown too hot to smother.
Soon, I foresee, we'll break with one another.
If I said otherwise, I should deceive you;
Sooner or later, I shall be forced to leave you,
And if I swore that we shall never part,
I should misread the omens of my heart.

CÉLIMÈNE

You kindly saw me home, it would appear,
So as to pour invectives in my ear.

ALCESTE

I've no desire to quarrel. But I deplore
Your inability to shut the door
On all these suitors who beset you so.
There's what annoys me, if you care to know.

[*Act Two · Scene One*]

CÉLIMÈNE

Is it my fault that all these men pursue me?
Am I to blame if they're attracted to me?
And when they gently beg an audience,
Ought I to take a stick and drive them hence?

ALCESTE

Madam, there's no necessity for a stick;
A less responsive heart would do the trick.
Of your attractiveness I don't complain;
But those your charms attract, you then detain
By a most melting and receptive manner,
And so enlist their hearts beneath your banner.
It's the agreeable hopes which you excite
That keep these lovers round you day and night;
Were they less liberally smiled upon,
That sighing troop would very soon be gone.
But tell me, Madam, why it is that lately
This man Clitandre interests you so greatly?
Because of what high merits do you deem
Him worthy of the honor of your esteem?
Is it that your admiring glances linger
On the splendidly long nail of his little finger?
Or do you share the general deep respect
For the blond wig he chooses to affect?
Are you in love with his embroidered hose?
Do you adore his ribbons and his bows?
Or is it that this paragon bewitches
Your tasteful eye with his vast German breeches?

198

Perhaps his giggle, or his falsetto voice,
Makes him the latest gallant of your choice?

CÉLIMÈNE

You're much mistaken to resent him so.
Why I put up with him you surely know:
My lawsuit's very shortly to be tried,
And I must have his influence on my side.

ALCESTE

Then lose your lawsuit, Madam, or let it drop;
Don't torture me by humoring such a fop.

CÉLIMÈNE

You're jealous of the whole world, Sir.

ALCESTE

                                    That's true,
Since the whole world is well-received by you.

CÉLIMÈNE

That my good nature is so unconfined
Should serve to pacify your jealous mind;
Were I to smile on one, and scorn the rest,
Then you might have some cause to be distressed.

199

[*Act Two* · *Scene One*]

ALCESTE

Well, if I mustn't be jealous, tell me, then,
Just how I'm better treated than other men.

CÉLIMÈNE

You know you have my love. Will that not do?

ALCESTE

What proof have I that what you say is true?

CÉLIMÈNE

I would expect, Sir, that my having said it
Might give the statement a sufficient credit.

ALCESTE

But how can I be sure that you don't tell
The selfsame thing to other men as well?

CÉLIMÈNE

What a gallant speech! How flattering to me!
What a sweet creature you make me out to be!
Well then, to save you from the pangs of doubt,
All that I've said I hereby cancel out;
Now, none but yourself shall make a monkey of you:
Are you content?

[*Act Two · Scene One*]

ALCESTE

Why, why am I doomed to love you?
I swear that I shall bless the blissful hour
When this poor heart's no longer in your power!
I make no secret of it: I've done my best
To exorcise this passion from my breast;
But thus far all in vain; it will not go;
It's for my sins that I must love you so.

CÉLIMÈNE

Your love for me is matchless, Sir; that's clear.

ALCESTE

Indeed, in all the world it has no peer;
Words can't describe the nature of my passion,
And no man ever loved in such a fashion.

CÉLIMÈNE

Yes, it's a brand-new fashion, I agree:
You show your love by castigating me,
And all your speeches are enraged and rude.
I've never been so furiously wooed.

ALCESTE

Yet you could calm that fury, if you chose.
Come, shall we bring our quarrels to a close?
Let's speak with open hearts, then, and begin . . .

201

SCENE TWO

CÉLIMÈNE

What is it?

BASQUE

Acaste is here.

CÉLIMÈNE

Well, send him in.

SCENE THREE

ALCESTE

What! Shall we never be alone at all?
You're always ready to receive a call,
And you can't bear, for ten ticks of the clock,
Not to keep open house for all who knock.

CÉLIMÈNE

I couldn't refuse him: he'd be most put out.

ALCESTE

Surely that's not worth worrying about.

CÉLIMÈNE

Acaste would never forgive me if he guessed
That I consider him a dreadful pest.

ALCESTE

If he's a pest, why bother with him then?

CÉLIMÈNE

Heavens! One can't antagonize such men;
Why, they're the chartered gossips of the court,
And have a say in things of every sort.
One must receive them, and be full of charm;
They're no great help, but they can do you harm,
And though your influence be ever so great,
They're hardly the best people to alienate.

important

ALCESTE

I see, dear lady, that you could make a case
For putting up with the whole human race;
These friendships that you calculate so nicely . . .

SCENE FOUR

ALCESTE, CÉLIMÈNE, BASQUE

BASQUE

Madam, Clitandre is here as well.

ALCESTE

Precisely.

CÉLIMÈNE

Where are you going?

ALCESTE

Elsewhere.

CÉLIMÈNE

Stay.

ALCESTE

No, no.

CÉLIMÈNE

Stay, Sir.

ALCESTE

I can't.

CÉLIMÈNE

I wish it.

ALCESTE

No, I must go.
I beg you, Madam, not to press the matter;
You know I have no taste for idle chatter.

CÉLIMÈNE

Stay: I command you.

ALCESTE

No, I cannot stay.

CÉLIMÈNE

Very well; you have my leave to go away.

SCENE FIVE

ELIANTE, PHILINTE, ACASTE, CLITANDRE, ALCESTE,
CÉLIMÈNE, BASQUE

ELIANTE, *to Célimène*

The Marquesses have kindly come to call.
Were they announced?

CÉLIMÈNE

Yes. Basque, bring chairs for all.
(*Basque provides the chairs, and exits.*)
(*To Alceste*)
You haven't gone?

ALCESTE

No; and I shan't depart
Till you decide who's foremost in your heart.

CÉLIMÈNE

Oh, hush.

ALCESTE

It's time to choose; take them, or me.

CÉLIMÈNE

You're mad.

ALCESTE

I'm not, as you shall shortly see.

CÉLIMÈNE

Oh?

ALCESTE

You'll decide.

CÉLIMÈNE

You're joking now, dear friend.

ALCESTE

No, no; you'll choose; my patience is at an end.

CLITANDRE

Madam, I come from court, where poor Cléonte
Behaved like a perfect fool, as is his wont.
Has he no friend to counsel him, I wonder,
And teach him less unerringly to blunder?

CÉLIMÈNE

It's true, the man's a most accomplished dunce;
His gauche behavior charms the eye at once;

And every time one sees him, on my word,
His manner's grown a trifle more absurd.

ACASTE

Speaking of dunces, I've just now conversed
With old Damon, who's one of the very worst;
I stood a lifetime in the broiling sun
Before his dreary monologue was done.

CÉLIMÈNE

Oh, he's a wondrous talker, and has the power
To tell you nothing hour after hour:
If, by mistake, he ever came to the point,
The shock would put his jawbone out of joint.

ELIANTE, *to Philinte*

The conversation takes its usual turn,
And all our dear friends' ears will shortly burn.

CLITANDRE

Timante's a character, Madam.

CÉLIMÈNE

                                    Isn't he, though?
A man of mystery from top to toe,
Who moves about in a romantic mist
On secret missions which do not exist.

His talk is full of eyebrows and grimaces;
How tired one gets of his momentous faces;
He's always whispering something confidential
Which turns out to be quite inconsequential;
Nothing's too slight for him to mystify;
He even whispers when he says "good-by."

ACASTE

Tell us about Géralde.

CÉLIMÈNE

                    That tiresome ass.
He mixes only with the titled class,
And fawns on dukes and princes, and is bored
With anyone who's not at least a lord.
The man's obsessed with rank, and his discourses
Are all of hounds and carriages and horses;
He uses Christian names with all the great,
And the word Milord, with him, is out of date.

CLITANDRE

He's very taken with Bélise, I hear.

CÉLIMÈNE

She is the dreariest company, poor dear.
Whenever she comes to call, I grope about
To find some topic which will draw her out,
But, owing to her dry and faint replies,

[*Act Two · Scene Five*]

The conversation wilts, and droops, and dies.
In vain one hopes to animate her face
By mentioning the ultimate commonplace;
But sun or shower, even hail or frost
Are matters she can instantly exhaust.
Meanwhile her visit, painful though it is,
Drags on and on through mute eternities,
And though you ask the time, and yawn, and yawn,
She sits there like a stone and won't be gone.

ACASTE

Now for Adraste.

CÉLIMÈNE

        Oh, that conceited elf
Has a gigantic passion for himself;
He rails against the court, and cannot bear it
That none will recognize his hidden merit;
All honors given to others give offense
To his imaginary excellence.

CLITANDRE

What about young Cléon? His house, they say,
Is full of the best society, night and day.

CÉLIMÈNE

His cook has made him popular, not he:
It's Cléon's table that people come to see.

[*Act Two · Scene Five*]

ELIANTE

He gives a splendid dinner, you must admit.

CÉLIMÈNE

But must he serve himself along with it?
For my taste, he's a most insipid dish
Whose presence sours the wine and spoils the fish.

PHILINTE

Damis, his uncle, is admired no end.
What's your opinion, Madam?

CÉLIMÈNE

                    Why, he's my friend.

PHILINTE

He seems a decent fellow, and rather clever.

CÉLIMÈNE

He works too hard at cleverness, however.
I hate to see him sweat and struggle so
To fill his conversation with bons mots.
Since he's decided to become a wit
His taste's so pure that nothing pleases it;
He scolds at all the latest books and plays,

[*Act Two · Scene Five*]

Thinking that wit must never stoop to praise,
That finding fault's a sign of intellect,
That all appreciation is abject,
And that by damning everything in sight
One shows oneself in a distinguished light.
He's scornful even of our conversations:
Their trivial nature sorely tries his patience;
He folds his arms, and stands above the battle,
And listens sadly to our childish prattle.

ACASTE

Wonderful, Madam! You've hit him off precisely.

CLITANDRE

No one can sketch a character so nicely.

ALCESTE

How bravely, Sirs, you cut and thrust at all
These absent fools, till one by one they fall:
But let one come in sight, and you'll at once
Embrace the man you lately called a dunce,
Telling him in a tone sincere and fervent
How proud you are to be his humble servant.

CLITANDRE

Why pick on us? Madame's been speaking, Sir,
And you should quarrel, if you must, with her.

213

[*Act Two* · *Scene Five*]

ALCESTE

No, no, by God, the fault is yours, because
You lead her on with laughter and applause,
And make her think that she's the more delightful
The more her talk is scandalous and spiteful.
Oh, she would stoop to malice far, far less
If no such claque approved her cleverness.
It's flatterers like you whose foolish praise
Nourishes all the vices of these days.

PHILINTE

But why protest when someone ridicules
Those you'd condemn, yourself, as knaves or fools?

CÉLIMÈNE

Why, Sir? Because he loves to make a fuss.
You don't expect him to agree with us,
When there's an opportunity to express
His heaven-sent spirit of contrariness?
What other people think, he can't abide;
Whatever they say, he's on the other side;
He lives in deadly terror of agreeing;
'Twould make him seem an ordinary being.
Indeed, he's so in love with contradiction,
He'll turn against his most profound conviction
And with a furious eloquence deplore it,
If only someone else is speaking for it.

214

[*Act Two · Scene Five*]

ALCESTE

Go on, dear lady, mock me as you please;
You have your audience in ecstasies.

PHILINTE

But what she says is true: you have a way
Of bridling at whatever people say;
Whether they praise or blame, your angry spirit
Is equally unsatisfied to hear it.

ALCESTE

Men, Sir, are always wrong, and that's the reason
That righteous anger's never out of season;
All that I hear in all their conversation
Is flattering praise or reckless condemnation.

CÉLIMÈNE

But . . .

ALCESTE

No, no, Madam, I am forced to state
That you have pleasures which I deprecate,
And that these others, here, are much to blame
For nourishing the faults which are your shame.

CLITANDRE

I shan't defend myself, Sir; but I vow
I'd thought this lady faultless until now.

215

ACASTE

I see her charms and graces, which are many;
But as for faults, I've never noticed any.

ALCESTE

I see them, Sir; and rather than ignore them,
I strenuously criticize her for them.
The more one loves, the more one should object
To every blemish, every least defect.
Were I this lady, I would soon get rid
Of lovers who approved of all I did,
And by their slack indulgence and applause
Endorsed my follies and excused my flaws.

CÉLIMÈNE

If all hearts beat according to your measure,
The dawn of love would be the end of pleasure;
And love would find its perfect consummation
In ecstasies of rage and reprobation.

ELIANTE

Love, as a rule, affects men otherwise,
And lovers rarely love to criticize.
They see their lady as a charming blur,
And find all things commendable in her.
If she has any blemish, fault, or shame,
They will redeem it by a pleasing name.
The pale-faced lady's lily-white, perforce;

The swarthy one's a sweet brunette, of course;
The spindly lady has a slender grace;
The fat one has a most majestic pace;
The plain one, with her dress in disarray,
They classify as *beauté négligée*;
The hulking one's a goddess in their eyes,
The dwarf, a concentrate of Paradise;
The haughty lady has a noble mind;
The mean one's witty, and the dull one's kind;
The chatterbox has liveliness and verve,
The mute one has a virtuous reserve.
So lovers manage, in their passion's cause,
To love their ladies even for their flaws.

ALCESTE

But I still say . . .

CÉLIMÈNE

     I think it would be nice
To stroll around the gallery once or twice.
What! You're not going, Sirs?

CLITANDRE AND ACASTE

      No, Madam, no.

ALCESTE

You seem to be in terror lest they go.
Do what you will, Sirs; leave, or linger on,
But I shan't go till after you are gone.

[*Act Two* · *Scene Five*]

ACASTE

I'm free to linger, unless I should perceive
Madame is tired, and wishes me to leave.

CLITANDRE

And as for me, I needn't go today
Until the hour of the King's *coucher.*

CÉLIMÈNE, *to Alceste*

You're joking, surely?

ALCESTE

Not in the least; we'll see
Whether you'd rather part with them, or me.

jealousy

SCENE SIX

ALCESTE, CÉLIMÈNE, ELIANTE, ACASTE, PHILINTE,
CLITANDRE, BASQUE

BASQUE, *to Alceste*

Sir, there's a fellow here who bids me state
That he must see you, and that it can't wait.

ALCESTE

Tell him that I have no such pressing affairs.

BASQUE

It's a long tailcoat that this fellow wears,
With gold all over.

CÉLIMÈNE, *to Alceste*

You'd best go down and see.
Or—have him enter.

SCENE SEVEN

ALCESTE, CÉLIMÈNE, ELIANTE, ACASTE, PHILINTE, CLITANDRE, A GUARD of the Marshalsea

ALCESTE, *confronting the guard*

Well, what do you want with me?
Come in, Sir.

GUARD

I've a word, Sir, for your ear.

ALCESTE

Speak it aloud, Sir; I shall strive to hear.

GUARD

The Marshals have instructed me to say
You must report to them without delay.

ALCESTE

Who? Me, Sir?

GUARD

Yes, Sir; you.

[*Act Two · Scene Seven*]

ALCESTE

But what do they want?

PHILINTE, *to Alceste*

To scotch your silly quarrel with Oronte.

CÉLIMÈNE, *to Philinte*

What quarrel?

PHILINTE

Oronte and he have fallen out
Over some verse he spoke his mind about;
The Marshals wish to arbitrate the matter.

ALCESTE

Never shall I equivocate or flatter!

PHILINTE

You'd best obey their summons; come, let's go.

ALCESTE

How can they mend our quarrel, I'd like to know?
Am I to make a cowardly retraction,
And praise those jingles to his satisfaction?
I'll not recant; I've judged that sonnet rightly.
It's bad.

PHILINTE

But you might say so more politely. . . .

ALCESTE

I'll not back down; his verses make me sick.

PHILINTE

If only you could be more politic!
But come, let's go.

ALCESTE

             I'll go, but I won't unsay
A single word.

PHILINTE

Well, let's be on our way.

ALCESTE

Till I am ordered by my lord the King
To praise that poem, I shall say the thing
Is scandalous, by God, and that the poet
Ought to be hanged for having the nerve to show it.
(*To Clitandre and Acaste, who are laughing*)
By heaven, Sirs, I really didn't know
That I was being humorous.

[*Act Two · Scene Seven*]

CÉLIMÈNE

Go, Sir, go;

Settle your business.

ALCESTE

I shall, and when I'm through,
I shall return to settle things with you.

Act 3

SCENE ONE

CLITANDRE

Dear Marquess, how contented you appear;
All things delight you, nothing mars your cheer.
Can you, in perfect honesty, declare
That you've a right to be so debonair?

ACASTE

By Jove, when I survey myself, I find
No cause whatever for distress of mind.
I'm young and rich; I can in modesty
Lay claim to an exalted pedigree;
And owing to my name and my condition
I shall not want for honors and position.
Then as to courage, that most precious trait,
I seem to have it, as was proved of late
Upon the field of honor, where my bearing,
They say, was very cool and rather daring.
I've wit, of course; and taste in such perfection
That I can judge without the least reflection,
And at the theater, which is my delight,
Can make or break a play on opening night,
And lead the crowd in hisses or bravos,

And generally be known as one who knows.
I'm clever, handsome, gracefully polite;
My waist is small, my teeth are strong and white;
As for my dress, the world's astonished eyes
Assure me that I bear away the prize.
I find myself in favor everywhere,
Honored by men, and worshiped by the fair;
And since these things are so, it seems to me
I'm justified in my complacency.

CLITANDRE

Well, if so many ladies hold you dear,
Why do you press a hopeless courtship here?

ACASTE

Hopeless, you say? I'm not the sort of fool
That likes his ladies difficult and cool.
Men who are awkward, shy, and peasantish
May pine for heartless beauties, if they wish,
Grovel before them, bear their cruelties,
Woo them with tears and sighs and bended knees,
And hope by dogged faithfulness to gain
What their poor merits never could obtain.
For men like me, however, it makes no sense
To love on trust, and foot the whole expense.
Whatever any lady's merits be,
I think, thank God, that I'm as choice as she;
That if my heart is kind enough to burn
For her, she owes me something in return;
And that in any proper love affair
The partners must invest an equal share.

[*Act Three · Scene One*]

CLITANDRE

You think, then, that our hostess favors you?

ACASTE

I've reason to believe that that is true.

CLITANDRE

How did you come to such a mad conclusion?
You're blind, dear fellow. This is sheer delusion.

ACASTE

All right, then: I'm deluded and I'm blind.

CLITANDRE

Whatever put the notion in your mind?

ACASTE

Delusion.

CLITANDRE

What persuades you that you're right?

ACASTE

I'm blind.

[*Act Three* · *Scene One*]

CLITANDRE

But have you any proofs to cite?

ACASTE

I tell you I'm deluded.

CLITANDRE

Have you, then,
Received some secret pledge from Célimène?

ACASTE

Oh, no: she scorns me.

CLITANDRE

Tell me the truth, I beg.

ACASTE

She just can't bear me.

CLITANDRE

Ah, don't pull my leg.
Tell me what hope she's given you, I pray.

[*Act Three* · *Scene One*]

ACASTE

I'm hopeless, and it's you who win the day.
She hates me thoroughly, and I'm so vexed *(exaggeration)*
I mean to hang myself on Tuesday next.

CLITANDRE

Dear Marquess, let us have an armistice
And make a treaty. What do you say to this?
If ever one of us can plainly prove
That Célimène encourages his love,
The other must abandon hope, and yield,
And leave him in possession of the field.

ACASTE

Now, there's a bargain that appeals to me;
With all my heart, dear Marquess, I agree.
But hush.

SCENE TWO

CÉLIMÈNE, ACASTE, CLITANDRE

CÉLIMÈNE

Still here?

CLITANDRE

T'was love that stayed our feet.

CÉLIMÈNE

I think I heard a carriage in the street.
Whose is it? D'you know?

SCENE THREE

CÉLIMÈNE, ACASTE, CLITANDRE, BASQUE

BASQUE

Arsinoé is here,
Madame.

CÉLIMÈNE

Arsinoé, you say? Oh, dear.

BASQUE

Eliante is entertaining her below.

CÉLIMÈNE

What brings the creature here, I'd like to know?

ACASTE

They say she's dreadfully prudish, but in fact
I think her piety . . .

[*Act Three · Scene Three*]

CÉLIMÈNE

It's all an act.
At heart she's worldly, and her poor success
In snaring men explains her prudishness.
It breaks her heart to see the beaux and gallants
Engrossed by other women's charms and talents,
And so she's always in a jealous rage
Against the faulty standards of the age.
She lets the world believe that she's a prude
To justify her loveless solitude,
And strives to put a brand of moral shame
On all the graces that she cannot claim.
But still she'd love a lover; and Alceste
Appears to be the one she'd love the best.
His visits here are poison to her pride;
She seems to think I've lured him from her side;
And everywhere, at court or in the town,
The spiteful, envious woman runs me down.
In short, she's just as stupid as can be,
Vicious and arrogant in the last degree,
And . . .

elaborat mocking traits of society

234

SCENE FOUR

ARSINOÉ, CÉLIMÈNE, CLITANDRE, ACASTE

CÉLIMÈNE

Ah! What happy chance has brought you here?
I've thought about you ever so much, my dear.

ARSINOÉ

I've come to tell you something you should know.

CÉLIMÈNE

How good of you to think of doing so!
                    (*Clitandre and Acaste go out, laughing.*)

SCENE FIVE

ARSINOÉ, CÉLIMÈNE

ARSINOÉ

It's just as well those gentlemen didn't tarry.

CÉLIMÈNE

Shall we sit down?

ARSINOÉ

                  That won't be necessary.
Madam, the flame of friendship ought to burn
Brightest in matters of the most concern,
And as there's nothing which concerns us more
Than honor, I have hastened to your door
To bring you, as your friend, some information
About the status of your reputation.
I visited, last night, some virtuous folk,
And, quite by chance, it was of you they spoke;
There was, I fear, no tendency to praise
Your light behavior and your dashing ways.
The quantity of gentlemen you see
And your by now notorious coquetry
Were both so vehemently criticized

236

By everyone, that I was much surprised.
Of course, I needn't tell you where I stood;
I came to your defense as best I could,
Assured them you were harmless, and declared
Your soul was absolutely unimpaired.
But there are some things, you must realize,
One can't excuse, however hard one tries,
And I was forced at last into conceding
That your behavior, Madam, is misleading,
That it makes a bad impression, giving rise
To ugly gossip and obscene surmise,
And that if you were more *overtly* good,
You wouldn't be so much misunderstood.
Not that I think you've been unchaste—no! no!
The saints preserve me from a thought so low!
But mere good conscience never did suffice:
One must avoid the outward show of vice.
Madam, you're too intelligent, I'm sure,
To think my motives anything but pure
In offering you this counsel—which I do
Out of a zealous interest in you.

CÉLIMÈNE

Madam, I haven't taken you amiss;
I'm very much obliged to you for this;
And I'll at once discharge the obligation
By telling you about *your* reputation.
You've been so friendly as to let me know
What certain people say of me, and so
I mean to follow your benign example
By offering you a somewhat similar sample.

The other day, I went to an affair
And found some most distinguished people there
Discussing piety, both false and true.
The conversation soon came round to you.
Alas! Your prudery and bustling zeal
Appeared to have a very slight appeal.
Your affectation of a grave demeanor,
Your endless talk of virtue and of honor,
The aptitude of your suspicious mind
For finding sin where there is none to find,
Your towering self-esteem, that pitying face
With which you contemplate the human race,
Your sermonizings and your sharp aspersions
On people's pure and innocent diversions—
All these were mentioned, Madam, and, in fact,
Were roundly and concertedly attacked.
"What good," they said, "are all these outward shows,
When everything belies her pious pose?
She prays incessantly; but then, they say,
She beats her maids and cheats them of their pay;
She shows her zeal in every holy place,
But still she's vain enough to paint her face;
She holds that naked statues are immoral,
But with a naked *man* she'd have no quarrel."
Of course, I said to everybody there
That they were being viciously unfair;
But still they were disposed to criticize you,
And all agreed that someone should advise you
To leave the morals of the world alone,
And worry rather more about your own.
They felt that one's self-knowledge should be great
Before one thinks of setting others straight;

That one should learn the art of living well
Before one threatens other men with hell,
And that the Church is best equipped, no doubt,
To guide our souls and root our vices out.
Madam, you're too intelligent, I'm sure,
To think my motives anything but pure
In offering you this counsel—which I do
Out of a zealous interest in you.

ARSINOÉ

I dared not hope for gratitude, but I
Did not expect so acid a reply;
I judge, since you've been so extremely tart,
That my good counsel pierced you to the heart.

CÉLIMÈNE

Far from it, Madam. Indeed, it seems to me
We ought to trade advice more frequently.
One's vision of oneself is so defective
That it would be an excellent corrective.
If you are willing, Madam, let's arrange
Shortly to have another frank exchange
In which we'll tell each other, *entre nous,*
What you've heard tell of me, and I of you.

ARSINOÉ

Oh, people never censure you, my dear;
It's me they criticize. Or so I hear.

CÉLIMÈNE

Madam, I think we either blame or praise
According to our taste and length of days.
There is a time of life for coquetry,
And there's a season, too, for prudery.
When all one's charms are gone, it is, I'm sure,
Good strategy to be devout and pure:
It makes one seem a little less forsaken.
Some day, perhaps, I'll take the road you've taken:
Time brings all things. But I have time aplenty,
And see no cause to be a prude at twenty.

good person ←

ARSINOÉ

You give your age in such a gloating tone
That one would think I was an ancient crone;
We're not so far apart, in sober truth,
That you can mock me with a boast of youth!
Madam, you baffle me. I wish I knew
What moves you to provoke me as you do.

CÉLIMÈNE

For my part, Madam, I should like to know
Why you abuse me everywhere you go.
Is it my fault, dear lady, that your hand
Is not, alas, in very great demand?
If men admire me, if they pay me court
And daily make me offers of the sort

240

[*Act Three · Scene Five*]

You'd dearly love to have them make to you,
How can I help it? What would you have me do?
If what you want is lovers, please feel free
To take as many as you can from me.

ARSINOÉ

Oh, come. D'you think the world is losing sleep
Over that flock of lovers which you keep,
Or that we find it difficult to guess
What price you pay for their devotedness?
Surely you don't expect us to suppose
Mere merit could attract so many beaux?
It's not your virtue that they're dazzled by;
Nor is it virtuous love for which they sigh.
You're fooling no one, Madam; the world's not blind;
There's many a lady heaven has designed
To call men's noblest, tenderest feelings out,
Who has no lovers dogging her about;
From which it's plain that lovers nowadays
Must be acquired in bold and shameless ways,
And only pay one court for such reward
As modesty and virtue can't afford.
Then don't be quite so puffed up, if you please,
About your tawdry little victories;
Try, if you can, to be a shade less vain,
And treat the world with somewhat less disdain.
If one were envious of your amours,
One soon could have a following like yours;
Lovers are no great trouble to collect
If one prefers them to one's self-respect.

241

CÉLIMÈNE

Collect them then, my dear; I'd love to see
You demonstrate that charming theory;
Who knows, you might . . .

ARSINOÉ

                Now, Madam, that will do;
It's time to end this trying interview.
My coach is late in coming to your door,
Or I'd have taken leave of you before.

CÉLIMÈNE

Oh, please don't feel that you must rush away;
I'd be delighted, Madam, if you'd stay.
However, lest my conversation bore you,
Let me provide some better company for you;
This gentleman, who comes most apropos,
Will please you more than I could do, I know.

SCENE SIX

ALCESTE, CÉLIMÈNE, ARSINOÉ

CÉLIMÈNE

Alceste, I have a little note to write
Which simply must go out before tonight;
Please entertain *Madame;* I'm sure that she
Will overlook my incivility.

SCENE SEVEN

quiproquo

ALCESTE, ARSINOÉ

ARSINOÉ

Well, Sir, our hostess graciously contrives
For us to chat until my coach arrives;
And I shall be forever in her debt
For granting me this little tête-à-tête.
We women very rightly give our hearts
To men of noble character and parts,
And your especial merits, dear Alceste,
Have roused the deepest sympathy in my breast.
Oh, how I wish they had sufficient sense
At court, to recognize your excellence!
They wrong you greatly, Sir. How it must hurt you
Never to be rewarded for your virtue!

ALCESTE

Why, Madam, what cause have I to feel aggrieved?
What great and brilliant thing have I achieved?
What service have I rendered to the King
That I should look to him for anything?

[*Act Three* · *Scene Seven*]

ARSINOÉ

Not everyone who's honored by the State
Has done great services. A man must wait
Till time and fortune offer him the chance.
Your merit, Sir, is obvious at a glance,
And . . .

ALCESTE

Ah, forget my merit; I'm not neglected.
The court, I think, can hardly be expected
To mine men's souls for merit, and unearth
Our hidden virtues and our secret worth.

ARSINOÉ

Some virtues, though, are far too bright to hide;
Yours are acknowledged, Sir, on every side.
Indeed, I've heard you warmly praised of late
By persons of considerable weight.

ALCESTE

This fawning age has praise for everyone,
And all distinctions, Madam, are undone.
All things have equal honor nowadays,
And no one should be gratified by praise.
To be admired, one only need exist,
And every lackey's on the honors list.

everyone is honoured

[*Act Three · Scene Seven*]

ARSINOÉ

I only wish, Sir, that you had your eye
On some position at court, however high;
You'd only have to hint at such a notion
For me to set the proper wheels in motion;
I've certain friendships I'd be glad to use
To get you any office you might choose.

ALCESTE

Madam, I fear that any such ambition
Is wholly foreign to my disposition.
The soul God gave me isn't of the sort
That prospers in the weather of a court.
It's all too obvious that I don't possess
The virtues necessary for success.
My one great talent is for speaking plain;
I've never learned to flatter or to feign;
And anyone so stupidly sincere
Had best not seek a courtier's career.
Outside the court, I know, one must dispense
With honors, privilege, and influence;
But still one gains the right, foregoing these,
Not to be tortured by the wish to please.
One needn't live in dread of snubs and slights,
Nor praise the verse that every idiot writes,
Nor humor silly Marquesses, nor bestow
Politic sighs on Madam So-and-So.

ARSINOÉ

Forget the court, then; let the matter rest.
But I've another cause to be distressed

About your present situation, Sir.
It's to your love affair that I refer.
She whom you love, and who pretends to love you,
Is, I regret to say, unworthy of you.

ALCESTE

Why, Madam! Can you seriously intend
To make so grave a charge against your friend?

ARSINOÉ

Alas, I must. I've stood aside too long
And let that lady do you grievous wrong;
But now my debt to conscience shall be paid:
I tell you that your love has been betrayed.

ALCESTE

I thank you, Madam; you're extremely kind.
Such words are soothing to a lover's mind.

ARSINOÉ

Yes, though she *is* my friend, I say again
You're very much too good for Célimène.
She's wantonly misled you from the start.

ALCESTE

You may be right; who knows another's heart?
But ask yourself if it's the part of charity
To shake my soul with doubts of her sincerity.

[*Act Three* · *Scene Seven*]

ARSINOÉ

Well, if you'd rather be a dupe than doubt her,
That's your affair. I'll say no more about her.

ALCESTE

Madam, you know that doubt and vague suspicion
Are painful to a man in my position;
It's most unkind to worry me this way
Unless you've some real proof of what you say.

ARSINOÉ

Sir, say no more: all doubt shall be removed,
And all that I've been saying shall be proved.
You've only to escort me home, and there
We'll look into the heart of this affair.
I've ocular evidence which will persuade you
Beyond a doubt, that Célimène's betrayed you.
Then, if you're saddened by that revelation,
Perhaps I can provide some consolation.

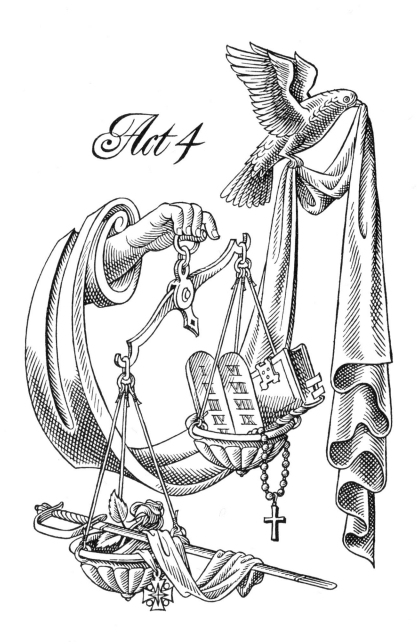

Act 4

SCENE ONE

ELIANTE, PHILINTE

PHILINTE

Madam, he acted like a stubborn child;
I thought they never would be reconciled;
In vain we reasoned, threatened, and appealed;
He stood his ground and simply would not yield.
The Marshals, I feel sure, have never heard
An argument so splendidly absurd.
"No, gentlemen," said he, "I'll not retract.
His verse is bad: extremely bad, in fact.
Surely it does the man no harm to know it.
Does it disgrace him, not to be a poet?
A gentleman may be respected still,
Whether he writes a sonnet well or ill.
That I dislike his verse should not offend him;
In all that touches honor, I commend him;
He's noble, brave, and virtuous—but I fear
He can't in truth be called a sonneteer.
I'll gladly praise his wardrobe; I'll endorse
His dancing, or the way he sits a horse;
But, gentlemen, I cannot praise his rhyme.
In fact, it ought to be a capital crime
For anyone so sadly unendowed
To write a sonnet, and read the thing aloud."

At length he fell into a gentler mood
And, striking a concessive attitude,
He paid Oronte the following courtesies:
"Sir, I regret that I'm so hard to please,
And I'm profoundly sorry that your lyric
Failed to provoke me to a panegyric."
After these curious words, the two embraced,
And then the hearing was adjourned—in haste.

ELIANTE

His conduct has been very singular lately;
Still, I confess that I respect him greatly.
The honesty in which he takes such pride
Has—to my mind—its noble, heroic side.
In this false age, such candor seems outrageous;
But I could wish that it were more contagious.

PHILINTE

What most intrigues me in our friend Alceste
Is the grand passion that rages in his breast.
The sullen humors he's compounded of
Should not, I think, dispose his heart to love;
But since they do, it puzzles me still more
That he should choose your cousin to adore.

ELIANTE

It does, indeed, belie the theory
That love is born of gentle sympathy,
And that the tender passion must be based
On sweet accords of temper and of taste.

[*Act Four* · *Scene One*]

PHILINTE

Does she return his love, do you suppose?

ELIANTE

Ah, that's a difficult question, Sir. Who knows?
How can we judge the truth of her devotion?
Her heart's a stranger to its own emotion.
Sometimes it thinks it loves, when no love's there;
At other times it loves quite unaware.

PHILINTE

I rather think Alceste is in for more
Distress and sorrow than he's bargained for;
Were he of my mind, Madam, his affection
Would turn in quite a different direction,
And we would see him more responsive to
The kind regard which he receives from you.

ELIANTE

Sir, I believe in frankness, and I'm inclined,
In matters of the heart, to speak my mind.
I don't oppose his love for her; indeed,
I hope with all my heart that he'll succeed,
And were it in my power, I'd rejoice
In giving him the lady of his choice.
But if, as happens frequently enough
In love affairs, he meets with a rebuff—
If Célimène should grant some rival's suit—

253

I'd gladly play the role of substitute;
Nor would his tender speeches please me less
Because they'd once been made without success.

PHILINTE

Well, Madam, as for me, I don't oppose
Your hopes in this affair; and heaven knows
That in my conversations with the man
I plead your cause as often as I can.
But if those two should marry, and so remove
All chance that he will offer you his love,
Then I'll declare my own, and hope to see
Your gracious favor pass from him to me.
In short, should you be cheated of Alceste,
I'd be most happy to be second best.

ELIANTE

Philinte, you're teasing.

PHILINTE

            Ah, Madam, never fear;
No words of mine were ever so sincere,
And I shall live in fretful expectation
Till I can make a fuller declaration.

SCENE TWO

ALCESTE, ELIANTE, PHILINTE

ALCESTE

Avenge me, Madam! I must have satisfaction,
Or this great wrong will drive me to distraction!

ELIANTE

Why, what's the matter? What's upset you so?

ALCESTE

Madam, I've had a mortal, mortal blow.
If Chaos repossessed the universe,
I swear I'd not be shaken any worse.
I'm ruined. . . . I can say no more. . . . My soul . . .

ELIANTE

Do try, Sir, to regain your self-control.

ALCESTE

Just heaven! Why were so much beauty and grace
Bestowed on one so vicious and so base?

[*Act Four · Scene Two*]

ELIANTE

Once more, Sir, tell us. . . .

ALCESTE

                My world has gone to wrack;
I'm—I'm betrayed; she's stabbed me in the back:
Yes, Célimène (who would have thought it of her?)
Is false to me, and has another lover.

ELIANTE

Are you quite certain? Can you prove these things?

PHILINTE

Lovers are prey to wild imaginings
And jealous fancies. No doubt there's some mistake. . . .

ALCESTE

Mind your own business, Sir, for heaven's sake.
(*To Eliante*)
Madam, I have the proof that you demand
Here in my pocket, penned by her own hand.
Yes, all the shameful evidence one could want
Lies in this letter written to Oronte—
Oronte! whom I felt sure she couldn't love,
And hardly bothered to be jealous of.

[*Act Four · Scene Two*]

PHILINTE

Still, in a letter, appearances may deceive;
This may not be so bad as you believe.

ALCESTE

Once more I beg you, Sir, to let me be;
Tend to your own affairs; leave mine to me.

ELIANTE

Compose yourself; this anguish that you feel . . .

ALCESTE

Is something, Madam, you alone can heal.
My outraged heart, beside itself with grief,
Appeals to you for comfort and relief.
Avenge me on your cousin, whose unjust
And faithless nature has deceived my trust;
Avenge a crime your pure soul must detest.

ELIANTE

But how, Sir?

ALCESTE

      Madam, this heart within my breast
Is yours; pray take it; redeem my heart from her,
And so avenge me on my torturer.

Let her be punished by the fond emotion,
The ardent love, the bottomless devotion,
The faithful worship which this heart of mine
Will offer up to yours as to a shrine.

ELIANTE

You have my sympathy, Sir, in all you suffer;
Nor do I scorn the noble heart you offer;
But I suspect you'll soon be mollified,
And this desire for vengeance will subside.
When some beloved hand has done us wrong
We thirst for retribution—but not for long;
However dark the deed that she's committed,
A lovely culprit's very soon acquitted.
Nothing's so stormy as an injured lover,
And yet no storm so quickly passes over.

ALCESTE

No, Madam, no—this is no lovers' spat;
I'll not forgive her; it's gone too far for that;
My mind's made up; I'll kill myself before
I waste my hopes upon her any more.
Ah, here she is. My wrath intensifies.
I shall confront her with her tricks and lies,
And crush her utterly, and bring you then
A heart no longer slave to Célimène.

SCENE THREE

ALCESTE, *aside*

Sweet heaven, help me to control my passion.

CÉLIMÈNE

(*Aside*)
        (*To Alceste*)
Oh, Lord. Why stand there staring in that fashion?
And what d'you mean by those dramatic sighs,
And that malignant glitter in your eyes?

ALCESTE

I mean that sins which cause the blood to freeze
Look innocent beside your treacheries;
That nothing Hell's or Heaven's wrath could do
Ever produced so bad a thing as you.

CÉLIMÈNE

Your compliments were always sweet and pretty.

ALCESTE

Madam, it's not the moment to be witty.
No, blush and hang your head; you've ample reason,
Since I've the fullest evidence of your treason.
Ah, this is what my sad heart prophesied;
Now all my anxious fears are verified;
My dark suspicion and my gloomy doubt
Divined the truth, and now the truth is out.
For all your trickery, I was not deceived;
It was my bitter stars that I believed.
But don't imagine that you'll go scot-free;
You shan't misuse me with impunity.
I know that love's irrational and blind;
I know the heart's not subject to the mind,
And can't be reasoned into beating faster;
I know each soul is free to choose its master;
Therefore had you but spoken from the heart,
Rejecting my attentions from the start,
I'd have no grievance, or at any rate
I could complain of nothing but my fate.
Ah, but so falsely to encourage me—
That was a treason and a treachery
For which you cannot suffer too severely,
And you shall pay for that behavior dearly.
Yes, now I have no pity, not a shred;
My temper's out of hand; I've lost my head;
Shocked by the knowledge of your double-dealings,
My reason can't restrain my savage feelings;
A righteous wrath deprives me of my senses,
And I won't answer for the consequences.

[*Act Four · Scene Three*]

CÉLIMÈNE

What does this outburst mean? Will you please explain?
Have you, by any chance, gone quite insane?

ALCESTE

Yes, yes, I went insane the day I fell
A victim to your black and fatal spell,
Thinking to meet with some sincerity
Among the treacherous charms that beckoned me.

CÉLIMÈNE

Pooh. Of what treachery can you complain?

ALCESTE

How sly you are, how cleverly you feign!
But you'll not victimize me any more.
Look: here's a document you've seen before.
This evidence, which I acquired today,
Leaves you, I think, without a thing to say.

CÉLIMÈNE

Is this what sent you into such a fit?

ALCESTE

You should be blushing at the sight of it.

CÉLIMÈNE

Ought I to blush? I truly don't see why.

ALCESTE

Ah, now you're being bold as well as sly;
Since there's no signature, perhaps you'll claim . . .

CÉLIMÈNE

I wrote it, whether or not it bears my name.

ALCESTE

And you can view with equanimity
This proof of your disloyalty to me!

CÉLIMÈNE

Oh, don't be so outrageous and extreme.

ALCESTE

You take this matter lightly, it would seem.
Was it no wrong to me, no shame to you,
That you should send Oronte this billet-doux?

CÉLIMÈNE

Oronte! Who said it was for him?

[*Act Four · Scene Three*]

ALCESTE

                              Why, those
Who brought me this example of your prose.
But what's the difference? If you wrote the letter
To someone else, it pleases me no better.
My grievance and your guilt remain the same.

CÉLIMÈNE

But need you rage, and need I blush for shame,
If this was written to a *woman* friend?

ALCESTE

Ah! Most ingenious. I'm impressed no end;
And after that incredible evasion
Your guilt is clear. I need no more persuasion.
How dare you try so clumsy a deception?
D'you think I'm wholly wanting in perception?
Come, come, let's see how brazenly you'll try
To bolster up so palpable a lie:
Kindly construe this ardent closing section
As nothing more than sisterly affection!
Here, let me read it. Tell me, if you dare to,
That this is for a woman . . .

CÉLIMÈNE

                              I don't care to.
What right have you to badger and berate me,
And so highhandedly interrogate me?

ALCESTE

Now, don't be angry; all I ask of you
Is that you justify a phrase or two . . .

CÉLIMÈNE

No, I shall not. I utterly refuse,
And you may take those phrases as you choose.

ALCESTE

Just show me how this letter could be meant
For a woman's eyes, and I shall be content.

CÉLIMÈNE

No, no, it's for Oronte; you're perfectly right.
I welcome his attentions with delight,
I prize his character and his intellect,
And everything is just as you suspect.
Come, do your worst now; give your rage free rein;
But kindly cease to bicker and complain.

ALCESTE, *aside*

Good God! Could anything be more inhuman?
Was ever a heart so mangled by a woman?
When I complain of how she has betrayed me,
She bridles, and commences to upbraid me!
She tries my tortured patience to the limit;
She won't deny her guilt; she glories in it!

And yet my heart's too faint and cowardly
To break these chains of passion, and be free,
To scorn her as it should, and rise above
This unrewarded, mad, and bitter love.
(*To Célimène*)
Ah, traitress, in how confident a fashion
You take advantage of my helpless passion,
And use my weakness for your faithless charms
To make me once again throw down my arms!
But do at least deny this black transgression;
Take back that mocking and perverse confession;
Defend this letter and your innocence,
And I, poor fool, will aid in your defense.
Pretend, pretend, that you are just and true,
And I shall make myself believe in you.

CÉLIMÈNE

Oh, stop it. Don't be such a jealous dunce,
Or I shall leave off loving you at once.
Just why should I *pretend?* What could impel me
To stoop so low as that? And kindly tell me
Why, if I loved another, I shouldn't merely
Inform you of it, simply and sincerely!
I've told you where you stand, and that admission
Should altogether clear me of suspicion;
After so generous a guarantee,
What right have you to harbor doubts of me?
Since women are (from natural reticence)
Reluctant to declare their sentiments,
And since the honor of our sex requires
That we conceal our amorous desires,

Ought any man for whom such laws are broken
To question what the oracle has spoken?
Should he not rather feel an obligation
To trust that most obliging declaration?
Enough, now. Your suspicions quite disgust me;
Why should I love a man who doesn't trust me?
I cannot understand why I continue,
Fool that I am, to take an interest in you.
I ought to choose a man less prone to doubt,
And give you something to be vexed about.

ALCESTE

Ah, what a poor enchanted fool I am;
These gentle words, no doubt, were all a sham;
But destiny requires me to entrust
My happiness to you, and so I must.
I'll love you to the bitter end, and see
How false and treacherous you dare to be.

CÉLIMÈNE

No, you don't really love me as you ought.

ALCESTE

I love you more than can be said or thought;
Indeed, I wish you were in such distress
That I might show my deep devotedness.
Yes, I could wish that you were wretchedly poor,
Unloved, uncherished, utterly obscure;
That fate had set you down upon the earth

Without possessions, rank, or gentle birth;
Then, by the offer of my heart, I might
Repair the great injustice of your plight;
I'd raise you from the dust, and proudly prove
The purity and vastness of my love.

CÉLIMÈNE

This is a strange benevolence indeed!
God grant that I may never be in need. . . .
Ah, here's Monsieur Dubois, in quaint disguise.

SCENE FOUR

CÉLIMÈNE, ALCESTE, DUBOIS

ALCESTE

Well, why this costume? Why those frightened eyes?
What ails you?

DUBOIS

Well, Sir, things are most mysterious.

ALCESTE

What do you mean?

DUBOIS

I fear they're very serious.

ALCESTE

What?

DUBOIS

Shall I speak more loudly?

[*Act Four · Scene Four*]

ALCESTE

Yes; speak out.

DUBOIS

Isn't there someone here, Sir?

ALCESTE

Speak, you lout!
Stop wasting time.

DUBOIS

Sir, we must slip away.

ALCESTE

How's that?

DUBOIS

We must decamp without delay.

ALCESTE

Explain yourself.

DUBOIS

I tell you we must fly.

[*Act Four · Scene Four*]

ALCESTE

What for?

DUBOIS

We mustn't pause to say good-by.

ALCESTE

Now what d'you mean by all of this, you clown?

DUBOIS

I mean, Sir, that we've got to leave this town.

ALCESTE

I'll tear you limb from limb and joint from joint
If you don't come more quickly to the point.

DUBOIS

Well, Sir, today a man in a black suit,
Who wore a black and ugly scowl to boot,
Left us a document scrawled in such a hand
As even Satan couldn't understand.

It bears upon your lawsuit, I don't doubt;
But all hell's devils couldn't make it out.

ALCESTE

Well, well, go on. What then? I fail to see
How this event obliges us to flee.

DUBOIS

Well, Sir: an hour later, hardly more,
A gentleman who's often called before
Came looking for you in an anxious way.
Not finding you, he asked me to convey
(Knowing I could be trusted with the same)
The following message. . . . Now, what *was* his name?

ALCESTE

Forget his name, you idiot. What did he say?

DUBOIS

Well, it was one of your friends, Sir, anyway.
He warned you to begone, and he suggested
That if you stay, you may well be arrested.

ALCESTE

What? Nothing more specific? Think, man, think!

[*Act Four · Scene Four*]

DUBOIS

No, Sir. He had me bring him pen and ink,
And dashed you off a letter which, I'm sure,
Will render things distinctly less obscure.

ALCESTE

Well—let me have it!

CÉLIMÈNE

What *is* this all about?

ALCESTE

God knows; but I have hopes of finding out.
How long am I to wait, you blitherer?

DUBOIS, *after a protracted search for the letter*

I must have left it on your table, Sir.

ALCESTE

I ought to . . .

CÉLIMÈNE

No, no, keep your self-control;
Go find out what's behind his rigmarole.

[*Act Four · Scene Four*]

ALCESTE

It seems that fate, no matter what I do,
Has sworn that I may not converse with you;
But, Madam, pray permit your faithful lover
To try once more before the day is over.

Act 5

SCENE ONE

ALCESTE

No, it's too much. My mind's made up, I tell you.

PHILINTE

Why should this blow, however hard, compel you . . .

ALCESTE

No, no, don't waste your breath in argument;
Nothing you say will alter my intent;
This age is vile, and I've made up my mind
To have no further commerce with mankind.
Did not truth, honor, decency, and the laws
Oppose my enemy and approve my cause?
My claims were justified in all men's sight;
I put my trust in equity and right;
Yet, to my horror and the world's disgrace,
Justice is mocked, and I have lost my case!
A scoundrel whose dishonesty is notorious
Emerges from another lie victorious!
Honor and right condone his brazen fraud,
While rectitude and decency applaud!

[Act Five · Scene One]

Before his smirking face, the truth stands charmed,
And virtue conquered, and the law disarmed!
His crime is sanctioned by a court decree!
And not content with what he's done to me,
The dog now seeks to ruin me by stating
That I composed a book now circulating,
A book so wholly criminal and vicious
That even to speak its title is seditious!
Meanwhile Oronte, my rival, lends his credit
To the same libelous tale, and helps to spread it!
Oronte! a man of honor and of rank,
With whom I've been entirely fair and frank;
Who sought me out and forced me, willy-nilly,
To judge some verse I found extremely silly;
And who, because I properly refused
To flatter him, or see the truth abused,
Abets my enemy in a rotten slander!
There's the reward of honesty and candor!
The man will hate me to the end of time
For failing to commend his wretched rhyme!
And not this man alone, but all humanity
Do what they do from interest and vanity;
They prate of honor, truth, and righteousness,
But lie, betray, and swindle nonetheless.
Come then: man's villainy is too much to bear;
Let's leave this jungle and this jackal's lair.
Yes! treacherous and savage race of men,
You shall not look upon my face again.

PHILINTE

Oh, don't rush into exile prematurely;
Things aren't as dreadful as you make them, surely.

278

[*Act Five · Scene One*]

It's rather obvious, since you're still at large,
That people don't believe your enemy's charge.
Indeed, his tale's so patently untrue
That it may do more harm to him than you.

ALCESTE

Nothing could do that scoundrel any harm:
His frank corruption is his greatest charm,
And, far from hurting him, a further shame
Would only serve to magnify his name.

PHILINTE

In any case, his bald prevarication
Has done no injury to your reputation,
And you may feel secure in that regard.
As for your lawsuit, it should not be hard
To have the case reopened, and contest
This judgment . . .

ALCESTE

            No, no, let the verdict rest.
Whatever cruel penalty it may bring,
I wouldn't have it changed for anything.
It shows the times' injustice with such clarity
That I shall pass it down to our posterity
As a great proof and signal demonstration
Of the black wickedness of this generation. condemning
It may cost twenty thousand francs; but I

279

[Act Five · Scene One]

Shall pay their twenty thousand, and gain thereby
The right to storm and rage at human evil,
And send the race of mankind to the devil.

Condemning

PHILINTE

Listen to me. . . .

ALCESTE

       Why? What can you possibly say?
Don't argue, Sir; your labor's thrown away.
Do you propose to offer lame excuses
For men's behavior and the times' abuses?

PHILINTE

No, all you say I'll readily concede:
This is a low, dishonest age indeed;
Nothing but trickery prospers nowadays,
And people ought to mend their shabby ways.
Yes, man's a beastly creature; but must we then
Abandon the society of men?
Here in the world, each human frailty
Provides occasion for philosophy,
And that is virtue's noblest exercise;
If honesty shone forth from all men's eyes,
If every heart were frank and kind and just,
What could our virtues do but gather dust
(Since their employment is to help us bear
The villainies of men without despair)?
A heart well-armed with virtue can endure. . . .

Complaining

[*Act Five* · *Scene One*]

ALCESTE

Sir, you're a matchless reasoner, to be sure;
Your words are fine and full of cogency;
But don't waste time and eloquence on me.
My reason bids me go, for my own good.
My tongue won't lie and flatter as it should;
God knows what frankness it might next commit,
And what I'd suffer on account of it.
Pray let me wait for Célimène's return
In peace and quiet. I shall shortly learn,
By her response to what I have in view,
Whether her love for me is feigned or true.

PHILINTE

Till then, let's visit Eliante upstairs.

ALCESTE

No, I am too weighed down with somber cares.
Go to her, do; and leave me with my gloom
Here in the darkened corner of this room.

PHILINTE

Why, that's no sort of company, my friend;
I'll see if Eliante will not descend.

SCENE TWO

CÉLIMÈNE, ORONTE, ALCESTE

ORONTE

Yes, Madam, if you wish me to remain
Your true and ardent lover, you must deign
To give me some more positive assurance.
All this suspense is quite beyond endurance.
If your heart shares the sweet desires of mine,
Show me as much by some convincing sign;
And here's the sign I urgently suggest:
That you no longer tolerate Alceste,
But sacrifice him to my love, and sever
All your relations with the man forever.

CÉLIMÈNE

Why do you suddenly dislike him so?
You praised him to the skies not long ago.

ORONTE

Madam, that's not the point. I'm here to find
Which way your tender feelings are inclined.
Choose, if you please, between Alceste and me,
And I shall stay or go accordingly.

[*Act Five · Scene Two*]

ALCESTE, *emerging from the corner*

Yes, Madam, choose; this gentleman's demand
Is wholly just, and I support his stand.
I too am true and ardent; I too am here
To ask you that you make your feelings clear.
No more delays, now; no equivocation;
The time has come to make your declaration.

ORONTE

Sir, I've no wish in any way to be
An obstacle to your felicity.

ALCESTE

Sir, I've no wish to share her heart with you;
That may sound jealous, but at least it's true.

ORONTE

If, weighing us, she leans in your direction . . .

ALCESTE

If she regards you with the least affection . . .

ORONTE

I swear I'll yield her to you there and then.

ALCESTE

I swear I'll never see her face again.

ORONTE

Now, Madam, tell us what we've come to hear.

ALCESTE

Madam, speak openly and have no fear.

ORONTE

Just say which one is to remain your lover.

ALCESTE

Just name one name, and it will all be over.

ORONTE

What! Is it possible that you're undecided?

ALCESTE

What! Can your feelings possibly be divided?

CÉLIMÈNE

Enough: this inquisition's gone too far:
How utterly unreasonable you are!
Not that I couldn't make the choice with ease;

[*Act Five · Scene Two*]

My heart has no conflicting sympathies;
I know full well which one of you I favor,
And you'd not see me hesitate or waver.
But how can you expect me to reveal
So cruelly and bluntly what I feel?
I think it altogether too unpleasant
To choose between two men when both are present;
One's heart has means more subtle and more kind
Of letting its affections be divined,
Nor need one be uncharitably plain
To let a lover know he loves in vain.

ORONTE

No, no, speak plainly; I for one can stand it.
I beg you to be frank.

ALCESTE

                    And I demand it.
The simple truth is what I wish to know,
And there's no need for softening the blow.
You've made an art of pleasing everyone,
But now your days of coquetry are done:
You have no choice now, Madam, but to choose,
For I'll know what to think if you refuse;
I'll take your silence for a clear admission
That I'm entitled to my worst suspicion.

ORONTE

I thank you for this ultimatum, Sir,
And I may say I heartily concur.

[*Act Five · Scene Two*]

CÉLIMÈNE

Really, this foolishness is very wearing:
Must you be so unjust and overbearing?
Haven't I told you why I must demur?
Ah, here's Eliante; I'll put the case to her.

SCENE THREE

ELIANTE, PHILINTE, CÉLIMÈNE, ORONTE, ALCESTE

CÉLIMÈNE

Cousin, I'm being persecuted here
By these two persons, who, it would appear,
Will not be satisfied till I confess
Which one I love the more, and which the less,
And tell the latter to his face that he
Is henceforth banished from my company.
Tell me, has ever such a thing been done?

ELIANTE

You'd best not turn to me; I'm not the one
To back you in a matter of this kind:
I'm all for those who frankly speak their mind.

ORONTE

Madam, you'll search in vain for a defender.

ALCESTE

You're beaten, Madam, and may as well surrender.

[*Act Five · Scene Three*]

ORONTE

Speak, speak, you must; and end this awful strain.

ALCESTE

Or don't, and your position will be plain.

ORONTE

A single word will close this painful scene.

ALCESTE

But if you're silent, I'll know what you mean.

SCENE FOUR

ARSINOÉ, CÉLIMÈNE, ELIANTE,
ALCESTE, PHILINTE,
ACASTE, CLITANDRE, ORONTE

ACASTE, *to Célimène*

Madam, with all due deference, we two
Have come to pick a little bone with you.

CLITANDRE, *to Oronte and Alceste*

I'm glad you're present, Sirs; as you'll soon learn,
Our business here is also your concern.

ARSINOÉ, *to Célimène*

Madam, I visit you so soon again
Only because of these two gentlemen,
Who came to me indignant and aggrieved
About a crime too base to be believed.
Knowing your virtue, having such confidence in it,
I couldn't think you guilty for a minute,
In spite of all their telling evidence;
And, rising above our little difference,
I've hastened here in friendship's name to see
You clear yourself of this great calumny.

[*Act Five · Scene Four*]

ACASTE

Yes, Madam, let us see with what composure
You'll manage to respond to this disclosure.
You lately sent Clitandre this tender note.

CLITANDRE

And this one, for Acaste, you also wrote.

ACASTE, *to Oronte and Alceste*

You'll recognize this writing, Sirs, I think;
The lady is so free with pen and ink
That you must know it all too well, I fear.
But listen: this is something you should hear.

"How absurd you are to condemn my lightheartedness in society, and to accuse me of being happiest in the company of others. Nothing could be more unjust; and if you do not come to me instantly and beg pardon for saying such a thing, I shall never forgive you as long as I live. Our big bumbling friend the Viscount . . ."

What a shame that he's not here.

"Our big bumbling friend the Viscount, whose name stands first in your complaint, is hardly a man to my taste; and ever since the day I watched him spend three-quarters of an hour spitting into a well, so as to make circles in the water, I have been unable to think highly of him. As for the little Marquess . . ."

In all modesty, gentlemen, that is I.

[*Act Five · Scene Four*]

"As for the little Marquess, who sat squeezing my hand for such a long while yesterday, I find him in all respects the most trifling creature alive; and the only things of value about him are his cape and his sword. As for the man with the green ribbons . . ."

(*To Alceste*)
It's your turn now, Sir.

"As for the man with the green ribbons, he amuses me now and then with his bluntness and his bearish ill-humor; but there are many times indeed when I think him the greatest bore in the world. And as for the sonneteer . . ."

(*To Oronte*)
Here's your helping.

"And as for the sonneteer, who has taken it into his head to be witty, and insists on being an author in the teeth of opinion, I simply cannot be bothered to listen to him, and his prose wearies me quite as much as his poetry. Be assured that I am not always so well-entertained as you suppose; that I long for your company, more than I dare to say, at all these entertainments to which people drag me; and that the presence of those one loves is the true and perfect seasoning to all one's pleasures."

CLITANDRE

And now for me.

"Clitandre, whom you mention, and who so pesters me with his saccharine speeches, is the last man on earth for whom I could feel any affection. He is quite mad to

suppose that I love him, and so are you, to doubt that
you are loved. Do come to your senses; exchange your
suppositions for his; and visit me as often as possible,
to help me bear the annoyance of his unwelcome attentions."

It's a sweet character that these letters show,
And what to call it, Madam, you well know.
Enough. We're off to make the world acquainted
With this sublime self-portrait that you've painted.

ACASTE

Madam, I'll make you no farewell oration;
No, you're not worthy of my indignation.
Far choicer hearts than yours, as you'll discover,
Would like this little Marquess for a lover.

SCENE FIVE

CÉLIMÈNE, ELIANTE, ARSINOÉ, ALCESTE,
ORONTE, PHILINTE

ORONTE

So! After all those loving letters you wrote,
You turn on me like this, and cut my throat!
And your dissembling, faithless heart, I find,
Has pledged itself by turns to all mankind!
How blind I've been! But now I clearly see;
I thank you, Madam, for enlightening me.
My heart is mine once more, and I'm content;
The loss of it shall be your punishment.
(*To Alceste*)
Sir, she is yours; I'll seek no more to stand
Between your wishes and this lady's hand.

SCENE SIX

CÉLIMÈNE, ELIANTE, ARSINOÉ, ALCESTE, PHILINTE

ARSINOÉ, *to Célimène*

Madam, I'm forced to speak. I'm far too stirred
To keep my counsel, after what I've heard.
I'm shocked and staggered by your want of morals.
It's not my way to mix in others' quarrels;
But really, when this fine and noble spirit,
This man of honor and surpassing merit,
Laid down the offering of his heart before you,
How *could* you . . .

ALCESTE

         Madam, permit me, I implore you,
To represent myself in this debate.
Don't bother, please, to be my advocate.
My heart, in any case, could not afford
To give your services their due reward;
And if I chose, for consolation's sake,
Some other lady, t'would not be you I'd take.

[*Act Five · Scene Six*]

ARSINOÉ

What makes you think you could, Sir? And how dare
    you
Imply that I've been trying to ensnare you?
If you can for a moment entertain
Such flattering fancies, you're extremely vain.
I'm not so interested as you suppose
In Célimène's discarded gigolos.
Get rid of that absurd illusion, do.
Women like me are not for such as you.
Stay with this creature, to whom you're so attached;
I've never seen two people better matched.

SCENE SEVEN

CÉLIMÈNE, ELIANTE, ALCESTE, PHILINTE

ALCESTE, *to Célimène*

Well, I've been still throughout this exposé,
Till everyone but me has said his say.
Come, have I shown sufficient self-restraint?
And may I now . . .

CÉLIMÈNE

Yes, make your just complaint.
Reproach me freely, call me what you will;
You've every right to say I've used you ill.
I've wronged you, I confess it; and in my shame
I'll make no effort to escape the blame.
The anger of those others I could despise;
My guilt toward you I sadly recognize.
Your wrath is wholly justified, I fear;
I know how culpable I must appear,
I know all things bespeak my treachery,
And that, in short, you've grounds for hating me.
Do so; I give you leave.

ALCESTE

Ah, traitress—how,
How should I cease to love you, even now?
Though mind and will were passionately bent
On hating you, my heart would not consent.
(*To Eliante and Philinte*)
Be witness to my madness, both of you;
See what infatuation drives one to;
But wait; my folly's only just begun,
And I shall prove to you before I'm done
How strange the human heart is, and how far
From rational we sorry creatures are.
(*To Célimène*)
Woman, I'm willing to forget your shame,
And clothe your treacheries in a sweeter name;
I'll call them youthful errors, instead of crimes,
And lay the blame on these corrupting times.
My one condition is that you agree
To share my chosen fate, and fly with me
To that wild, trackless, solitary place
In which I shall forget the human race.
Only by such a course can you atone
For those atrocious letters; by that alone
Can you remove my present horror of you,
And make it possible for me to love you.

CÉLIMÈNE

What! *I* renounce the world at my young age,
And die of boredom in some hermitage?

ALCESTE

Ah, if you really loved me as you ought,
You wouldn't give the world a moment's thought;
Must you have me, and all the world beside?

CÉLIMÈNE

Alas, at twenty one is terrified
Of solitude. I fear I lack the force
And depth of soul to take so stern a course.
But if my hand in marriage will content you,
Why, there's a plan which I might well consent to,
And . . .

ALCESTE

        No, I detest you now. I could excuse
Everything else, but since you thus refuse
To love me wholly, as a wife should do,
And see the world in me, as I in you,
Go! I reject your hand, and disenthrall
My heart from your enchantments, once for all.

SCENE EIGHT

ELIANTE, ALCESTE, PHILINTE

ALCESTE, *to Eliante*

Madam, your virtuous beauty has no peer;
Of all this world, you only are sincere;
I've long esteemed you highly, as you know;
Permit me ever to esteem you so,
And if I do not now request your hand,
Forgive me, Madam, and try to understand.
I feel unworthy of it; I sense that fate
Does not intend me for the married state,
That I should do you wrong by offering you
My shattered heart's unhappy residue,
And that in short . . .

ELIANTE

     Your argument's well taken:
Nor need you fear that I shall feel forsaken.
Were I to offer him this hand of mine,
Your friend Philinte, I think, would not decline.

[*Act Five · Scene Eight*]

PHILINTE

Ah, Madam, that's my heart's most cherished goal,
For which I'd gladly give my life and soul.

ALCESTE, *to Eliante and Philinte*

May you be true to all you now profess,
And so deserve unending happiness.
Meanwhile, betrayed and wronged in everything,
I'll flee this bitter world where vice is king,
And seek some spot unpeopled and apart
Where I'll be free to have an honest heart.

PHILINTE

Come, Madam, let's do everything we can
To change the mind of this unhappy man.

Tartuffe

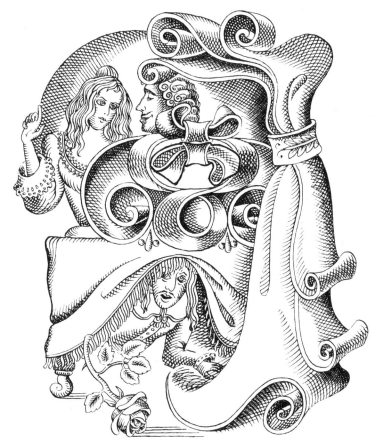

COMEDY IN FIVE ACTS, 1669

Drawings by Igor Tulipanov

For my brother Lawrence

INTRODUCTION

There may be people who deny comedy the right to be serious, and think it improper for any but trivial themes to consort with laughter. It would take people of that kind to find in *Tartuffe* anything offensive to religion. The warped characters of the play express an obviously warped religious attitude, which is corrected by the reasonable orthodoxy of Cléante, the wholesomeness of Dorine, and the entire testimony of the action. The play is not a satire on religion, as those held who kept it off the boards for five years. Is it, then, a satire on religious hypocrisy, as Molière claimed in his polemical preface of 1669?

The play speaks often of religious hypocrisy, displays it in action, and sometimes seems to be gesturing toward its practitioners in seventeenth-century French society. Tartuffe is made to recommend, more than once, those Jesuitical techniques for easing the conscience which Pascal attacked in the *Provincial Letters*. Cléante makes a long speech against people who feign piety for the sake of preferment or political advantage. And yet no one in the play can be said to be a religious hypocrite in any representative sense. Tartuffe may at times suggest or symbolize the slippery casuist, or the sort of hypocrite denounced by Cléante, but he is not himself such a person. He is a versatile parasite or confidence man, with a very long criminal record, and to pose as a holy man is not his only *modus operandi*: we see him, in the last act, shifting easily from the role of saint to that of hundred-percenter. As for the other major characters who might qualify, Madame Pernelle is simply a nasty bigot, while the religious attitudes of her son Orgon are, for all their underlying corruption, quite sincere.

[Introduction]

Tartuffe is only incidentally satiric; what we experience in reading or seeing it, as several modern critics have argued, is not a satire but a "deep" comedy in which (1) a knave tries to control life by cold chicanery, (2) a fool tries to oppress life by unconscious misuse of the highest values, and (3) life, happily, will not have it.

Orgon, the central character of the play, is a rich bourgeois of middle age, with two grown children by his first wife. His second wife, Elmire, is attractive, young, and socially clever. We gather from the maid Dorine that Orgon has until lately seemed a good and sensible man, but the Orgon whom we meet in Act I, Scene 4 has become a fool. What has happened to him? It appears that he, like many another middle-aged man, has been alarmed by a sense of failing powers and failing authority, and that he has compensated by adopting an extreme religious severity. In this he is comparable to the aging coquette described by Dorine, who "quits a world which fast is quitting her," and saves face by becoming a censorious prude.

Orgon's resort to bigotry has coincided with his discovery of Tartuffe, a wily opportunist who imposes upon him by a pretense of sanctity, and is soon established in Orgon's house as honored guest, spiritual guide, and moral censor. Tartuffe's attitude toward Orgon is perfectly simple: he regards his benefactor as a dupe, and proposes to swindle him as badly as he can. Orgon's attitude toward Tartuffe is more complex and far less conscious. It consists, in part, of an unnatural fondness or "crush" about which the clear-sighted Dorine is explicit:

> *He pets and pampers him with love more tender*
> *Than any pretty mistress could engender. . . .*

It also involves, in the strict sense of the word, idolatry: Orgon's febrile religious emotions are all related to Tartuffe

and appear to terminate in him. Finally, and least con-
sciously, Orgon cherishes Tartuffe because, with the sanc-
tion of the latter's austere precepts, he can tyrannize over
his family and punish them for possessing what he feels
himself to be losing: youth, gaiety, strong natural desires.
This punitive motive comes to the surface, looking like
plain sadism, when Orgon orders his daughter to

> *Marry Tartuffe, and mortify your flesh!*

Orgon is thus both Tartuffe's victim and his unconscious
exploiter; once we apprehend this, we can better understand Orgon's stubborn refusal to see Tartuffe for the fraud
that he is.

When Orgon says to Cléante,

> *My mother, children, brother and wife could die,*
> *And I'd not feel a single moment's pain,*

he is parodying or perverting a Christian idea which derives
from the Gospels and rings out purely in Luther's "A
Mighty Fortress is Our God":

> *Let goods and kindred go,*
> *This mortal life also. . . .*

The trouble with Orgon's high spirituality is that one cannot
obey the first commandment without obeying the second
also. Orgon has withdrawn all proper feeling from those
about him, and his vicious fatuity creates an atmosphere
which is the comic equivalent of *King Lear*'s. All natural
bonds of love and trust are strained or broken; evil is taken
for good; truth must to kennel. Cléante's reasonings, the
rebellious protests of Damis, the entreaties of Mariane, and
the mockeries of Dorine are ineffectual against Orgon's
folly; he must see Tartuffe paw at his wife, and hear Tartuffe speak contemptuously of him, before he is willing to

part with the sponsor of his spiteful piety. How little "religion" there has been in Orgon's behavior, how much it has arisen from infatuation and bitterness, we may judge by his indiscriminate outburst in the fifth act:

> *Enough, by God! I'm through with pious men!*
> *Henceforth I'll hate the whole false brotherhood,*
> *And persecute them worse than Satan could.*

By the time Orgon is made to see Tartuffe's duplicity, the latter has accomplished his swindle, and is in a position to bring about Orgon's material ruin. It takes Louis XIV himself to save the day, in a conclusion which may seem both forced and flattering, but which serves to contrast a judicious, humane and forgiving ruler with the domestic tyrant Orgon. The King's moral insight is Tartuffe's final undoing; nevertheless there is an earlier scene in which we are given better assurance of the invincibility of the natural and sane. I refer to Tartuffe's first conversation with Elmire, in which passion compels the hypocrite recklessly to abandon his role. What comes out of Tartuffe in that scene is an expression of helpless lust, couched in an appalling mixture of the languages of gallantry and devotion. It is not attractive; and yet one is profoundly satisfied to discover that, as W. G. Moore puts it, "Tartuffe's human nature escapes his calculation." To be flawlessly monstrous is, thank heaven, not easy.

In translating *Tartuffe* I have tried, as with *The Misanthrope* some years ago, to reproduce with all possible fidelity both Molière's words and his poetic form. The necessity of keeping verse and rhyme, in such plays as these, was argued at some length in an introduction to the earlier translation, and I shall not repeat all those arguments here. It is true that *Tartuffe* presents an upper-bourgeois rather than a courtly milieu; there is less deliberate wit and elegance than in the dialogue of *The Misanthrope*, and consequently there is less call for the couplet as a conveyor of epigrammatic effects. Yet there are such effects in *Tartuffe*, and rhyme and verse are required here for other good reasons: to pay out the long speeches with clarifying emphasis, and at an assimilable rate; to couple farcical sequences to passages of greater weight and resonance; and to give a purely formal pleasure, as when balancing verse-patterns support the "ballet" movement of the close of Act II. My convictions being what they are, I am happy to report what a number of productions of the *Misanthrope* translation have shown: that contemporary audiences are quite willing to put up with rhymed verse on the stage.

I thank Messrs. Jacques Barzun and Eric Bentley for encouraging me to undertake this translation; Messrs. Harry Levin, Frederic Musser and Edward Williamson for suggesting improvements in the text; and the Ford and Philadelphia Community Foundations for their support of the project.

CHARACTERS

MME PERNELLE, Orgon's mother
ORGON, Elmire's husband
ELMIRE, Orgon's wife
DAMIS, Orgon's son, Elmire's stepson
MARIANE, Orgon's daughter, Elmire's stepdaughter,
    in love with Valère
VALÈRE, in love with Mariane
CLÉANTE, Orgon's brother-in-law
TARTUFFE, a hypocrite
DORINE, Mariane's lady's-maid
M. LOYAL, a bailiff
A POLICE OFFICER
FLIPOTE, Mme Pernelle's maid

The scene throughout: Orgon's house in Paris

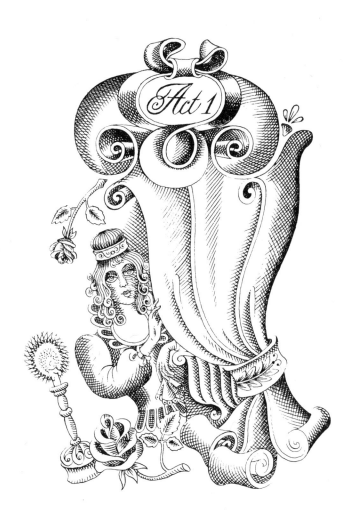

SCENE ONE

MADAME PERNELLE *and* FLIPOTE, *her maid*, ELMIRE,
MARIANE, DORINE, DAMIS, CLÉANTE

MADAME PERNELLE

Come, come, Flipote; it's time I left this place.

ELMIRE

I can't keep up, you walk at such a pace.

MADAME PERNELLE

Don't trouble, child; no need to show me out.
It's not your manners I'm concerned about.

ELMIRE

We merely pay you the respect we owe.
But, Mother, why this hurry? Must you go?

MADAME PERNELLE

I must. This house appals me. No one in it
Will pay attention for a single minute.

[*Act One · Scene One*]

Children, I take my leave much vexed in spirit.
I offer good advice, but you won't hear it.
You all break in and chatter on and on.
It's like a madhouse with the keeper gone.

DORINE

If . . .

MADAME PERNELLE

Girl, you talk too much, and I'm afraid
You're far too saucy for a lady's-maid.
You push in everywhere and have your say.

girl's role

DAMIS

But . . .

Madame starts criticisms of everybody around her

MADAME PERNELLE

You, boy, grow more foolish every day.
To think my grandson should be such a dunce!
I've said a hundred times, if I've said it once,
That if you keep the course on which you've started,
You'll leave your worthy father broken-hearted.

grandson

MARIANE

I think . . .

[*Act One · Scene One*]

MADAME PERNELLE

And you, his sister, seem so pure,
So shy, so innocent, and so demure.
But you know what they say about still waters.
I pity parents with secretive daughters.

ELMIRE

Now, Mother . . .

MADAME PERNELLE

And as for you, child, let me add
That your behavior is extremely bad,
And a poor example for these children, too.
Their dear, dead mother did far better than you.
You're much too free with money, and I'm distressed
To see you so elaborately dressed.
When it's one's husband that one aims to please,
One has no need of costly fripperies.

CLÉANTE

Oh, Madam, really . . .

MADAME PERNELLE

You are her brother, Sir,
And I respect and love you; yet if I were
My son, this lady's good and pious spouse,
I wouldn't make you welcome in my house.

315

You're full of worldly counsels which, I fear,
Aren't suitable for decent folk to hear.
I've spoken bluntly, Sir; but it behooves us
Not to mince words when righteous fervor moves us.

DAMIS

Your man Tartuffe is full of holy speeches . . .

MADAME PERNELLE

And practises precisely what he preaches.
He's a fine man, and should be listened to.
I will not hear him mocked by fools like you.

DAMIS

Good God! Do you expect me to submit
To the tyranny of that carping hypocrite?
Must we forgo all joys and satisfactions
Because that bigot censures all our actions?

religious excentricism

DORINE

To hear him talk—and he talks all the time—
There's nothing one can do that's not a crime.
He rails at everything, your dear Tartuffe.

MADAME PERNELLE

Whatever he reproves deserves reproof.
He's out to save your souls, and all of you
Must love him, as my son would have you do.

[*Act One · Scene One*]

DAMIS

Ah no, Grandmother, I could never take
To such a rascal, even for my father's sake.
That's how I feel, and I shall not dissemble.
His every action makes me seethe and tremble
With helpless anger, and I have no doubt
That he and I will shortly have it out.

DORINE

Surely it is a shame and a disgrace
To see this man usurp the master's place—
To see this beggar who, when first he came,
Had not a shoe or shoestring to his name
So far forget himself that he behaves
As if the house were his, and we his slaves.

MADAME PERNELLE

Well, mark my words, your souls would fare far better
If you obeyed his precepts to the letter.

DORINE

You see him as a saint. I'm far less awed;
In fact, I see right through him. He's a fraud.

MADAME PERNELLE

Nonsense!

DORINE

His man Laurent's the same, or worse;
I'd not trust either with a penny purse.

MADAME PERNELLE

I can't say what his servant's morals may be;
His own great goodness I can guarantee.
You all regard him with distaste and fear
Because he tells you what you're loath to hear,
Condemns your sins, points out your moral flaws,
And humbly strives to further Heaven's cause.

DORINE

If sin is all that bothers him, why is it
He's so upset when folk drop in to visit?
Is Heaven so outraged by a social call
That he must prophesy against us all?
I'll tell you what I think: if you ask me,
He's jealous of my mistress' company.

MADAME PERNELLE

Rubbish! (*To Elmire:*) He's not alone, child, in com-
    plaining
Of all of your promiscuous entertaining.
Why, the whole neighborhood's upset, I know,
By all these carriages that come and go,

With crowds of guests parading in and out
And noisy servants loitering about.
In all of this, I'm sure there's nothing vicious;
But why give people cause to be suspicious?

CLÉANTE

They need no cause; they'll talk in any case.
Madam, this world would be a joyless place
If, fearing what malicious tongues might say,
We locked our doors and turned our friends away.
And even if one did so dreary a thing,
D'you think those tongues would cease their chattering?
One can't fight slander; it's a losing battle;
Let us instead ignore their tittle-tattle.
Let's strive to live by conscience' clear decrees,
And let the gossips gossip as they please.

DORINE

If there is talk against us, I know the source:
It's Daphne and her little husband, of course.
Those who have greatest cause for guilt and shame
Are quickest to besmirch a neighbor's name.
When there's a chance for libel, they never miss it;
When something can be made to seem illicit
They're off at once to spread the joyous news,
Adding to fact what fantasies they choose.
By talking up their neighbor's indiscretions
They seek to camouflage their own transgressions,

319

Hoping that others' innocent affairs
Will lend a hue of innocence to theirs,
Or that their own black guilt will come to seem
Part of a general shady color-scheme.

MADAME PERNELLE

All that is quite irrelevant. I doubt
That anyone's more virtuous and devout
Than dear Orante; and I'm informed that she
Condemns your mode of life most vehemently.

DORINE

Oh, yes, she's strict, devout, and has no taint
Of worldliness; in short, she seems a saint.
But it was time which taught her that disguise;
She's thus because she can't be otherwise.
So long as her attractions could enthrall,
She flounced and flirted and enjoyed it all,
But now that they're no longer what they were
She quits a world which fast is quitting her,
And wears a veil of virtue to conceal
Her bankrupt beauty and her lost appeal.
That's what becomes of old coquettes today:
Distressed when all their lovers fall away,
They see no recourse but to play the prude,
And so confer a style on solitude.
Thereafter, they're severe with everyone,
Condemning all our actions, pardoning none,

320

And claiming to be pure, austere, and zealous
When, if the truth were known, they're merely jealous,
And cannot bear to see another know
The pleasures time has forced them to forgo.

MADAME PERNELLE (*Initially to Elmire:*)

That sort of talk is what you like to hear;
Therefore you'd have us all keep still, my dear,
While Madam rattles on the livelong day.
Nevertheless, I mean to have my say.
I tell you that you're blest to have Tartuffe
Dwelling, as my son's guest, beneath this roof;
That Heaven has sent him to forestall its wrath
By leading you, once more, to the true path;
That all he reprehends its reprehensible,
And that you'd better heed him, and be sensible.
These visits, balls, and parties in which you revel
Are nothing but inventions of the Devil.
One never hears a word that's edifying:
Nothing but chaff and foolishness and lying,
As well as vicious gossip in which one's neighbor
Is cut to bits with epee, foil, and saber.
People of sense are driven half-insane
At such affairs, where noise and folly reign
And reputations perish thick and fast.
As a wise preacher said on Sunday last,
Parties are Towers of Babylon, because
The guests all babble on with never a pause;
And then he told a story which, I think . . .
(*To Cléante:*)
I heard that laugh, Sir, and I saw that wink!

[*Act One · Scene One*]

Go find your silly friends and laugh some more!
Enough; I'm going; don't show me to the door.
I leave this household much dismayed and vexed;
I cannot say when I shall see you next.

(*Slapping Flipote:*)

Wake up, don't stand there gaping into space!
I'll slap some sense into that stupid face.
Move, move, you slut.

difference between ancient & modern

322

SCENE TWO

CLÉANTE

I think I'll stay behind;
I want no further pieces of her mind.
How that old lady . . .

DORINE

Oh, what wouldn't she say
If she could hear you speak of her that way!
She'd thank you for the *lady*, but I'm sure
She'd find the *old* a little premature.

CLÉANTE

My, what a scene she made, and what a din!
And how this man Tartuffe has taken her in!

DORINE

Yes, but her son is even worse deceived;
His folly must be seen to be believed.

[*Act One · Scene Two*]

In the late troubles, he played an able part
And served his king with wise and loyal heart,
But he's quite lost his senses since he fell
Beneath Tartuffe's infatuating spell.
He calls him brother, and loves him as his life,
Preferring him to mother, child, or wife.
In him and him alone will he confide;
He's made him his confessor and his guide;
He pets and pampers him with love more tender
Than any pretty mistress could engender,
Gives him the place of honor when they dine,
Delights to see him gorging like a swine,
Stuffs him with dainties till his guts distend,
And when he belches, cries "God bless you, friend!"
In short, he's mad; he worships him; he dotes;
His deeds he marvels at, his words he quotes,
Thinking each act a miracle, each word
Oracular as those that Moses heard.
Tartuffe, much pleased to find so easy a victim,
Has in a hundred ways beguiled and tricked him,
Milked him of money, and with his permission
Established here a sort of Inquisition.
Even Laurent, his lackey, dares to give
Us arrogant advice on how to live;
He sermonizes us in thundering tones
And confiscates our ribbons and colognes.
Last week he tore a kerchief into pieces
Because he found it pressed in a *Life of Jesus:*
He said it was a sin to juxtapose
Unholy vanities and holy prose.

SCENE THREE

ELMIRE, MARIANE, DAMIS, CLÉANTE, DORINE

ELMIRE (*To Cléante:*)

You did well not to follow; she stood in the door
And said *verbatim* all she'd said before.
I saw my husband coming. I think I'd best
Go upstairs now, and take a little rest.

CLÉANTE

I'll wait and greet him here; then I must go.
I've really only time to say hello.

DAMIS

Sound him about my sister's wedding, please.
I think Tartuffe's against it, and that he's
Been urging Father to withdraw his blessing.
As you well know, I'd find that most distressing.
Unless my sister and Valère can marry,
My hopes to wed *his* sister will miscarry,
And I'm determined . . .

DORINE

He's coming.

325

SCENE FOUR

ORGON, CLÉANTE, DORINE

ORGON

Ah, Brother, good-day.

CLÉANTE

Well, welcome back. I'm sorry I can't stay.
How was the country? Blooming, I trust, and green?

ORGON

Excuse me, Brother; just one moment.
(*To Dorine:*)

Dorine . . .
(*To Cléante:*)
To put my mind at rest, I always learn
The household news the moment I return.
(*To Dorine:*)
Has all been well, these two days I've been gone?
How are the family? What's been going on?

[*Act One · Scene Four*]

Your wife, two days ago, had a bad fever,
And a fierce headache which refused to leave her.

ORGON

Ah. And Tartuffe?

DORINE

                Tartuffe? Why, he's round and red,
Bursting with health, and excellently fed.

ORGON

Poor fellow!

DORINE

           That night, the mistress was unable
To take a single bite at the dinner-table.
Her headache-pains, she said, were simply hellish.

ORGON

Ah. And Tartuffe?

327

[*Act One · Scene Four*]

DORINE

He ate his meal with relish,
And zealously devoured in her presence
A leg of mutton and a brace of pheasants.

ORGON

Poor fellow!

DORINE

Well, the pains continued strong,
And so she tossed and tossed the whole night long,
Now icy-cold, now burning like a flame.
We sat beside her bed till morning came.

ORGON

Ah. And Tartuffe?

DORINE

Why, having eaten, he rose
And sought his room, already in a doze,
Got into his warm bed, and snored away
In perfect peace until the break of day.

ORGON

Poor fellow!

328

[*Act One · Scene Four*]

DORINE

After much ado, we talked her
Into dispatching someone for the doctor.
He bled her, and the fever quickly fell.

ORGON

Ah. And Tartuffe?

DORINE

He bore it very well.
To keep his cheerfulness at any cost,
And make up for the blood *Madame* had lost,
He drank, at lunch, four beakers full of port.

ORGON

Poor fellow!

DORINE

Both are doing well, in short.
I'll go and tell *Madame* that you've expressed
Keen sympathy and anxious interest.

SCENE FIVE

ORGON, CLÉANTE

CLÉANTE

That girl was laughing in your face, and though
I've no wish to offend you, even so
I'm bound to say that she had some excuse.
How can you possibly be such a goose?
Are you so dazed by this man's hocus-pocus
That all the world, save him, is out of focus?
You've given him clothing, shelter, food, and care;
Why must you also . . .

ORGON

                Brother, stop right there.
You do not know the man of whom you speak.

CLÉANTE

I grant you that. But my judgment's not so weak
That I can't tell, by his effect on others . . .

[*Act One* · *Scene Five*]

ORGON

Ah, when you meet him, you two will be like brothers!
There's been no loftier soul since time began.
He is a man who . . . a man who . . . an excellent man.
To keep his precepts is to be reborn,
And view this dunghill of a world with scorn.
Yes, thanks to him I'm a changed man indeed.
Under his tutelage my soul's been freed
From earthly loves, and every human tie:
My mother, children, brother, and wife could die,
And I'd not feel a single moment's pain.

CLÉANTE

That's a fine sentiment, Brother; most humane.

ORGON

Oh, had you seen Tartuffe as I first knew him,
Your heart, like mine, would have surrendered to him.
He used to come into our church each day
And humbly kneel nearby, and start to pray.
He'd draw the eyes of everybody there
By the deep fervor of his heartfelt prayer;
He'd sigh and weep, and sometimes with a sound
Of rapture he would bend and kiss the ground;
And when I rose to go, he'd run before
To offer me holy-water at the door.
His serving-man, no less devout than he,
Informed me of his master's poverty;

I gave him gifts, but in his humbleness
He'd beg me every time to give him less.
"Oh, that's too much," he'd cry, "too much by twice!
I don't deserve it. The half, Sir, would suffice."
And when I wouldn't take it back, he'd share
Half of it with the poor, right then and there.
At length, Heaven prompted me to take him in
To dwell with us, and free our souls from sin.
He guides our lives, and to protect my honor
Stays by my wife, and keeps an eye upon her;
He tells me whom she sees, and all she does,
And seems more jealous than I ever was!
And how austere he is! Why, he can detect
A mortal sin where you would least suspect;
In smallest trifles, he's extremely strict.
Last week, his conscience was severely pricked
Because, while praying, he had caught a flea
And killed it, so he felt, too wrathfully.

CLÉANTE

Good God, man! Have you lost your common sense—
Or is this all some joke at my expense?
How can you stand there and in all sobriety . . .

ORGON

Brother, your language savors of impiety.
Too much free-thinking's made your faith unsteady,
And as I've warned you many times already,
'Twill get you into trouble before you're through.

[*Act One · Scene Five*]

CLÉANTE

So I've been told before by dupes like you:
Being blind, you'd have all others blind as well;
The clear-eyed man you call an infidel,
And he who sees through humbug and pretense
Is charged, by you, with want of reverence.
Spare me your warnings, Brother; I have no fear
Of speaking out, for you and Heaven to hear,
Against affected zeal and pious knavery.
There's true and false in piety, as in bravery,
And just as those whose courage shines the most
In battle, are the least inclined to boast,
So those whose hearts are truly pure and lowly
Don't make a flashy show of being holy.
There's a vast difference, so it seems to me,
Between true piety and hypocrisy:
How do you fail to see it, may I ask?
Is not a face quite different from a mask?
Cannot sincerity and cunning art,
Reality and semblance, be told apart?
Are scarecrows just like men, and do you hold
That a false coin is just as good as gold?
Ah, Brother, man's a strangely fashioned creature
Who seldom is content to follow Nature,
But recklessly pursues his inclination
Beyond the narrow bounds of moderation,
And often, by transgressing Reason's laws,
Perverts a lofty aim or noble cause.
A passing observation, but it applies.

333

[*Act One · Scene Five*]

ORGON

I see, dear Brother, that you're profoundly wise;
You harbor all the insight of the age.
You are our one clear mind, our only sage,
The era's oracle, its Cato too,
And all mankind are fools compared to you.

CLÉANTE

Brother, I don't pretend to be a sage,
Nor have I all the wisdom of the age.
There's just one insight I would dare to claim:
I know that true and false are not the same;
And just as there is nothing I more revere
Than a soul whose faith is steadfast and sincere,
Nothing that I more cherish and admire
Than honest zeal and true religious fire,
So there is nothing that I find more base
Than specious piety's dishonest face—
Than these bold mountebanks, these histrios
Whose impious mummeries and hollow shows
Exploit our love of Heaven, and make a jest
Of all that men think holiest and best;
These calculating souls who offer prayers
Not to their Maker, but as public wares,
And seek to buy respect and reputation
With lifted eyes and sighs of exaltation;
These charlatans, I say, whose pilgrim souls
Proceed, by way of Heaven, toward earthly goals,
Who weep and pray and swindle and extort,

334

[*Act One · Scene Five*]

Who preach the monkish life, but haunt the court,
Who make their zeal the partner of their vice—
Such men are vengeful, sly, and cold as ice,
And when there is an enemy to defame
They cloak their spite in fair religion's name,
Their private spleen and malice being made
To seem a high and virtuous crusade,
Until, to mankind's reverent applause,
They crucify their foe in Heaven's cause.
Such knaves are all too common; yet, for the wise,
True piety isn't hard to recognize,
And, happily, these present times provide us
With bright examples to instruct and guide us.
Consider Ariston and Périandre;
Look at Oronte, Alcidamas, Clitandre;
Their virtue is acknowledged; who could doubt it?
But you won't hear them beat the drum about it.
They're never ostentatious, never vain,
And their religion's moderate and humane;
It's not their way to criticize and chide:
They think censoriousness a mark of pride,
And therefore, letting others preach and rave,
They show, by deeds, how Christians should behave.
They think no evil of their fellow man,
But judge of him as kindly as they can.
They don't intrigue and wangle and conspire;
To lead a good life is their one desire;
The sinner wakes no rancorous hate in them;
It is the sin alone which they condemn;
Nor do they try to show a fiercer zeal
For Heaven's cause than Heaven itself could feel.
These men I honor, these men I advocate

As models for us all to emulate.
Your man is not their sort at all, I fear:
And, while your praise of him is quite sincere,
I think that you've been dreadfully deluded.

ORGON

Now then, dear Brother, is your speech concluded?

CLÉANTE

Why, yes.

ORGON

Your servant, Sir. (*He turns to go.*)

CLÉANTE

                              No, Brother; wait.
There's one more matter. You agreed of late
That young Valère might have your daughter's hand.

ORGON

I did.

CLÉANTE

And set the date, I understand.

336

[*Act One · Scene Five*]

ORGON

Quite so.

CLÉANTE

You've now postponed it; is that true?

ORGON

No doubt.

CLÉANTE

The match no longer pleases you?

ORGON

Who knows?

CLÉANTE

D'you mean to go back on your word?

ORGON

I won't say that.

CLÉANTE

Has anything occurred
Which might entitle you to break your pledge?

337

[*Act One · Scene Five*]

ORGON

Perhaps.

CLÉANTE

Why must you hem, and haw, and hedge?
The boy asked me to sound you in this affair . . .

ORGON

It's been a pleasure.

CLÉANTE

But what shall I tell Valère?

ORGON

Whatever you like.

CLÉANTE

But what have you decided?
What are your plans?

ORGON

I plan, Sir, to be guided
By Heaven's will.

[*Act One · Scene Five*]

CLÉANTE

Come, Brother, don't talk rot.
You've given Valère your word; will you keep it, or not?

ORGON

Good day.

CLÉANTE

This looks like poor Valère's undoing;
I'll go and warn him that there's trouble brewing.

Act 2

SCENE ONE

ORGON, MARIANE

ORGON

Mariane.

MARIANE

Yes, Father?

ORGON

A word with you; come here.

MARIANE

What are you looking for?

ORGON (*Peering into a small closet:*)

                    Eavesdroppers, dear.
I'm making sure we shan't be overheard.
Someone in there could catch our every word.
Ah, good, we're safe. Now, Mariane, my child,
You're a sweet girl who's tractable and mild,
Whom I hold dear, and think most highly of.

343

[*Act Two · Scene One*]

MARIANE

I'm deeply grateful, Father, for your love.

ORGON

That's well said, Daughter; and you can repay me
If, in all things, you'll cheerfully obey me.

MARIANE

To please you, Sir, is what delights me best.

ORGON

Good, good. Now, what d'you think of Tartuffe, our
 guest?

MARIANE

I, Sir?

ORGON

Yes. Weigh your answer; think it through.

MARIANE

Oh, dear. I'll say whatever you wish me to.

344

[*Act Two · Scene One*]

ORGON

That's wisely said, my Daughter. Say of him, then,
That he's the very worthiest of men,
And that you're fond of him, and would rejoice
In being his wife, if that should be my choice.
Well?

MARIANE

What?

ORGON

What's that?

MARIANE

I ...

ORGON

Well?

MARIANE

Forgive me, pray.

ORGON

Did you not hear me?

[*Act Two · Scene One*]

MARIANE

Of *whom*, Sir, must I say
That I am fond of him, and would rejoice
In being his wife, if that should be your choice?

ORGON

Why, of Tartuffe.

MARIANE

But, Father, that's false, you know.
Why would you have me say what isn't so?

ORGON

Because I am resolved it shall be true.
That it's my wish should be enough for you.

MARIANE

You can't mean, Father . . .

ORGON

Yes, Tartuffe shall be
Allied by marriage to this family,
And he's to be your husband, is that clear?
It's a father's privilege . . .

346

SCENE TWO

DORINE, ORGON, MARIANE

ORGON (*To Dorine:*)

What are you doing in here?
Is curiosity so fierce a passion
With you, that you must eavesdrop in this fashion?

DORINE

There's lately been a rumor going about—
Based on some hunch or chance remark, no doubt—
That you mean Mariane to wed Tartuffe.
I've laughed it off, of course, as just a spoof.

ORGON

You find it so incredible?

DORINE

Yes, I do.
I won't accept that story, even from you.

347

[*Act Two · Scene Two*]

ORGON

Well, you'll believe it when the thing is done.

DORINE

Yes, yes, of course. Go on and have your fun.

ORGON

I've never been more serious in my life.

DORINE

Ha!

ORGON

Daughter, I mean it; you're to be his wife.

DORINE

No, don't believe your father; it's all a hoax.

ORGON

See here, young woman . . .

DORINE

Come, Sir, no more jokes;
You can't fool us.

[*Act Two · Scene Two*]

ORGON

How dare you talk that way?

DORINE

All right, then: we believe you, sad to say.
But how a man like you, who looks so wise
And wears a moustache of such splendid size,
Can be so foolish as to . . .

ORGON

Silence, please!
My girl, you take too many liberties.
I'm master here, as you must not forget.

DORINE

Do let's discuss this calmly; don't be upset.
You can't be serious, Sir, about this plan.
What should that bigot want with Mariane?
Praying and fasting ought to keep him busy.
And then, in terms of wealth and rank, what is he?
Why should a man of property like you
Pick out a beggar son-in-law?

ORGON

That will do.
Speak of his poverty with reverence.
His is a pure and saintly indigence

Which far transcends all worldly pride and pelf.
He lost his fortune, as he says himself,
Because he cared for Heaven alone, and so
Was careless of his interests here below.
I mean to get him out of his present straits
And help him to recover his estates—
Which, in his part of the world, have no small fame.
Poor though he is, he's a gentleman just the same.

DORINE

Yes, so he tells us; and, Sir, it seems to me
Such pride goes very ill with piety.
A man whose spirit spurns this dungy earth
Ought not to brag of lands and noble birth;
Such worldly arrogance will hardly square
With meek devotion and the life of prayer.
. . . But this approach, I see, has drawn a blank;
Let's speak, then, of his person, not his rank.
Doesn't it seem to you a trifle grim
To give a girl like her to a man like him?
When two are so ill-suited, can't you see
What the sad consequence is bound to be?
A young girl's virtue is imperilled, Sir,
When such a marriage is imposed on her;
For if one's bridegroom isn't to one's taste,
It's hardly an inducement to be chaste,
And many a man with horns upon his brow
Has made his wife the thing that she is now.
It's hard to be a faithful wife, in short,
To certain husbands of a certain sort,

And he who gives his daughter to a man she hates
Must answer for her sins at Heaven's gates.
Think, Sir, before you play so risky a role.

ORGON

This servant-girl presumes to save my soul!

DORINE

You would do well to ponder what I've said.

ORGON

Daughter, we'll disregard this dunderhead.
Just trust your father's judgment. Oh, I'm aware
That I once promised you to young Valère;
But now I hear he gambles, which greatly shocks me;
What's more, I've doubts about his orthodoxy.
His visits to church, I note, are very few.

DORINE

Would you have him go at the same hours as you,
And kneel nearby, to be sure of being seen?

ORGON

I can dispense with such remarks, Dorine.
(*To Mariane:*)
Tartuffe, however, is sure of Heaven's blessing,
And that's the only treasure worth possessing.

[*Act Two · Scene Two*]

This match will bring you joys beyond all measure;
Your cup will overflow with every pleasure;
You two will interchange your faithful loves
Like two sweet cherubs, or two turtle-doves.
No harsh word shall be heard, no frown be seen,
And he shall make you happy as a queen.

DORINE

And she'll make him a cuckold, just wait and see.

ORGON

What language!

DORINE

                    Oh, he's a man of destiny;
He's *made* for horns, and what the stars demand
Your daughter's virtue surely can't withstand.

ORGON

Don't interrupt me further. Why can't you learn
That certain things are none of your concern?

DORINE

It's for your own sake that I interfere.
        (*She repeatedly interrupts Orgon just as he is turn-
        ing to speak to his daughter:*)

[*Act Two · Scene Two*]

ORGON

Most kind of you. Now, hold your tongue, d'you hear?

DORINE

If I didn't love you . . .

ORGON

Spare me your affection.

DORINE

I'll love you, Sir, in spite of your objection.

ORGON

Blast!

DORINE

I can't bear, Sir, for your honor's sake,
To let you make this ludicrous mistake.

ORGON

You mean to go on talking?

DORINE

If I didn't protest
This sinful marriage, my conscience couldn't rest.

[Act Two · Scene Two]

ORGON

If you don't hold your tongue, you little shrew . . .

DORINE

What, lost your temper? A pious man like you?

ORGON

Yes! Yes! You talk and talk. I'm maddened by it.
Once and for all, I tell you to be quiet.

DORINE

Well, I'll be quiet. But I'll be thinking hard.

ORGON

Think all you like, but you had better guard
That saucy tongue of yours, or I'll . . .
                    (*Turning back to Mariane:*)
                                        Now, child,
I've weighed this matter fully.

DORINE (*Aside:*)

                              It drives me wild
That I can't speak.
        (*Orgon turns his head, and she is silent.*)

354

[*Act Two · Scene Two*]

ORGON

       Tartuffe is no young dandy,
But, still, his person . . .

DORINE (*Aside:*)

       Is as sweet as candy.

ORGON

Is such that, even if you shouldn't care
For his other merits . . .
   (*He turns and stands facing Dorine, arms crossed.*)

DORINE (*Aside:*)

       They'll make a lovely pair.
If I were she, no man would marry me
Against my inclination, and go scot-free.
He'd learn, before the wedding-day was over,
How readily a wife can find a lover.

ORGON (*To Dorine:*)

It seems you treat my orders as a joke.

DORINE

Why, what's the matter? 'Twas not to you I spoke.

355

[Act Two · Scene Two]

ORGON

What *were* you doing?

DORINE

Talking to myself, that's all.

ORGON

Ah! (*Aside:*) One more bit of impudence and gall,
And I shall give her a good slap in the face.
(*He puts himself in position to slap her; Dorine,
whenever he glances at her, stands immobile and
silent:*)
Daughter, you shall accept, and with good grace,
The husband I've selected . . . Your wedding-day . . .
(*To Dorine:*)
Why don't you talk to yourself?

DORINE

I've nothing to say.

ORGON

Come, just one word.

DORINE

No thank you, Sir. I pass.

356

[*Act Two · Scene Two*]

ORGON

Come, speak; I'm waiting.

DORINE

I'd not be such an ass.

ORGON (*Turning to Mariane:*)

In short, dear Daughter, I mean to be obeyed,
And you must bow to the sound choice I've made.

DORINE (*Moving away:*)

I'd not wed such a monster, even in jest.
    (*Orgon attempts to slap her, but misses.*)

ORGON

Daughter, that maid of yours is a thorough pest;
She makes me sinfully annoyed and nettled.
I can't speak further; my nerves are too unsettled.
She's so upset me by her insolent talk,
I'll calm myself by going for a walk.

SCENE THREE

DORINE, MARIANE

DORINE (*Returning:*)

Well, have you lost your tongue, girl? Must I play
Your part, and say the lines you ought to say?
Faced with a fate so hideous and absurd,
Can you not utter one dissenting word?

MARIANE

What good would it do? A father's power is great.

DORINE

Resist him now, or it will be too late.

MARIANE

But . . .

DORINE

Tell him one cannot love at a father's whim;
That you shall marry for yourself, not him;

358

That since it's you who are to be the bride,
It's you, not he, who must be satisfied;
And that if his Tartuffe is so sublime,
He's free to marry him at any time.

MARIANE

I've bowed so long to Father's strict control,
I couldn't oppose him now, to save my soul.

DORINE

Come, come, Mariane. Do listen to reason, won't you?
Valère has asked your hand. Do you love him, or don't
    you?

MARIANE

Oh, how unjust of you! What can you mean
By asking such a question, dear Dorine?
You know the depth of my affection for him;
I've told you a hundred times how I adore him.

DORINE

I don't believe in everything I hear;
Who knows if your professions were sincere?

MARIANE

They were, Dorine, and you do me wrong to doubt it;
Heaven knows that I've been all too frank about it.

DORINE

You love him, then?

MARIANE

Oh, more than I can express.

DORINE

And he, I take it, cares for you no less?

MARIANE

I think so.

DORINE

And you both, with equal fire,
Burn to be married?

MARIANE

That is our one desire.

DORINE

What of Tartuffe, then? What of your father's plan?

MARIANE

I'll kill myself, if I'm forced to wed that man.

[*Act Two · Scene Three*]

DORINE

I hadn't thought of that recourse. How splendid!
Just die, and all your troubles will be ended!
A fine solution. Oh, it maddens me
To hear you talk in that self-pitying key.

MARIANE

Dorine, how harsh you are! It's most unfair.
You have no sympathy for my despair.

DORINE

I've none at all for people who talk drivel
And, faced with difficulties, whine and snivel.

MARIANE

No doubt I'm timid, but it would be wrong . . .

DORINE

True love requires a heart that's firm and strong.

MARIANE

I'm strong in my affection for Valère,
But coping with my father is his affair.

DORINE

But if your father's brain has grown so cracked
Over his dear Tartuffe that he can retract
His blessing, though your wedding-day was named,
It's surely not Valère who's to be blamed.

MARIANE

If I defied my father, as you suggest,
Would it not seem unmaidenly, at best?
Shall I defend my love at the expense
Of brazenness and disobedience?
Shall I parade my heart's desires, and flaunt . . .

DORINE

No, I ask nothing of you. Clearly you want
To be Madame Tartuffe, and I feel bound
Not to oppose a wish so very sound.
What right have I to criticize the match?
Indeed, my dear, the man's a brilliant catch.
Monsieur Tartuffe! Now, there's a man of weight!
Yes, yes, Monsieur Tartuffe, I'm bound to state,
Is quite a person; that's not to be denied;
'Twill be no little thing to be his bride.
The world already rings with his renown;
He's a great noble—in his native town;
His ears are red, he has a pink complexion,
And all in all, he'll suit you to perfection.

MARIANE

Dear God!

DORINE

Oh, how triumphant you will feel
At having caught a husband so ideal!

MARIANE

Oh, do stop teasing, and use your cleverness
To get me out of this appalling mess.
Advise me, and I'll do whatever you say.

DORINE

Ah no, a dutiful daughter must obey
Her father, even if he weds her to an ape.
You've a bright future; why struggle to escape?
Tartuffe will take you back where his family lives,
To a small town aswarm with relatives—
Uncles and cousins whom you'll be charmed to meet.
You'll be received at once by the elite,
Calling upon the bailiff's wife, no less—
Even, perhaps, upon the mayoress,
Who'll sit you down in the *best* kitchen chair.
Then, once a year, you'll dance at the village fair
To the drone of bagpipes—two of them, in fact—
And see a puppet-show, or an animal act.
Your husband . . .

[*Act Two · Scene Three*]

MARIANE

Oh, you turn my blood to ice!
Stop torturing me, and give me your advice.

DORINE (*Threatening to go:*)

Your servant, Madam.

MARIANE

Dorine, I beg of you . . .

DORINE

No, you deserve it; this marriage must go through.

MARIANE

Dorine!

DORINE

No.

MARIANE

Not Tartuffe! You know I think him . . .

DORINE

Tartuffe's your cup of tea, and you shall drink him.

364

[*Act Two · Scene Three*]

MARIANE

I've always told you everything, and relied . . .

DORINE

No. You deserve to be tartuffified. → creation of words

MARIANE

Well, since you mock me and refuse to care,
I'll henceforth seek my solace in despair:
Despair shall be my counsellor and friend,
And help me bring my sorrows to an end.
                    (*She starts to leave.*)

DORINE

There now, come back; my anger has subsided.
You do deserve some pity, I've decided.

MARIANE

Dorine, if Father makes me undergo
This dreadful martyrdom, I'll die, I know.

DORINE

Don't fret; it won't be difficult to discover
Some plan of action . . . But here's Valère, your lover.

365

SCENE FOUR

VALÈRE, MARIANE, DORINE

VALÈRE

Madam, I've just received some wondrous news
Regarding which I'd like to hear your views.

MARIANE

What news?

VALÈRE

You're marrying Tartuffe.

MARIANE

                              I find
That Father does have such a match in mind.

VALÈRE

Your father, Madam . . .

[*Act Two · Scene Four*]

MARIANE

. . . has just this minute said
That it's Tartuffe he wishes me to wed.

VALÈRE

Can he be serious?

MARIANE

Oh, indeed he can;
He's clearly set his heart upon the plan.

VALÈRE

And what position do you propose to take,
Madam?

MARIANE

Why—I don't know.

VALÈRE

For heaven's sake—
You don't know?

MARIANE

No.

[*Act Two · Scene Four*]

VALÈRE

Well, well!

MARIANE

Advise me, do.

VALÈRE

Marry the man. That's my advice to you.

MARIANE

That's your advice?

VALÈRE

Yes.

MARIANE

Truly?

VALÈRE

Oh, absolutely.
You couldn't choose more wisely, more astutely.

MARIANE

Thanks for this counsel; I'll follow it, of course.

368

[Act Two · Scene Four]

VALÈRE

Do, do; I'm sure 'twill cost you no remorse.

MARIANE

To give it didn't cause your heart to break.

VALÈRE

I gave it, Madam, only for your sake.

MARIANE

And it's for your sake that I take it, Sir.

DORINE (*Withdrawing to the rear of the stage:*)

Let's see which fool will prove the stubborner.

VALÈRE

So! I am nothing to you, and it was flat
Deception when you . . .

MARIANE

            Please, enough of that.
You've told me plainly that I should agree
To wed the man my father's chosen for me,
And since you've deigned to counsel me so wisely,
I promise, Sir, to do as you advise me.

[handwritten margin note: word games — saying what they didn't mean]

VALÈRE

Ah, no, 'twas not by me that you were swayed.
No, your decision was already made;
Though now, to save appearances, you protest
That you're betraying me at my behest.

MARIANE

Just as you say.

VALÈRE

Quite so. And I now see
That you were never truly in love with me.

MARIANE

Alas, you're free to think so if you choose.

VALÈRE

I choose to think so, and here's a bit of news:
You've spurned my hand, but I know where to turn
For kinder treatment, as you shall quickly learn.

MARIANE

I'm sure you do. Your noble qualities
Inspire affection . . .

[*Act Two · Scene Four*]

VALÈRE

Forget my qualities, please.
They don't inspire you overmuch, I find.
But there's another lady I have in mind
Whose sweet and generous nature will not scorn
To compensate me for the loss I've borne.

MARIANE

I'm no great loss, and I'm sure that you'll transfer
Your heart quite painlessly from me to her.

VALÈRE

I'll do my best to take it in my stride.
The pain I feel at being cast aside
Time and forgetfulness may put an end to.
Or if I can't forget, I shall pretend to.
No self-respecting person is expected
To go on loving once he's been rejected.

MARIANE

Now, that's a fine, high-minded sentiment.

VALÈRE

One to which any sane man would assent.
Would you prefer it if I pined away
In hopeless passion till my dying day?

Am I to yield you to a rival's arms
And not console myself with other charms?

MARIANE

Go then: console yourself; don't hesitate.
I wish you to; indeed, I cannot wait.

VALÈRE

You wish me to?

MARIANE

Yes.

VALÈRE

That's the final straw.
Madam, farewell. Your wish shall be my law.
(*He starts to leave, and then returns: this repeatedly:*)

MARIANE

Splendid.

VALÈRE (*Coming back again:*)

This breach, remember, is of your making;
It's you who've driven me to the step I'm taking.

372

[*Act Two · Scene Four*]

MARIANE

Of course.

VALÈRE (*Coming back again:*)

Remember, too, that I am merely
Following your example.

MARIANE

I see that clearly.

VALÈRE

Enough. I'll go and do your bidding, then.

MARIANE

Good.

VALÈRE (*Coming back again:*)

You shall never see my face again.

MARIANE

Excellent.

VALÈRE (*Walking to the door, then turning about:*)

Yes?

373

MARIANE

What?

VALÈRE

What's that? What did you say?

MARIANE

Nothing. You're dreaming.

VALÈRE

Ah. Well, I'm on my way.
Farewell, *Madame*.
(*He moves slowly away.*)

MARIANE

Farewell.

DORINE (*To Mariane:*)

If you ask me,
Both of you are as mad as mad can be.
Do stop this nonsense, now. I've only let you
Squabble so long to see where it would get you.
Whoa there, Monsieure Valère!
(*She goes and seizes Valère by the arm; he makes a
great show of resistance.*)

[*Act Two · Scene Four*]

VALÈRE

What's this, Dorine?

DORINE

Come here.

VALÈRE

No, no, my heart's too full of spleen.
Don't hold me back; her wish must be obeyed.

DORINE

Stop!

VALÈRE

It's too late now; my decision's made.

DORINE

Oh, pooh!

MARIANE (*Aside:*)

He hates the sight of me, that's plain.
I'll go, and so deliver him from pain.

[*Act Two · Scene Four*]

DORINE (*Leaving Valère, running after Mariane:*)

And now *you* run away! Come back.

MARIANE

No, no.
Nothing you say will keep me here. Let go!

VALÈRE (*Aside:*)

She cannot bear my presence, I perceive.
To spare her further torment, I shall leave.

DORINE (*Leaving Mariane, running after Valère:*)

Again! You'll not escape, Sir; don't you try it.
Come here, you two. Stop fussing, and be quiet.
    (*She takes Valère by the hand, then Mariane, and
    draws them together.*)

VALÈRE (*To Dorine:*)

What do you want of me?

MARIANE (*To Dorine:*)

What is the point of this?

DORINE

We're going to have a little armistice.

(*To Valère:*)
Now, weren't you silly to get so overheated?

VALÈRE

Didn't you see how badly I was treated?

DORINE (*To Mariane:*)

Aren't you a simpleton, to have lost your head?

MARIANE

Didn't you hear the hateful things he said?

DORINE (*To Valère:*)

You're both great fools. Her sole desire, Valère,
Is to be yours in marriage. To that I'll swear.
(*To Mariane:*)
He loves you only, and he wants no wife
But you, Mariane. On that I'll stake my life.

MARIANE (*To Valère:*)

Then why you advised me so, I cannot see.

VALÈRE (*To Mariane:*)

On such a question, why ask advice of *me?*

[*Act Two · Scene Four*]

DORINE

Oh, you're impossible. Give me your hands, you two.
(*To Valère:*)
Yours first.

VALÈRE (*Giving Dorine his hand:*)

But why?

DORINE (*To Mariane:*)

And now a hand from you.

MARIANE (*Also giving Dorine her hand:*)

What are you doing?

DORINE

There: a perfect fit.
You suit each other better than you'll admit.
(*Valère and Mariane hold hands for some time with-
out looking at each other.*)

VALÈRE (*Turning toward Mariane:*)

Ah, come, don't be so haughty. Give a man
A look of kindness, won't you, Mariane?
(*Mariane turns toward Valère and smiles.*)

378

DORINE

I tell you, lovers are completely mad!

VALÈRE (*To Mariane:*)

Now come, confess that you were very bad
To hurt my feelings as you did just now.
I have a just complaint, you must allow.

MARIANE

You must allow that you were most unpleasant . . .

DORINE

Let's table that discussion for the present;
Your father has a plan which must be stopped.

MARIANE

Advise us, then; what means must we adopt?

DORINE

We'll use all manner of means, and all at once.
(*To Mariane:*)
Your father's addled; he's acting like a dunce.
Therefore you'd better humor the old fossil.
Pretend to yield to him, be sweet and docile,
And then postpone, as often as necessary,

379

pretend to
agree, (like
l'avare)

The day on which you have agreed to marry.
You'll thus gain time, and time will turn the trick.
Sometimes, for instance, you'll be taken sick,
And that will seem good reason for delay;
Or some bad omen will make you change the day—
You'll dream of muddy water, or you'll pass
A dead man's hearse, or break a looking-glass.
If all else fails, no man can marry you
Unless you take his ring and say "I do."
But now, let's separate. If they should find
Us talking here, our plot might be divined.
(*To Valère:*)
Go to your friends, and tell them what's occurred,
And have them urge her father to keep his word.
Meanwhile, we'll stir her brother into action,
And get Elmire, as well, to join our faction.
Good-bye.

VALÈRE (*To Mariane:*)

Though each of us will do his best,
It's your true heart on which my hopes shall rest.

MARIANE (*To Valère:*)

Regardless of what Father may decide,
None but Valère shall claim me as his bride.

VALÈRE

Oh, how those words content me! Come what will . . .

DORINE

Oh, lovers, lovers! Their tongues are never still.
Be off, now.

VALÈRE (*Turning to go, then turning back:*)

One last word . . .

DORINE

No time to chat:
You leave by this door; and *you* leave by that.
(*Dorine pushes them, by the shoulders, toward op-
posing doors.*)

SCENE ONE

DAMIS

May lightning strike me even as I speak,
May all men call me cowardly and weak,
If any fear or scruple holds me back
From settling things, at once, with that great quack!

DORINE

Now, don't give way to violent emotion.
Your father's merely talked about this notion,
And words and deeds are far from being one.
Much that is talked about is left undone.

DAMIS

No, I must stop that scoundrel's machinations;
I'll go and tell him off; I'm out of patience.

DORINE

Do calm down and be practical. I had rather
My mistress dealt with him—and with your father.

385

She has some influence with Tartuffe, I've noted.
He hangs upon her words, seems most devoted,
And may, indeed, be smitten by her charm.
Pray Heaven it's true! 'Twould do our cause no harm.
She sent for him, just now, to sound him out
On this affair you're so incensed about;
She'll find out where he stands, and tell him, too,
What dreadful strife and trouble will ensue
If he lends countenance to your father's plan.
I couldn't get in to see him, but his man
Says that he's almost finished with his prayers.
Go, now. I'll catch him when he comes downstairs.

DAMIS

I want to hear this conference, and I will.

DORINE

No, they must be alone.

DAMIS

Oh, I'll keep still.

DORINE

Not you. I know your temper. You'd start a brawl,
And shout and stamp your foot and spoil it all.
Go on.

[*Act Three · Scene One*]

DAMIS

I won't; I have a perfect right . . .

DORINE

Lord, you're a nuisance! He's coming; get out of sight.
   (*Damis conceals himself in a closet at the rear of the stage.*)

SCENE TWO

TARTUFFE, DORINE

TARTUFFE (*Observing Dorine, and calling to his
manservant offstage:*)

Hang up my hair-shirt, put my scourge in place,
And pray, Laurent, for Heaven's perpetual grace.
I'm going to the prison now, to share
My last few coins with the poor wretches there.

DORINE (*Aside:*)

Dear God, what affectation! What a fake!

TARTUFFE

You wished to see me?

DORINE

Yes . . .

TARTUFFE (*Taking a handkerchief from his pocket:*)

For mercy's sake,
Please take this handkerchief, before you speak.

DORINE

What?

TARTUFFE

Cover that bosom, girl. The flesh is weak,
And unclean thoughts are difficult to control.
Such sights as that can undermine the soul.

DORINE

Your soul, it seems, has very poor defenses,
And flesh makes quite an impact on your senses.
It's strange that you're so easily excited;
My own desires are not so soon ignited,
And if I saw you naked as a beast,
Not all your hide would tempt me in the least.

TARTUFFE

Girl, speak more modestly; unless you do,
I shall be forced to take my leave of you.

DORINE

Oh, no, it's I who must be on my way;
I've just one little message to convey.
Madame is coming down, and begs you, Sir,
To wait and have a word or two with her.

[*Act Three · Scene Two*]

TARTUFFE

Gladly.

DORINE (*Aside:*)

That had a softening effect!
I think my guess about him was correct.

TARTUFFE

Will she be long?

DORINE

No: that's her step I hear.
Ah, here she is, and I shall disappear.

SCENE THREE

TARTUFFE

May Heaven, whose infinite goodness we adore,
Preserve your body and soul forevermore,
And bless your days, and answer thus the plea
Of one who is its humblest votary.

ELMIRE

I thank you for that pious wish. But please,
Do take a chair and let's be more at ease.
                    (*They sit down.*)

TARTUFFE

I trust that you are once more well and strong?

ELMIRE

Oh, yes: the fever didn't last for long.

391

TARTUFFE

My prayers are too unworthy, I am sure,
To have gained from Heaven this most gracious cure;
But lately, Madam, my every supplication
Has had for object your recuperation.

ELMIRE

You shouldn't have troubled so. I don't deserve it.

TARTUFFE

Your health is priceless, Madam, and to preserve it
I'd gladly give my own, in all sincerity.

ELMIRE

Sir, you outdo us all in Christian charity.
You've been most kind. I count myself your debtor.

TARTUFFE

'Twas nothing, Madam. I long to serve you better.

ELMIRE

There's a private matter I'm anxious to discuss.
I'm glad there's no one here to hinder us.

TARTUFFE

I too am glad; it floods my heart with bliss
To find myself alone with you like this.
For just this chance I've prayed with all my power—
But prayed in vain, until this happy hour.

ELMIRE

This won't take long, Sir, and I hope you'll be
Entirely frank and unconstrained with me.

TARTUFFE

Indeed, there's nothing I had rather do
Than bare my inmost heart and soul to you.
First, let me say that what remarks I've made
About the constant visits you are paid
Were prompted not by any mean emotion,
But rather by a pure and deep devotion,
A fervent zeal . . .

ELMIRE

No need for explanation.
Your sole concern, I'm sure, was my salvation.

TARTUFFE (*Taking Elmire's hand and pressing her fingertips:*)

Quite so; and such great fervor do I feel . . .

[*Act Three · Scene Three*]

ELMIRE

Ooh! Please! You're pinching!

TARTUFFE

'Twas from excess of zeal.
I never meant to cause you pain, I swear.
I'd rather . . .
(*He places his hand on Elmire's knee.*)

ELMIRE

What can your hand be doing there?

TARTUFFE

Feeling your gown; what soft, fine-woven stuff!

ELMIRE

Please, I'm extremely ticklish. That's enough.
(*She draws her chair away; Tartuffe pulls his after her.*)

TARTUFFE (*Fondling the lace collar of her gown:*)

My, my, what lovely lacework on your dress!
The workmanship's miraculous, no less.
I've not seen anything to equal it.

[*Act Three · Scene Three*]

ELMIRE

Yes, quite. But let's talk business for a bit.
They say my husband means to break his word
And give his daughter to you, Sir. Had you heard?

TARTUFFE

He did once mention it. But I confess
I dream of quite a different happiness.
It's elsewhere, Madam, that my eyes discern
The promise of that bliss for which I yearn.

ELMIRE

I see: you care for nothing here below.

TARTUFFE

Ah, well—my heart's not made of stone, you know.

ELMIRE

All your desires mount heavenward, I'm sure,
In scorn of all that's earthly and impure.

TARTUFFE

A love of heavenly beauty does not preclude
A proper love for earthly pulchritude;
Our senses are quite rightly captivated
By perfect works our Maker has created.

395

Some glory clings to all that Heaven has made;
In you, all Heaven's marvels are displayed.
On that fair face, such beauties have been lavished,
The eyes are dazzled and the heart is ravished;
How could I look on you, O flawless creature,
And not adore the Author of all Nature,
Feeling a love both passionate and pure
For you, his triumph of self-portraiture?
At first, I trembled lest that love should be
A subtle snare that Hell had laid for me;
I vowed to flee the sight of you, eschewing
A rapture that might prove my soul's undoing;
But soon, fair being, I became aware
That my deep passion could be made to square
With rectitude, and with my bounden duty.
I thereupon surrendered to your beauty.
It is, I know, presumptuous on my part
To bring you this poor offering of my heart,
And it is not my merit, Heaven knows,
But your compassion on which my hopes repose.
You are my peace, my solace, my salvation;
On you depends my bliss—or desolation;
I bide your judgment and, as you think best,
I shall be either miserable or blest.

ELMIRE

Your declaration is most gallant, Sir,
But don't you think it's out of character?
You'd have done better to restrain your passion
And think before you spoke in such a fashion.
It ill becomes a pious man like you . . .

396

TARTUFFE

I may be pious, but I'm human too:
With your celestial charms before his eyes,
A man has not the power to be wise.
I know such words sound strangely, coming from me,
But I'm no angel, nor was meant to be,
And if you blame my passion, you must needs
Reproach as well the charms on which it feeds.
Your loveliness I had no sooner seen
Than you became my soul's unrivalled queen;
Before your seraph glance, divinely sweet,
My heart's defenses crumbled in defeat,
And nothing fasting, prayer, or tears might do
Could stay my spirit from adoring you.
My eyes, my sighs have told you in the past
What now my lips make bold to say at last,
And if, in your great goodness, you will deign
To look upon your slave, and ease his pain,—
If, in compassion for my soul's distress,
You'll stoop to comfort my unworthiness,
I'll raise to you, in thanks for that sweet manna,
An endless hymn, an infinite hosanna.
With me, of course, there need be no anxiety,
No fear of scandal or of notoriety.
These young court gallants, whom all the ladies fancy,
Are vain in speech, in action rash and chancy;
When they succeed in love, the world soon knows it;
No favor's granted them but they disclose it
And by the looseness of their tongues profane
The very altar where their hearts have lain.

Men of my sort, however, love discreetly,
And one may trust our reticence completely.
My keen concern for my good name insures
The absolute security of yours;
In short, I offer you, my dear Elmire,
Love without scandal, pleasure without fear.

ELMIRE

I've heard your well-turned speeches to the end,
And what you urge I clearly apprehend.
Aren't you afraid that I may take a notion
To tell my husband of your warm devotion,
And that, supposing he were duly told,
His feelings toward you might grow rather cold?

TARTUFFE

I know, dear lady, that your exceeding charity
Will lead your heart to pardon my temerity;
That you'll excuse my violent affection
As human weakness, human imperfection;
And that—O fairest!—you will bear in mind
That I'm but flesh and blood, and am not blind.

ELMIRE

Some women might do otherwise, perhaps,
But I shall be discreet about your lapse;
I'll tell my husband nothing of what's occurred
If, in return, you'll give your solemn word

To advocate as forcefully as you can
The marriage of Valère and Mariane,
Renouncing all desire to dispossess
Another of his rightful happiness,
And . . .

trickery

SCENE FOUR

DAMIS, ELMIRE, TARTUFFE

DAMIS (*Emerging from the closet where he has been hiding:*)

No! We'll not hush up this vile affair;
I heard it all inside that closet there,
Where Heaven, in order to confound the pride
Of this great rascal, prompted me to hide.
Ah, now I have my long-awaited chance
To punish his deceit and arrogance,
And give my father clear and shocking proof
Of the black character of his dear Tartuffe.

ELMIRE

Ah no, Damis; I'll be content if he
Will study to deserve my leniency.
I've promised silence—don't make me break my word;
To make a scandal would be too absurd.
Good wives laugh off such trifles, and forget them;
Why should they tell their husbands, and upset them?

[*Act Three* · *Scene Four*]

DAMIS

You have your reasons for taking such a course,
And I have reasons, too, of equal force.
To spare him now would be insanely wrong.
I've swallowed my just wrath for far too long
And watched this insolent bigot bringing strife
And bitterness into our family life.
Too long he's meddled in my father's affairs,
Thwarting my marriage-hopes, and poor Valère's.
It's high time that my father was undeceived,
And now I've proof that can't be disbelieved—
Proof that was furnished me by Heaven above.
It's too good not to take advantage of.
This is my chance, and I deserve to lose it
If, for one moment, I hesitate to use it.

ELMIRE

Damis . . .

DAMIS

      No, I must do what I think right.
Madam, my heart is bursting with delight,
And, say whatever you will, I'll not consent
To lose the sweet revenge on which I'm bent.
I'll settle matters without more ado;
And here, most opportunely, is my cue.

SCENE FIVE

ORGON, DAMIS, TARTUFFE, ELMIRE

DAMIS

Father, I'm glad you've joined us. Let us advise you
Of some fresh news which doubtless will surprise you.
You've just now been repaid with interest
For all your loving-kindness to our guest.
He's proved his warm and grateful feelings toward you;
It's with a pair of horns he would reward you.
Yes, I surprised him with your wife, and heard
His whole adulterous offer, every word.
She, with her all too gentle disposition,
Would not have told you of his proposition;
But I shall not make terms with brazen lechery,
And feel that not to tell you would be treachery.

ELMIRE

And I hold that one's husband's peace of mind
Should not be spoilt by tattle of this kind.
One's honor doesn't require it: to be proficient
In keeping men at bay is quite sufficient.
These are my sentiments, and I wish, Damis,
That you had heeded me and held your peace.

402

SCENE SIX

ORGON

Can it be true, this dreadful thing I hear?

TARTUFFE

Yes, Brother, I'm a wicked man, I fear:
A wretched sinner, all depraved and twisted,
The greatest villain that has ever existed.
My life's one heap of crimes, which grows each minute;
There's naught but foulness and corruption in it;
And I perceive that Heaven, outraged by me,
Has chosen this occasion to mortify me.
Charge me with any deed you wish to name;
I'll not defend myself, but take the blame.
Believe what you are told, and drive Tartuffe
Like some base criminal from beneath your roof;
Yes, drive me hence, and with a parting curse:
I shan't protest, for I deserve far worse.

ORGON (*To Damis:*)

Ah, you deceitful boy, how dare you try
To stain his purity with so foul a lie?

DAMIS

What! Are you taken in by such a bluff?
Did you not hear . . . ?

ORGON

Enough, you rogue, enough!

TARTUFFE

Ah, Brother, let him speak: you're being unjust.
Believe his story; the boy deserves your trust.
Why, after all, should you have faith in me?
How can you know what I might do, or be?
Is it on my good actions that you base
Your favor? Do you trust my pious face?
Ah, no, don't be deceived by hollow shows;
I'm far, alas, from being what men suppose;
Though the world takes me for a man of worth,
I'm truly the most worthless man on earth.
            (*To Damis:*)
Yes, my dear son, speak out now: call me the chief
Of sinners, a wretch, a murderer, a thief;
Load me with all the names men most abhor;
I'll not complain; I've earned them all, and more;
I'll kneel here while you pour them on my head
As a just punishment for the life I've led.

ORGON (*To Tartuffe:*)

This is too much, dear Brother.

word game

404

[*Act Three · Scene Six*]
(*To Damis:*)
Have you no heart?

DAMIS

Are you so hoodwinked by this rascal's art . . . ?

ORGON

Be still, you monster.
(*To Tartuffe:*)
Brother, I pray you, rise.
(*To Damis:*)
Villain!

DAMIS

But . . .

ORGON

Silence!

DAMIS

Can't you realize . . . ?

ORGON

Just one word more, and I'll tear you limb from limb.

TARTUFFE

In God's name, Brother, don't be harsh with him.
I'd rather far be tortured at the stake
Than see him bear one scratch for my poor sake.

ORGON (*To Damis:*)

Ingrate!

TARTUFFE

If I must beg you, on bended knee,
To pardon him . . .

ORGON (*Falling to his knees, addressing Tartuffe:*)

Such goodness cannot be!
(*To Damis:*)
Now, *there's* true charity!

DAMIS

What, you . . . ?

ORGON

Villain, be still!
I know your motives; I know you wish him ill:
Yes, all of you—wife, children, servants, all—
Conspire against him and desire his fall,

Employing every shameful trick you can
To alienate me from this saintly man.
Ah, but the more you seek to drive him away,
The more I'll do to keep him. Without delay,
I'll spite this household and confound its pride
By giving him my daughter as his bride.

DAMIS

You're going to force her to accept his hand?

ORGON

Yes, and this very night, d'you understand?
I shall defy you all, and make it clear
That I'm the one who gives the orders here.
Come, wretch, kneel down and clasp his blessed feet,
And ask his pardon for your black deceit.

DAMIS

I ask that swindler's pardon? Why, I'd rather . . .

ORGON

So! You insult him, and defy your father!
A stick! A stick! (*To Tartuffe:*) No, no—release me, do.
                    (*To Damis:*)
Out of my house this minute! Be off with you,
And never dare set foot in it again.

[*Act Three · Scene Six*]

DAMIS

Well, I shall go, but . . .

ORGON

        Well, go quickly, then.
I disinherit you; an empty purse
Is all you'll get from me—except my curse!

SCENE SEVEN

ORGON, TARTUFFE

ORGON

How he blasphemed your goodness! What a son!

TARTUFFE

Forgive him, Lord, as I've already done.
(*To Orgon:*)
You can't know how it hurts when someone tries
To blacken me in my dear Brother's eyes.

ORGON

Ahh!

TARTUFFE

The mere thought of such ingratitude
Plunges my soul into so dark a mood . . .
Such horror grips my heart . . . I gasp for breath,
And cannot speak, and feel myself near death.

ORGON

(*He runs, in tears, to the door through which he
has just driven his son.*)

You blackguard! Why did I spare you? Why did I not
Break you in little pieces on the spot?
Compose yourself, and don't be hurt, dear friend.

TARTUFFE

These scenes, these dreadful quarrels, have got to end.
I've much upset your household, and I perceive
That the best thing will be for me to leave.

ORGON

What are you saying!

TARTUFFE

                   They're all against me here;
They'd have you think me false and insincere.

ORGON

Ah, what of that? Have I ceased believing in you?

TARTUFFE

Their adverse talk will certainly continue,
And charges which you now repudiate
You may find credible at a later date.

[Act Three · Scene Seven]

ORGON

No, Brother, never.

TARTUFFE

Brother, a wife can sway
Her husband's mind in many a subtle way.

ORGON

No, no.

TARTUFFE

To leave at once is the solution;
Thus only can I end their persecution.

ORGON

No, no, I'll not allow it; you shall remain.

TARTUFFE

Ah, well; 'twill mean much martyrdom and pain,
But if you wish it . . .

ORGON

Ah!

411

TARTUFFE

Enough; so be it.
But one thing must be settled, as I see it.
For your dear honor, and for our friendship's sake,
There's one precaution I feel bound to take.
I shall avoid your wife, and keep away . . .

ORGON

No, you shall not, whatever they may say.
It pleases me to vex them, and for spite
I'd have them see you with her day and night.
What's more, I'm going to drive them to despair
By making you my only son and heir;
This very day, I'll give to you alone
Clear deed and title to everything I own.
A dear, good friend and son-in-law-to-be
Is more than wife, or child, or kin to me.
Will you accept my offer, dearest son?

TARTUFFE

In all things, let the will of Heaven be done.

ORGON

Poor fellow! Come, we'll go draw up the deed.
Then let them burst with disappointed greed!

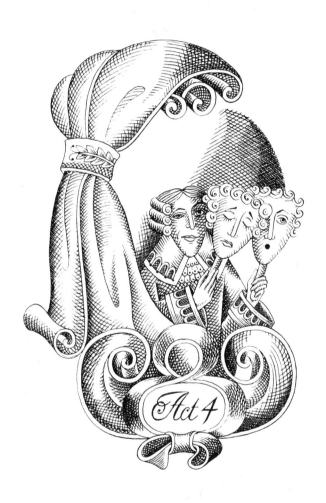

Act 4

SCENE ONE

CLÉANTE, TARTUFFE

CLÉANTE

Yes, all the town's discussing it, and truly,
Their comments do not flatter you unduly.
I'm glad we've met, Sir, and I'll give my view
Of this sad matter in a word or two.
As for who's guilty, that I shan't discuss;
Let's say it was Damis who caused the fuss;
Assuming, then, that you have been ill-used
By young Damis, and groundlessly accused,
Ought not a Christian to forgive, and ought
He not to stifle every vengeful thought?
Should you stand by and watch a father make
His only son an exile for your sake?
Again I tell you frankly, be advised:
The whole town, high and low, is scandalized;
This quarrel must be mended, and my advice is
Not to push matters to a further crisis.
No, sacrifice your wrath to God above,
And help Damis regain his father's love.

415

[*Act Four · Scene One*]

TARTUFFE

Alas, for my part I should take great joy
In doing so. I've nothing against the boy.
I pardon all, I harbor no resentment;
To serve him would afford me much contentment.
But Heaven's interest will not have it so:
If he comes back, then I shall have to go.
After his conduct—so extreme, so vicious—
Our further intercourse would look suspicious.
God knows what people would think! Why, they'd
    describe
My goodness to him as a sort of bribe;
They'd say that out of guilt I made pretense
Of loving-kindness and benevolence—
That, fearing my accuser's tongue, I strove
To buy his silence with a show of love.

CLÉANTE

Your reasoning is badly warped and stretched,
And these excuses, Sir, are most far-fetched.
Why put yourself in charge of Heaven's cause?
Does Heaven need our help to enforce its laws?
Leave vengeance to the Lord, Sir; while we live,
Our duty's not to punish, but forgive;
And what the Lord commands, we should obey
Without regard to what the world may say.
What! Shall the fear of being misunderstood
Prevent our doing what is right and good?
No, no; let's simply do what Heaven ordains,
And let no other thoughts perplex our brains.

416

TARTUFFE

Again, Sir, let me say that I've forgiven
Damis, and thus obeyed the laws of Heaven;
But I am not commanded by the Bible
To live with one who smears my name with libel.

CLÉANTE

Were you commanded, Sir, to indulge the whim
Of poor Orgon, and to encourage him
In suddenly transferring to your name
A large estate to which you have no claim?

TARTUFFE

'Twould never occur to those who know me best
To think I acted from self-interest.
The treasures of this world I quite despise;
Their specious glitter does not charm my eyes;
And if I have resigned myself to taking
The gift which my dear Brother insists on making,
I do so only, as he well understands,
Lest so much wealth fall into wicked hands,
Lest those to whom it might descend in time
Turn it to purposes of sin and crime,
And not, as I shall do, make use of it
For Heaven's glory and mankind's benefit.

CLÉANTE

Forget these trumped-up fears. Your argument
Is one the rightful heir might well resent;

417

It *is* a moral burden to inherit
Such wealth, but give Damis a chance to bear it.
And would it not be worse to be accused
Of swindling, than to see that wealth misused?
I'm shocked that you allowed Orgon to broach
This matter, and that you feel no self-reproach;
Does true religion teach that lawful heirs
May freely be deprived of what is theirs?
And if the Lord has told you in your heart
That you and young Damis must dwell apart,
Would it not be the decent thing to beat
A generous and honorable retreat,
Rather than let the son of the house be sent,
For your convenience, into banishment?
Sir, if you wish to prove the honesty
Of your intentions . . .

TARTUFFE

       Sir, it is half-past three.
I've certain pious duties to attend to,
And hope my prompt departure won't offend you.

CLÉANTE (*Alone:*)

Damn.

SCENE TWO

ELMIRE, MARIANE, CLÉANTE, DORINE

DORINE

Stay, Sir, and help Mariane, for Heaven's sake!
She's suffering so, I fear her heart will break.
Her father's plan to marry her off tonight
Has put the poor child in a desperate plight.
I hear him coming. Let's stand together, now,
And see if we can't change his mind, somehow,
About this match we all deplore and fear.

SCENE THREE

ORGON, ELMIRE, MARIANE, CLÉANTE, DORINE

ORGON

Hah! Glad to find you all assembled here.
(*To Mariane:*)
This contract, child, contains your happiness,
And what it says I think your heart can guess.

MARIANE (*Falling to her knees:*)

Sir, by that Heaven which sees me here distressed,
And by whatever else can move your breast,
Do not employ a father's power, I pray you,
To crush my heart and force it to obey you,
Nor by your harsh commands oppress me so
That I'll begrudge the duty which I owe—
And do not so embitter and enslave me
That I shall hate the very life you gave me.
If my sweet hopes must perish, if you refuse
To give me to the one I've dared to choose,
Spare me at least—I beg you, I implore—
The pain of wedding one whom I abhor;
And do not, by a heartless use of force,
Drive me to contemplate some desperate course.

[*Act Four · Scene Three*]

ORGON (*Feeling himself touched by her:*)

Be firm, my soul. No human weakness, now.

MARIANE

I don't resent your love for him. Allow
Your heart free rein, Sir; give him your property,
And if that's not enough, take mine from me;
He's welcome to my money; take it, do,
But don't, I pray, include my person too.
Spare me, I beg you; and let me end the tale
Of my sad days behind a convent veil.

ORGON

A convent! Hah! When crossed in their amours,
All lovesick girls have the same thought as yours.
Get up! The more you loathe the man, and dread him,
The more ennobling it will be to wed him.
Marry Tartuffe, and mortify your flesh!
Enough; don't start that whimpering afresh.

DORINE

But why . . . ?

ORGON

Be still, there. Speak when you're spoken to.
Not one more bit of impudence out of you.

[*Act Four · Scene Three*]

CLÉANTE

If I may offer a word of counsel here . . .

ORGON

Brother, in counseling you have no peer;
All your advice is forceful, sound, and clever;
I don't propose to follow it, however.

ELMIRE (*To Orgon:*)

I am amazed, and don't know what to say;
Your blindness simply takes my breath away.
You are indeed bewitched, to take no warning
From our account of what occurred this morning.

ORGON

Madam, I know a few plain facts, and one
Is that you're partial to my rascal son;
Hence, when he sought to make Tartuffe the victim
Of a base lie, you dared not contradict him.
Ah, but you underplayed your part, my pet;
You should have looked more angry, more upset.

ELMIRE

When men make overtures, must we reply
With righteous anger and a battle-cry?
Must we turn back their amorous advances
With sharp reproaches and with fiery glances?

Myself, I find such offers merely amusing,
And make no scenes and fusses in refusing;
My taste is for good-natured rectitude,
And I dislike the savage sort of prude
Who guards her virtue with her teeth and claws,
And tears men's eyes out for the slightest cause:
The Lord preserve me from such honor as that,
Which bites and scratches like an alley-cat!
I've found that a polite and cool rebuff
Discourages a lover quite enough.

ORGON

I know the facts, and I shall not be shaken.

ELMIRE

I marvel at your power to be mistaken. —Word games
Would it, I wonder, carry weight with you
If I could *show* you that our tale was true?

ORGON

Show me?

ELMIRE

Yes.

ORGON

Rot.

[Act Four · Scene Three]

ELMIRE

Come, what if I found a way
To make you see the facts as plain as day?

ORGON

Nonsense.

ELMIRE

Do answer me; don't be absurd.
I'm not now asking you to trust our word.
Suppose that from some hiding-place in here
You learned the whole sad truth by eye and ear—
What would you say of your good friend, after that?

ORGON

Why, I'd say . . . nothing, by Jehoshaphat!
It can't be true.

ELMIRE

You've been too long deceived,
And I'm quite tired of being disbelieved.
Come now: let's put my statements to the test,
And you shall see the truth made manifest.

ORGON

I'll take that challenge. Now do your uttermost.
We'll see how you make good your empty boast.

[Act Four · Scene Three]

ELMIRE (*To Dorine:*)

Send him to me.

DORINE

He's crafty; it may be hard
To catch the cunning scoundrel off his guard.

ELMIRE

No, amorous men are gullible. Their conceit
So blinds them that they're never hard to cheat.
Have him come down (*To Cléante & Mariane:*) Please
   leave us, for a bit.

SCENE FOUR

ELMIRE, ORGON

ELMIRE

Pull up this table, and get under it.

ORGON

What?

ELMIRE

It's essential that you be well-hidden.

ORGON

Why there?

ELMIRE

Oh, Heavens! Just do as you are bidden.
I have my plans; we'll soon see how they fare.
Under the table, now; and once you're there,
Take care that you are neither seen nor heard.

[*Act Four · Scene Four*]

ORGON

Well, I'll indulge you, since I gave my word
To see you through this infantile charade.

ELMIRE

Once it is over, you'll be glad we played.
    (*To her husband, who is now under the table:*)
I'm going to act quite strangely, now, and you
Must not be shocked at anything I do.
Whatever I may say, you must excuse
As part of that deceit I'm forced to use.
I shall employ sweet speeches in the task
Of making that imposter drop his mask;
I'll give encouragement to his bold desires,
And furnish fuel to his amorous fires.
Since it's for your sake, and for his destruction,
That I shall seem to yield to his seduction,
I'll gladly stop whenever you decide
That all your doubts are fully satisfied.
I'll count on you, as soon as you have seen
What sort of man he is, to intervene,
And not expose me to his odious lust
One moment longer than you feel you must.
Remember: you're to save me from my plight
Whenever . . . He's coming! Hush! Keep out of sight!

SCENE FIVE

TARTUFFE, ELMIRE, ORGON

TARTUFFE

You wish to have a word with me, I'm told.

ELMIRE

Yes. I've a little secret to unfold.
Before I speak, however, it would be wise
To close that door, and look about for spies.
    (*Tartuffe goes to the door, closes it, and returns.*)
The very last thing that must happen now
Is a repetition of this morning's row.
I've never been so badly caught off guard.
Oh, how I feared for you! You saw how hard
I tried to make that troublesome Damis
Control his dreadful temper, and hold his peace.
In my confusion, I didn't have the sense
Simply to contradict his evidence;
But as it happened, that was for the best,
And all has worked out in our interest.
This storm has only bettered your position;
My husband doesn't have the least suspicion,
And now, in mockery of those who do,
He bids me be continually with you.

428

[*Act Four · Scene Five*]

And that is why, quite fearless of reproof,
I now can be alone with my Tartuffe,
And why my heart—perhaps too quick to yield—
Feels free to let its passion be revealed.

TARTUFFE

Madam, your words confuse me. Not long ago,
You spoke in quite a different style, you know.

ELMIRE

Ah, Sir, if that refusal made you smart,
It's little that you know of woman's heart,
Or what that heart is trying to convey
When it resists in such a feeble way!
Always, at first, our modesty prevents
The frank avowal of tender sentiments;
However high the passion which inflames us,
Still, to confess its power somehow shames us.
Thus we reluct, at first, yet in a tone
Which tells you that our heart is overthrown,
That what our lips deny, our pulse confesses,
And that, in time, all noes will turn to yesses.
I fear my words are all too frank and free,
And a poor proof of woman's modesty;
But since I'm started, tell me, if you will—
Would I have tried to make Damis be still,
Would I have listened, calm and unoffended,
Until your lengthy offer of love was ended,
And been so very mild in my reaction,
Had your sweet words not given me satisfaction?

And when I tried to force you to undo
The marriage-plans my husband has in view,
What did my urgent pleading signify
If not that I admired you, and that I
Deplored the thought that someone else might own
Part of a heart I wished for mine alone?

TARTUFFE

Madam, no happiness is so complete
As when, from lips we love, come words so sweet;
Their nectar floods my every sense, and drains
In honeyed rivulets through all my veins.
To please you is my joy, my only goal;
Your love is the restorer of my soul;
And yet I must beg leave, now, to confess
Some lingering doubts as to my happiness.
Might this not be a trick? Might not the catch
Be that you wish me to break off the match
With Mariane, and so have feigned to love me?
I shan't quite trust your fond opinion of me
Until the feelings you've expressed so sweetly
Are demonstrated somewhat more concretely,
And you have shown, by certain kind concessions,
That I may put my faith in your professions.

ELMIRE (*She coughs, to warn her husband.*)

Why be in such a hurry? Must my heart
Exhaust its bounty at the very start?
To make that sweet admission cost me dear,
But you'll not be content, it would appear,

430

[*Act Four · Scene Five*]

Unless my store of favors is disbursed
To the last farthing, and at the very first.

TARTUFFE

The less we merit, the less we dare to hope,
And with our doubts, mere words can never cope.
We trust no promised bliss till we receive it;
Not till a joy is ours can we believe it.
I, who so little merit your esteem,
Can't credit this fulfillment of my dream,
And shan't believe it, Madam, until I savor
Some palpable assurance of your favor.

ELMIRE

My, how tyrannical your love can be,
And how it flusters and perplexes me!
How furiously you take one's heart in hand,
And make your every wish a fierce command!
Come, must you hound and harry me to death?
Will you not give me time to catch my breath?
Can it be right to press me with such force,
Give me no quarter, show me no remorse,
And take advantage, by your stern insistence,
Of the fond feelings which weaken my resistance?

TARTUFFE

Well, if you look with favor upon my love,
Why, then, begrudge me some clear proof thereof?

[*Act Four · Scene Five*]

ELMIRE

But how can I consent without offense
To Heaven, toward which you feel such reverence?

TARTUFFE

If Heaven is all that holds you back, don't worry.
I can remove that hindrance in a hurry.
Nothing of that sort need obstruct our path.

ELMIRE

Must one not be afraid of Heaven's wrath?

TARTUFFE

Madam, forget such fears, and be my pupil,
And I shall teach you how to conquer scruple.
Some joys, it's true, are wrong in Heaven's eyes;
Yet Heaven is not averse to compromise;
There is a science, lately formulated,
Whereby one's conscience may be liberated,
And any wrongful act you care to mention
May be redeemed by purity of intention.
I'll teach you, Madam, the secrets of that science;
Meanwhile, just place on me your full reliance.
Assuage my keen desires, and feel no dread:
The sin, if any, shall be on my head.
            (*Elmire coughs, this time more loudly*.)
You've a bad cough.

[*Act Four · Scene Five*]

ELMIRE

Yes, yes. It's bad indeed.

TARTUFFE (*Producing a little paper bag:*)

A bit of licorice may be what you need.

ELMIRE

No, I've a stubborn cold, it seems. I'm sure it
Will take much more than licorice to cure it.

TARTUFFE

How aggravating.

ELMIRE

Oh, more than I can say.

TARTUFFE

If you're still troubled, think of things this way:
No one shall know our joys, save us alone,
And there's no evil till the act is known;
It's scandal, Madam, which makes it an offense, hypocracy
And it's no sin to sin in confidence.

ELMIRE (*Having coughed once more:*)

Well, clearly I must do as you require,
And yield to your importunate desire.

433

It is apparent, now, that nothing less
Will satisfy you, and so I acquiesce.
To go so far is much against my will;
I'm vexed that it should come to this; but still,
Since you are so determined on it, since you
Will not allow mere language to convince you,
And since you ask for concrete evidence, I
See nothing for it, now, but to comply.
If this is sinful, if I'm wrong to do it,
So much the worse for him who drove me to it.
The fault can surely not be charged to me.

TARTUFFE

Madam, the fault is mine, if fault there be,
And . . .

ELMIRE

Open the door a little, and peek out;
I wouldn't want my husband poking about.

TARTUFFE

Why worry about the man? Each day he grows
More gullible; one can lead him by the nose.
To find us here would fill him with delight,
And if he saw the worst, he'd doubt his sight.

ELMIRE

Nevertheless, do step out for a minute
Into the hall, and see that no one's in it.

434

SCENE SIX

ORGON, ELMIRE

ORGON (*Coming out from under the table:*)

That man's a perfect monster, I must admit!
I'm simply stunned. I can't get over it.

ELMIRE

What, coming out so soon? How premature!
Get back in hiding, and wait until you're sure.
Stay till the end, and be convinced completely;
We mustn't stop till things are proved concretely.

ORGON

Hell never harbored anything so vicious!

ELMIRE

Tut, don't be hasty. Try to be judicious.
Wait, and be certain that there's no mistake.
No jumping to conclusions, for Heaven's sake!
  (*She places Orgon behind her, as Tartuffe re-enters.*)

435

SCENE SEVEN

TARTUFFE, ELMIRE, ORGON

TARTUFFE (*Not seeing Orgon:*)

Madam, all things have worked out to perfection;
I've given the neighboring rooms a full inspection;
No one's about; and now I may at last . . .

ORGON (*Intercepting him:*)

Hold on, my passionate fellow, not so fast!
I should advise a little more restraint.
Well, so you thought you'd fool me, my dear saint!
How soon you wearied of the saintly life—
Wedding my daughter, and coveting my wife!
I've long suspected you, and had a feeling
That soon I'd catch you at your double-dealing.
Just now, you've given me evidence galore;
It's quite enough; I have no wish for more.

ELMIRE (*To Tartuffe:*)

I'm sorry to have treated you so slyly,
But circumstances forced me to be wily.

[*Act Four · Scene Seven*]

TARTUFFE

Brother, you can't think . . .

ORGON

                 No more talk from you;
Just leave this household, without more ado.

TARTUFFE

What I intended . . .

ORGON

             That seems fairly clear.
Spare me your falsehoods and get out of here.

TARTUFFE

No, I'm the master, and you're the one to go!
This house belongs to me, I'll have you know,
And I shall show you that you can't hurt *me*
By this contemptible conspiracy,
That those who cross me know not what they do,
And that I've means to expose and punish you,
Avenge offended Heaven, and make you grieve
That ever you dared order me to leave.

SCENE EIGHT

ELMIRE

What was the point of all that angry chatter?

ORGON

Dear God, I'm worried. This is no laughing matter.

ELMIRE

How so?

ORGON

I fear I understood his drift.
I'm much disturbed about that deed of gift.

ELMIRE

You gave him . . . ?

438

[*Act Four · Scene Eight*]

ORGON

         Yes, it's all been drawn and signed.
But one thing more is weighing on my mind.

ELMIRE

What's that?

ORGON

         I'll tell you; but first let's see if there's
A certain strong-box in his room upstairs.

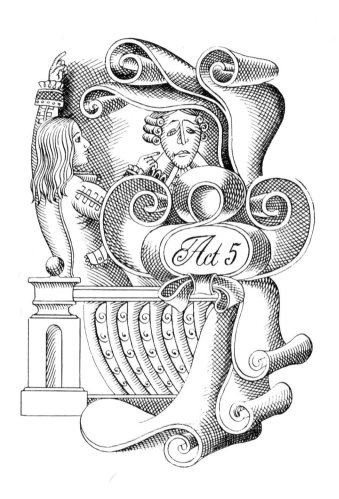

SCENE ONE

ORGON, CLÉANTE

CLÉANTE

Where are you going so fast?

ORGON

God knows!

CLÉANTE

Then wait;

Let's have a conference, and deliberate
On how this situation's to be met.

ORGON

That strong-box has me utterly upset;
This is the worst of many, many shocks.

CLÉANTE

Is there some fearful mystery in that box?

[*Act Five · Scene One*]

ORGON

My poor friend Argas brought that box to me
With his own hands, in utmost secrecy;
'Twas on the very morning of his flight.
It's full of papers which, if they came to light,
Would ruin him—or such is my impression.

CLÉANTE

Then why did you let it out of your possession?

ORGON

Those papers vexed my conscience, and it seemed best
To ask the counsel of my pious guest.
The cunning scoundrel got me to agree
To leave the strong-box in his custody,
So that, in case of an investigation,
I could employ a slight equivocation
And swear I didn't have it, and thereby,
At no expense to conscience, tell a lie.

CLÉANTE

It looks to me as if you're out on a limb.
Trusting him with that box, and offering him
That deed of gift, were actions of a kind
Which scarcely indicate a prudent mind.
With two such weapons, he has the upper hand,
And since you're vulnerable, as matters stand,
You erred once more in bringing him to bay.
You should have acted in some subtler way.

[*Act Five · Scene One*]

ORGON

Just think of it: behind that fervent face,
A heart so wicked, and a soul so base!
I took him in, a hungry beggar, and then . . .
Enough, by God! I'm through with pious men:
Henceforth I'll hate the whole false brotherhood,
And persecute them worse than Satan could.

CLÉANTE

Ah, there you go—extravagant as ever!
Why can you not be rational? You never
Manage to take the middle course, it seems,
But jump, instead, between absurd extremes.
You've recognized your recent grave mistake
In falling victim to a pious fake;
Now, to correct that error, must you embrace
An even greater error in its place,
And judge our worthy neighbors as a whole
By what you've learned of one corrupted soul?
Come, just because one rascal made you swallow
A show of zeal which turned out to be hollow,
Shall you conclude that all men are deceivers,
And that, today, there are no true believers?
Let atheists make that foolish inference;
Learn to distinguish virtue from pretense,
Be cautious in bestowing admiration,
And cultivate a sober moderation.
Don't humor fraud, but also don't asperse
True piety; the latter fault is worse,
And it is best to err, if err one must,
As you have done, upon the side of trust.

445

SCENE TWO

DAMIS

Father, I hear that scoundrel's uttered threats
Against you; that he pridefully forgets
How, in his need, he was befriended by you,
And means to use your gifts to crucify you.

ORGON

It's true, my boy. I'm too distressed for tears.

DAMIS

Leave it to me, Sir; let me trim his ears.
Faced with such insolence, we must not waver.
I shall rejoice in doing you the favor
Of cutting short his life, and your distress.

CLÉANTE

What a display of young hotheadedness!
Do learn to moderate your fits of rage.
In this just kingdom, this enlightened age,
One does not settle things by violence.

SCENE THREE

MADAME PERNELLE, MARIANE, ELMIRE, DORINE, DAMIS,
ORGON, CLÉANTE

MADAME PERNELLE

I hear strange tales of very strange events.

ORGON

Yes, strange events which these two eyes beheld.
The man's ingratitude is unparalleled.
I save a wretched pauper from starvation,
House him, and treat him like a blood relation,
Shower him every day with my largesse,
Give him my daughter, and all that I possess;
And meanwhile the unconscionable knave
Tries to induce my wife to misbehave;
And not content with such extreme rascality,
Now threatens me with my own liberality,
And aims, by taking base advantage of
The gifts I gave him out of Christian love,
To drive me from my house, a ruined man,
And make me end a pauper, as he began.

DORINE

Poor fellow!

447

[Act Five · Scene Three]

MADAME PERNELLE

No, my son, I'll never bring
Myself to think him guilty of such a thing.

ORGON

How's that?

MADAME PERNELLE

The righteous always were maligned.

ORGON

Speak clearly, Mother. Say what's on your mind.

MADAME PERNELLE

I mean that I can smell a rat, my dear.
You know how everybody hates him, here.

ORGON

That has no bearing on the case at all.

MADAME PERNELLE

I told you a hundred times, when you were small,
That virtue in this world is hated ever;
Malicious men may die, but malice never.

[*Act Five · Scene Three*]

ORGON

No doubt that's true, but how does it apply?

MADAME PERNELLE

They've turned you against him by a clever lie.

ORGON

I've told you, I was there and saw it done.

MADAME PERNELLE

Ah, slanderers will stop at nothing, Son.

ORGON

Mother, I'll lose my temper . . . For the last time,
I tell you I was witness to the crime.

MADAME PERNELLE

The tongues of spite are busy night and noon,
And to their venom no man is immune.

ORGON

You're talking nonsense. Can't you realize
I saw it; saw it; saw it with my eyes?
Saw, do you understand me? Must I shout it
Into your ears before you'll cease to doubt it?

449

[*Act Five · Scene Three*]

MADAME PERNELLE

Appearances can deceive, my son. Dear me,
We cannot always judge by what we see.

ORGON

Drat! Drat!

MADAME PERNELLE

One often interprets things awry;
Good can seem evil to a suspicious eye.

ORGON

Was I to see his pawing at Elmire
As an act of charity?

MADAME PERNELLE

Till his guilt is clear,
A man deserves the benefit of the doubt.
You should have waited, to see how things turned out.

ORGON

Great God in Heaven, what more proof did I need?
Was I to sit there, watching, until he'd . . .
You drive me to the brink of impropriety.

MADAME PERNELLE

No, no, a man of such surpassing piety
Could not do such a thing. You cannot shake me.
I don't believe it, and you shall not make me.

ORGON

You vex me so that, if you weren't my mother,
I'd say to you . . . some dreadful thing or other.

DORINE

It's your turn now, Sir, not to be listened to;
You'd not trust us, and now she won't trust you.

CLÉANTE

My friends, we're wasting time which should be spent
In facing up to our predicament.
I fear that scoundrel's threats weren't made in sport.

DAMIS

Do you think he'd have the nerve to go to court?

ELMIRE

I'm sure he won't: they'd find it all too crude
A case of swindling and ingratitude.

[*Act Five · Scene Three*]

CLÉANTE

Don't be too sure. He won't be at a loss
To give his claims a high and righteous gloss;
And clever rogues with far less valid cause
Have trapped their victims in a web of laws.
I say again that to antagonize
A man so strongly armed was most unwise.

ORGON

I know it; but the man's appalling cheek
Outraged me so, I couldn't control my pique.

CLÉANTE

I wish to Heaven that we could devise
Some truce between you, or some compromise.

ELMIRE

If I had known what cards he held, I'd not
Have roused his anger by my little plot.

ORGON (*To Dorine, as M. Loyal enters:*)

What is that fellow looking for? Who is he?
Go talk to him—and tell him that I'm busy.

SCENE FOUR

MONSIEUR LOYAL, MADAME PERNELLE, ORGON, DAMIS,
MARIANE, DORINE, ELMIRE, CLÉANTE

MONSIEUR LOYAL

Good day, dear sister. Kindly let me see
Your master.

DORINE

He's involved with company,
And cannot be disturbed just now, I fear.

MONSIEUR LOYAL

I hate to intrude; but what has brought me here
Will not disturb your master, in any event.
Indeed, my news will make him most content.

DORINE

Your name?

MONSIEUR LOYAL

Just say that I bring greetings from
Monsieur Tartuffe, on whose behalf I've come.

DORINE (*To Orgon:*)

Sir, he's a very gracious man, and bears
A message from Tartuffe, which, he declares,
Will make you most content.

CLÉANTE

     Upon my word,
I think this man had best be seen, and heard.

ORGON

Perhaps he has some settlement to suggest.
How shall I treat him? What manner would be best?

CLÉANTE

Control your anger, and if he should mention
Some fair adjustment, give him your full attention.

MONSIEUR LOYAL

Good health to you, good Sir. May Heaven confound
Your enemies, and may your joys abound.

ORGON (*Aside, to Cléante:*)

A gentle salutation: it confirms
My guess that he is here to offer terms.

454

[*Act Five · Scene Four*]

MONSIEUR LOYAL

I've always held your family most dear;
I served your father, Sir, for many a year.

ORGON

Sir, I must ask your pardon; to my shame,
I cannot now recall your face or name.

MONSIEUR LOYAL

Loyal's my name; I come from Normandy,
And I'm a bailiff, in all modesty.
For forty years, praise God, it's been my boast
To serve with honor in that vital post,
And I am here, Sir, if you will permit
The liberty, to serve you with this writ . . .

ORGON

To—*what?*

MONSIEUR LOYAL

　　　Now, please, Sir, let us have no friction:
It's nothing but an order of eviction.
You are to move your goods and family out
And make way for new occupants, without
Deferment or delay, and give the keys . . .

[*Act Five · Scene Four*]

ORGON

I? Leave this house?

MONSIEUR LOYAL

        Why yes, Sir, if you please.
This house, Sir, from the cellar to the roof,
Belongs now to the good Monsieur Tartuffe,
And he is lord and master of your estate
By virtue of a deed of present date,
Drawn in due form, with clearest legal phrasing . . .

DAMIS

Your insolence is utterly amazing!

MONSIEUR LOYAL

Young man, my business here is not with you,
But with your wise and temperate father, who,
Like every worthy citizen, stands in awe
Of justice, and would never obstruct the law.

ORGON

But . . .

MONSIEUR LOYAL

        Not for a million, Sir, would you rebel
Against authority; I know that well.
You'll not make trouble, Sir, or interfere
With the execution of my duties here.

[*Act Five · Scene Four*]

DAMIS

Someone may execute a smart tattoo
On that black jacket of yours, before you're through.

MONSIEUR LOYAL

Sir, bid your son be silent. I'd much regret
Having to mention such a nasty threat
Of violence, in writing my report.

DORINE (*Aside:*)

This man Loyal's a most disloyal sort!

MONSIEUR LOYAL

I love all men of upright character,
And when I agreed to serve these papers, Sir,
It was your feelings that I had in mind.
I couldn't bear to see the case assigned
To someone else, who might esteem you less
And so subject you to unpleasantness.

ORGON

What's more unpleasant than telling a man to leave
His house and home?

MONSIEUR LOYAL

      You'd like a short reprieve?
If you desire it, Sir, I shall not press you,
But wait until tomorrow to dispossess you.

Splendid. I'll come and spend the night here, then,
Most quietly, with half a score of men.
For form's sake, you might bring me, just before
You go to bed, the keys to the front door.
My men, I promise, will be on their best
Behavior, and will not disturb your rest.
But bright and early, Sir, you must be quick
And move out all your furniture, every stick:
The men I've chosen are both young and strong,
And with their help it shouldn't take you long.
In short, I'll make things pleasant and convenient,
And since I'm being so extremely lenient,
Please show me, Sir, a like consideration,
And give me your entire cooperation.

ORGON (*Aside:*)

I may be all but bankrupt, but I vow
I'd give a hundred louis, here and now,
Just for the pleasure of landing one good clout
Right on the end of that complacent snout.

CLÉANTE

Careful; don't make things worse.

DAMIS

My bootsole itches
To give that beggar a good kick in the breeches.

[*Act Five · Scene Four*]

DORINE

Monsieur Loyal, I'd love to hear the whack
Of a stout stick across your fine broad back.

MONSIEUR LOYAL

Take care: a woman too may go to jail if
She uses threatening language to a bailiff.

CLÉANTE

Enough, enough, Sir. This must not go on.
Give me that paper, please, and then begone.

MONSIEUR LOYAL

Well, *au revoir*. God give you all good cheer!

ORGON

May God confound you, and him who sent you here!

SCENE FIVE

ORGON, CLÉANTE, MARIANE, ELMIRE, MADAME PERNELLE,
DORINE, DAMIS

ORGON

Now, Mother, was I right or not? This writ
Should change your notion of Tartuffe a bit.
Do you perceive his villainy at last?

MADAME PERNELLE

I'm thunderstruck. I'm utterly aghast.

DORINE

Oh, come, be fair. You mustn't take offense
At this new proof of his benevolence.
He's acting out of selfless love, I know.
Material things enslave the soul, and so
He kindly has arranged your liberation
From all that might endanger your salvation.

ORGON

Will you not ever hold your tongue, you dunce?

460

[*Act Five · Scene Five*]

CLÉANTE

Come, you must take some action, and at once.

ELMIRE

Go tell the world of the low trick he's tried.
The deed of gift is surely nullified
By such behavior, and public rage will not
Permit the wretch to carry out his plot.

SCENE SIX

VALÈRE, ORGON, CLÉANTE, ELMIRE, MARIANE,
MADAME PERNELLE, DAMIS, DORINE

VALÈRE

Sir, though I hate to bring you more bad news,
Such is the danger that I cannot choose.
A friend who is extremely close to me
And knows my interest in your family
Has, for my sake, presumed to violate
The secrecy that's due to things of state,
And sends me word that you are in a plight
From which your one salvation lies in flight.
That scoundrel who's imposed upon you so
Denounced you to the King an hour ago
And, as supporting evidence, displayed
The strong-box of a certain renegade
Whose secret papers, so he testified,
You had disloyally agreed to hide.
I don't know just what charges may be pressed,
But there's a warrant out for your arrest;
Tartuffe has been instructed, furthermore,
To guide the arresting officer to your door.

[*Act Five · Scene Six*]

CLÉANTE

He's clearly done this to facilitate
His seizure of your house and your estate.

ORGON

That man, I must say, is a vicious beast!

VALÈRE

Quick, Sir; you mustn't tarry in the least.
My carriage is outside, to take you hence;
This thousand louis should cover all expense.
Let's lose no time, or you shall be undone;
The sole defense, in this case, is to run.
I shall go with you all the way, and place you
In a safe refuge to which they'll never trace you.

ORGON

Alas, dear boy, I wish that I could show you
My gratitude for everything I owe you.
But now is not the time; I pray the Lord
That I may live to give you your reward.
Farewell, my dears; be careful . . .

CLÉANTE

                       Brother, hurry.
We shall take care of things; you needn't worry.

463

SCENE SEVEN

THE OFFICER, TARTUFFE, VALÈRE, ORGON, ELMIRE,
MARIANE, MADAME PERNELLE, DORINE, CLÉANTE, DAMIS

TARTUFFE

Gently, Sir, gently; stay right where you are.
No need for haste; your lodging isn't far.
You're off to prison, by order of the Prince.

ORGON

This is the crowning blow, you wretch; and since
It means my total ruin and defeat,
Your villainy is now at last complete.

TARTUFFE

You needn't try to provoke me; it's no use.
Those who serve Heaven must expect abuse.

CLÉANTE

You are indeed most patient, sweet, and blameless.

464

[*Act Five · Scene Seven*]

DAMIS

How he exploits the name of Heaven! It's shameless.

TARTUFFE

Your taunts and mockeries are all for naught;
To do my duty is my only thought.

MARIANE

Your love of duty is most meritorious,
And what you've done is little short of glorious.

TARTUFFE

All deeds are glorious, Madam, which obey
The sovereign prince who sent me here today.

ORGON

I rescued you when you were destitute;
Have you forgotten that, you thankless brute?

TARTUFFE

No, no, I well remember everything;
But my first duty is to serve my King.
That obligation is so paramount
That other claims, beside it, do not count;

And for it I would sacrifice my wife,
My family, my friend, or my own life.

ELMIRE

Hypocrite!

DORINE

     All that we most revere, he uses
To cloak his plots and camouflage his ruses.

CLÉANTE

If it is true that you are animated
By pure and loyal zeal, as you have stated,
Why was this zeal not roused until you'd sought
To make Orgon a cuckold, and been caught?
Why weren't you moved to give your evidence
Until your outraged host had driven you hence?
I shan't say that the gift of all his treasure
Ought to have damped your zeal in any measure;
But if he is a traitor, as you declare,
How could you condescend to be his heir?

TARTUFFE (*To the Officer:*)

Sir, spare me all this clamor; it's growing shrill.
Please carry out your orders, if you will.

OFFICER

Yes, I've delayed too long, Sir. Thank you kindly.
You're just the proper person to remind me.
Come, you are off to join the other boarders
In the King's prison, according to his orders.

TARTUFFE

Who? I, Sir?

OFFICER

Yes.

TARTUFFE

To prison? This can't be true!

OFFICER

I owe an explanation, but not to you.
(*To Orgon:*)
Sir, all is well; rest easy, and be grateful.
We serve a Prince to whom all sham is hateful,
A Prince who sees into our inmost hearts,
And can't be fooled by any trickster's arts.
His royal soul, though generous and human,
Views all things with discernment and acumen;
His sovereign reason is not lightly swayed,
And all his judgments are discreetly weighed.

He honors righteous men of every kind,
And yet his zeal for virtue is not blind,
Nor does his love of piety numb his wits
And make him tolerant of hypocrites.
'Twas hardly likely that this man could cozen
A King who's foiled such liars by the dozen.
With one keen glance, the King perceived the whole
Perverseness and corruption of his soul,
And thus high Heaven's justice was displayed:
Betraying you, the rogue stood self-betrayed.
The King soon recognized Tartuffe as one
Notorious by another name, who'd done
So many vicious crimes that one could fill
Ten volumes with them, and be writing still.
But to be brief: our sovereign was appalled
By this man's treachery toward you, which he called
The last, worst villainy of a vile career,
And bade me follow the impostor here
To see how gross his impudence could be,
And force him to restore your property.
Your private papers, by the King's command,
I hereby seize and give into your hand.
The King, by royal order, invalidates
The deed which gave this rascal your estates,
And pardons, furthermore, your grave offense
In harboring an exile's documents.
By these decrees, our Prince rewards you for
Your loyal deeds in the late civil war,
And shows how heartfelt is his satisfaction
In recompensing any worthy action,
How much he prizes merit, and how he makes
More of men's virtues than of their mistakes.

[*Act Five · Scene Seven*]

DORINE

Heaven be praised!

MADAME PERNELLE

I breathe again, at last.

ELMIRE

We're safe.

MARIANE

I can't believe the danger's past.

ORGON (*To Tartuffe:*)

Well, traitor, now you see . . .

CLÉANTE

                    Ah, Brother, please,
Let's not descend to such indignities.
Leave the poor wretch to his unhappy fate,
And don't say anything to aggravate
His present woes; but rather hope that he
Will soon embrace an honest piety,
And mend his ways, and by a true repentance
Move our just King to moderate his sentence.
Meanwhile, go kneel before your sovereign's throne
And thank him for the mercies he has shown.

[*Act Five · Scene Seven*]

ORGON

vvell said: let's go at once and, gladly kneeling,
Express the gratitude which all are feeling.
Then, when that first great duty has been done,
We'll turn with pleasure to a second one,
And give Valère, whose love has proven so true,
The wedded happiness which is his due.

The Learned Ladies

COMEDY IN FIVE ACTS, 1672

Drawings by Enrico Arno

For Gilbert Parker

INTRODUCTION

The Learned Ladies resembles *Tartuffe* in that it is the drama of a bourgeois household which has lost its harmony and balance through some recent change. In the case of *Tartuffe*, what has changed is that the head of the house, Orgon, who was formerly a sound and solid man, has succumbed to a sort of specious and menopausal religious frenzy. The whole action of the play follows from this aberration of Orgon's, and the whole familial fabric of affections and responsibilities is shaken before the action is over. In *The Learned Ladies* it is once more—though less obviously—the head of the house to whom the disruption of normal relationships may be traced. Chrysale is a soft, comfort-loving person who speaks too often of "my collars" and "my roast of beef." He considers himself peace-loving and gentle, and his daughter Henriette is so kind as to describe his weakness as good nature; but in fact he is an ineffectual man, given to dreaming of his youth, who has always avoided the unpleasantness of exercising his authority as husband and father. The power vacuum thus created has been fully occupied, not long before the play begins, by Chrysale's wilful wife, Philaminte.

It was an unnatural thing, in the view of Molière's audience, for a wife to assume the husband's dominant role, and this is plainly illustrated by the fact that, in early productions of *Les femmes savantes*, the part of Philaminte was played by a male actor. In usurping the headship of the household, Philaminte has become an unsexed woman or the caricature of a man: instead of quiet authority, she has a vain and impatient coerciveness, and her domestic rule amounts to a reign of terror. Her ambition, and a measure of intelligence, lead her to become a bluestocking and, in emulation of certain great ladies, to turn her house into an academy and salon. She enlists in this program her unmarried sister-in-law, Bélise, and her elder daughter, Armande. The spirited and sensible younger daughter, Henriette, declines to be recruited.

In *Les précieuses ridicules* (1659), Molière had made farcical fun of middle-class young women who aspired to salon life, with its refinements of speech and manner, its witticisms, its "spiritual" gallantries, its madrigals and *bouts-rimés*. As the century grew older, salon habitués became concerned with science and philosophy as well, so that Molière's Learned Ladies of 1672 keep a telescope in the attic and make references to Descartes and Epicurus. The atmosphere, *chez* Philaminte, is above all Platonic. Mind and soul are exalted, the body is scorned, and marriage is viewed with contempt. This ambiance is emotionally convenient for Bélise, who adopts the fantasy that all men are secretly and ethereally in love with her, and who also appeases her balked maternal instinct by schooling the servants in elementary grammar and science. For Armande, membership in her mother's "academy" is a less comfortable fate. Following Philaminte's example, she proclaims a pure devotion to spirit and intellect, and a horror of material and bodily things; but in fact she can neither satisfy herself with intellectual activity nor detach herself from the flesh. She would be a touching figure, as many are who suffer from imperfect idealism, were it not for her pretentiousness and for her jealous spite toward those who enjoy what she has renounced.

The abdication of Chrysale, in other words, has precipitated an abnormal situation in which all of the main characters suffer deformity or strain. Bélise is pacified by her chimeras, but at the cost of a complete divorce from the real feelings of others: when Henriette's suitor, Clitandre, turns to her for help in the play's fourth scene, he might as well be addressing a dead woman. Armande, saddled with an aspiration which is too much for her, is condemned to imposture and envy. Philaminte's bullying insistence on creating an intellectual environment arises not from a true thirst for knowledge but from a desire for personal glory, as well as a rancorous wish (which she shares with Armande) to show men that

> women may be learnèd if they please,
> And found, like men, their own academies.

Because of the ruthless egoism of her project, and its spirit of revenge, Philaminte suppresses in herself the magnanimity which truly belongs to her nature, and which flashes out briefly in the final scene of the play. Her vanity may also be blamed for the blindness with which she admires the egregious pedant Trissotin,

and the heartlessness with which she presses Henriette to marry
him against her wishes.

And what of Henriette? Is she, as one French critic has said,
a "hateful girl" given to false humility, cutting ironies, and banal
conceptions of life? Certainly not. I am of Arthur Tilley's
opinion, that "her simplicity, her directness, and above all, her
sense of humor, make her the most delightful of Molière's young
women." She is far more intelligent and witty than her high-
falutin sister, Armande; she is filial without being spiritless;
independent without being rebellious; admirable in accepting
the fact that she is her lover's second choice; noble in her readi-
ness to release him from what temporarily seems a bad bargain.
To find any of her speeches abrasive is to forget her embattled
and near-desperate position as a younger daughter under pressure
from three variously demented women. We must judge her as
we would a noncollaborative citizen of some occupied country.
Defending herself against Armande, she banters and teases; with
her mother, she sometimes plays dumb or dull; to Clitandre, she
gives blunt and practical strategic advice; in her bold confronta-
tion with Trissotin, she proves a cunning debater, and concludes
with an understandable asperity. In all of this, she shows her
resourcefulness and pluck, but each tactic necessarily entails a
temporary distortion of her nature in reaction to circumstances.
Of Clitandre, too, it may be supposed that the situation exag-
gerates some of his attitudes, and turns him into more of a ranter
than he would usually be.

The Learned Ladies comes as close to being a satiric play as
does anything in Molière's *oeuvre*; yet here as everywhere he
subordinates satire to the comic spirit, which is less interested in
excoriating human error than in affirming the fullness of life. As
always in Molière, there lies in the background of the play a clear
and actual France: it is an absolute monarchy with a Catholic
culture and a powerful Church; it is characterized by strong
class distinctions; in it, all social or familial roles, such as the
father's ruling function in any household, are plain matters of
natural law; it is a highly centralized state, and life at court or in
Paris is very different from life in the provinces. Other basic
aspects of Molière's France might be cited; suffice it, however,
to add that behind this particular play (as behind *The Misanthrope*) there also lies the Paris of social and literary cliques and

salons, an élite world which considered itself more elegant than the court. Our understanding of the characters in *The Learned Ladies* is partially shaped by an awareness of the real France beyond them: we note, for instance, that for the upper-middle-class Philaminte the conducting of a salon is a form of social climbing, and that it gratifies her to hear Trissotin recite under her roof a sonnet which has lately pleased "a certain princess." The life of the characters does *not*, however, consist in the satiric indication of real persons belonging to the salon world of Paris; their vitality and depth result, as I have been trying to suggest, from their intense interplay with each other, and from the way in which an unbalanced family situation has warped, divided, or challenged their personalities. We look *at* and *into* Philaminte or Armande, not *through* them.

To this rule there are a couple of apparent exceptions. The name of Philaminte's salon guest Trissotin was, for the seventeenth-century ear, inevitably suggestive of Molière's contemporary Charles Cotin. A member of the French Academy and a frequenter of the most brilliant salons, the Abbé Cotin was a prolific writer of occasional verse, who had more than once satirically attacked Molière and his friend Boileau. Molière avenged himself by naming an unattractive character Trissotin ("thrice-a-fool"), and also by having that character recite as his own work two vulnerably arch poems of Cotin's composition. In Vadius, with whom Trissotin has a literary spat in Act III, audiences easily recognized a reference to the distinguished scholar Gilles Ménage, who made verses in French, Italian, Latin, and Greek, and had once, by several accounts, quarreled with Cotin over the merits of one of the latter's poems. Vadius and Trissotin resemble Ménage and Cotin in the above respects, and one might add that Ménage was well known for the peremptoriness of his aesthetic judgments, and Cotin for being vain of his literary productions. But there the resemblances stop. When *Les femmes savantes* was first acted, Cotin was a sixty-eight-year-old man in holy orders, and could not possibly be confused with the fortune-hunting Trissotin of Act V. No more was Vadius intended as a true portrait of Ménage. Though French audiences of 1672 could enjoy Molière's incidental thrusts as we cannot, the figures of Trissotin and Vadius were finally for them, as for us, two fictional sketches of salon wits. Satire, then, is a secondary and local effect in this play, and the two wits, though less complex than certain other characters, share the same fictional world with them, and serve the same plot and theme.

Plot, in Molière, is best not taken too hard. We should not hold our breaths, toward the close of *Tartuffe*, over the danger that Orgon will lose his property; Molière was not, after all, writing bourgeois melodrama. And neither *The School for Wives* nor *The Learned Ladies* should make us bite our nails for fear that Agnès or Henriette will be forced to marry the wrong man. The use of plot in Molière is, as W. G. Moore has said, "to present an abstract issue in concrete pictures"; the plot is there to shuffle the characters around, providing us with all the confrontations and revelations that are necessary to depict a comic deformity and to define it by contrast to saner behaviors. From this transpires the play's question or theme—which is, in the case of *The Learned Ladies*, the right relation of art and learning to everyday life.

Every major figure in the play, whether male or female, somehow embodies that theme, and the men have their fair share of odiousness and folly. Chrysale, expressing an attitude that many of his original audience would have endorsed, holds that women's "only study and philosophy" should be the rearing of children, the training of servants, the keeping of household accounts, and the making of trousseaus. Nor is he more intellectually ambitious for himself: while there may be nothing scandalous about his indifference to the revolutions of Saturn, he is thoroughly philistine in his scorn of all books save the heavy Plutarch in which he presses his collars. Chrysale's brother, Ariste, is actually more of a catalyst than a character, but one or two of his speeches share Chrysale's distaste for pedantry and for "besotted" intellectuality in women; and the kitchen maid, Martine, vehemently supports her master's aversion to having a bookworm for a son-in-law. None of these persons, of course, speaks for Molière: Ariste's remarks are conditioned by his role as Clitandre's advocate; Chrysale is self-centered and hidebound, and appeals to us only through his wholesome sympathy with young love; Martine has a certain instinctual wisdom, but can scarcely be trusted to appreciate the value that education might have for her betters. And yet we side with this faction, and second what is valid in their speeches, because the "learned ladies" are so ill-motivated and their heroes—Trissotin and Vadius—so appalling. Philaminte, Bélise, and Armande lack, as I have said, any real vocation for the life of the mind, and Act III demonstrates this in numerous ways. By their continual interruption of Trissotin's verses, the ladies show that they have small interest in poetry proper; by their fatuous praise of Trissotin's verses, they show that they have no taste. The "learning" they display is skimpy and ludicrous, and their dreams of an academy have less to do with knowledge than with self-assertion and celebrity. Finally, the scenes with Trissotin and Vadius are so full of coquetry, so charged with repressed sexuality, as to prove the ladies unfitted to be vestals of science and of the spirit. All this being the case, Philaminte and her associates represent a false and fruitless intellectual pretension which entails neglect of all the normal self-realizations and responsibilities of bourgeois women. As for Trissotin's relation to the theme of this play, he is someone for whom learning, or, rather, a literary career, has become the whole of life. Regarding the poems which he dedicates to "Irises and Phyllises," he assures Henriette that

My mind speaks in those verses, not my heart.

But in fact this desiccated man has no heart, and for all his mixing in society, he is perfectly antisocial in the sense of being perfectly selfish; all of his attentions and flatteries to Philaminte's circle, all of his intrigues for dowry or pension, are for the benefit of a self which consists wholly of literary vanity and the pursuit of reputation. Literature and thought, for such a man, are unreal because unrelated to human feeling; in consequence, his life is vicious and his verse is dead.

The healthiest attitudes toward the play's theme are embodied in, and expressed by, Clitandre and Henriette. In respect of two repeated topics, spirituality and language, they represent an agreeable median position. Philaminte and Armande urge a life of pure intellect, and Bélise will have nothing to do with "extended substance"; Chrysale, at the other extreme, identifies himself with his body (*mon corps est moi-même*); but in Act IV, Scene 2, Clitandre firmly tells Armande that he has "both a body and a spirit," and Henriette has already proven the same of herself in the first scene of the play. In regard to language, we have at one extreme the pungent, direct, but limited and ungrammatical speech of Martine; at the other, we have the stifling or prissy rules of the proposed academy, the substanceless flatteries and phrase-making of Trissotin and Vadius, and the absolute dissociation of style and function in Philaminte's proposal that a French marriage contract express the dowry "in talent and drachma," and be dated in "ides and calends." (Since Philaminte twice upbraids the notary for his barbaric style, it is amusing that she is here proposing the use of literal barbarisms.) Though Henriette's speech is at times strategically flat, and though Clitandre, when aroused, can rattle on for thirty lines like Hotspur, their discourse is, on the whole, straightforward, pithy, sprightly, and graceful, and amounts to the best employment of language in the play. The virtues of Clitandre and Henriette are not all to be discovered in some middle ground, however: for instance, despite all the high-minded talk of others, it is they who, in the final scene, represent the extreme of active unselfishness in *Les femmes savantes.*

It is possible to exaggerate the play's anti-intellectualism. One should remember that the action takes place not in the university, the church, a great salon, or the manor house of Madame de Sévigné, but in an upper-bourgeois milieu, where an ill-founded pursuit of the semblance of culture can pervert all of the norms of life. Molière does not deny that there may be truly learned men and women, or true literati like Boileau, and he has Clitandre speak of persons of genuine wit and brain who are not unwelcome at the court. If the pseudo-intellectuality of the "learned ladies" were not so flamboyant, and Clitandre and Henriette so occupied with resisting it, one would more readily notice that the young lovers are literate people who read poetry (Trissotin's, for example) and judge it with some accuracy. Clitandre, it should be observed, is not unfamiliar with the scholarship of Rasius and Baldus, and is capable of criticizing the Platonic separation of body and soul. He and Henriette are in fact witty, intelligent, tasteful, and independent-minded; yet they do not feel that the cultivation of the mind should estrange one from life's basic fulfillments and duties. Neither, clearly, does Molière.

Clitandre's assertion that "A woman should know something . . . / Of every subject" was a quite liberal sentiment for its day, but we will not now recognize it as such unless *The Learned Ladies* is read (or mounted) quite strictly "in period."

[*Introduction*]

Molière is a timeless author in the sense that his art, owing to its clarity and its concern with human fundamentals, is not only readily enjoyed by readers and audiences three centuries after his death, but is often, I think, taken pretty much as it was meant to be taken. This freshness of Molière, his present accessibility, has lately misled some theatrical companies into detaching his art from its temporal background, and giving it the kind of "updating" which involves absurd anachronisms and the loss of meaning through the loss of a credible social frame. Not long ago, I saw a production that aimed to make *Tartuffe* "relevant" by dressing the title character in the sheets and beads of a guru, and having the action take place around a family swimming pool in California. The attempt at topicality was, of course, doomed from the start: it was young people who, in the latter 1960's, were succumbing to the influence of gurus, whereas in Molière's play that is not the situation at all: the children, Damis and Mariane, regard Tartuffe as a fraud, and it is their middle-aged father who is taken in. Not only did the production not mesh with current events, as the director had hoped it would seem to do; it was also miserably confusing, amongst other things, to hear a guru uttering Tartuffe's speeches, which are full of Christian scriptural and liturgical echoes, as well as seventeenth-century Jesuit terminology. More recently, a Boston company based a regrettable "modern-dress" production of *The Misanthrope* on the supposition that Alceste's demand for frankness in social intercourse resembles the demand, lately made by our youth culture, that one "tell it like it is." As a result, the play began with Alceste's entering a twentieth-century American living room in hippie attire, a ten-speed bicycle under his arm. The reader will imagine how implausibly such a figure inhabited the world of the text, where people are addressed as Sir and Madam, where duelling is a serious matter, and where continual reference is made to viscounts, marquesses, and the court of Versailles. I hope that no presenter of this new translation will wish, by means of contemporary costume and set, to attempt a violent conflation of Molière's drama with the current women's movement. And I hope that all readers of this text will envision it in a just historical perspective: Clitandre's liberalism, Henriette's attractively balanced nature, the grotesqueness of the bluestockings, and every nuance of this excellent comedy will then be there to be seen.

Sincere thanks are owed to my colleague Morton Briggs, who urged me to undertake this translation and was so kind as to read it over. I must also thank my wife, and Sonja and William Jay Smith, for their goodness in criticizing both the text and these remarks.

CHARACTERS

CHRYSALE, a well-to-do bourgeois

PHILAMINTE, Chrysale's wife

ARMANDE and ⎱ daughters of Chrysale
HENRIETTE ⎰ and Philaminte

ARISTE, Chrysale's brother

BÉLISE, Chrysale's sister

CLITANDRE, Henriette's suitor

TRISSOTIN, a wit

VADIUS, a scholar

MARTINE, kitchen-maid

LÉPINE, a servant

JULIEN, valet to Vadius

A NOTARY

The scene: Chrysale's house in Paris

ACT 1

SCENE ONE

ARMANDE

What, Sister! Are you truly of a mind
To leave your precious maidenhood behind,
And give yourself in marriage to a man?
Can you be harboring such a vulgar plan?

HENRIETTE

Yes, Sister.

ARMANDE

Yes, you say! When have I heard
So odious and sickening a word?

HENRIETTE

Why does the thought of marriage so repel you?

ARMANDE

Fie, fie! For shame!

HENRIETTE

But what—

487

ARMANDE

                    For shame, I tell you!
Can you deny what sordid scenes are brought
To the mind's eye by that distasteful thought,
What coarse, degrading images arise,
What shocking things it makes one visualize?
Do you not shudder, Sister, and grow pale
At what this thought you're thinking would entail?

HENRIETTE

It would entail, as I conceive it, one
Husband, some children, and a house to run;
In all of which, it may as well be said,
I find no cause for loathing or for dread.

ARMANDE

Alas! Such bondage truly appeals to you?

HENRIETTE

At my young age, what better could I do
Than join myself in wedded harmony
To one I love, and who in turn loves me,
And through the deepening bond of man and wife
Enjoy a blameless and contented life?
Does such a union offer no attractions?

ARMANDE

Oh dear, you crave such squalid satisfactions!
How can you choose to play a petty role,
Dull and domestic, and content your soul
With joys no loftier than keeping house
And raising brats, and pampering a spouse?

Let common natures, vulgarly inclined,
Concern themselves with trifles of that kind.
Aspire to nobler objects, seek to attain
To keener joys upon a higher plane,
And, scorning gross material things as naught,
Devote yourself, as we have done, to thought.
We have a mother to whom all pay honor
For erudition; model yourself upon her;
Yes, prove yourself her daughter, as I have done,
Join in the quest for truth that she's begun,
And learn how love of study can impart
A sweet enlargement to the mind and heart.
Why marry, and be the slave of him you wed?
Be married to philosophy instead,
Which lifts us up above mankind, and gives
All power to reason's pure imperatives,
Thus rendering our bestial natures tame
And mastering those lusts which lead to shame.
A love of reason, a passion for the truth,
Should quite suffice one's heart in age or youth,
And I am moved to pity when I note
On what low objects certain women dote.

HENRIETTE

But Heaven, in its wise omnipotence,
Endows us all with differing gifts and bents,
And all souls are not fashioned, I'm afraid,
Of the stuff of which philosophers are made.
If yours was born for soaring to the heights
Of learning, and for speculative flights,
My own weak spirit, Sister, has from birth
Clung to the homelier pleasures of the earth.
Let's not oppose what Heaven has decreed,
But simply follow where our instincts lead.
You, through the towering genius you possess,
Shall dwell in philosophic loftiness,

While my prosaic nature, here below,
Shall taste such joys as marriage can bestow.
Thus, though our lives contrast with one another,
We each shall emulate our worthy mother—
You, in your quest for rational excellence,
I, in the less refined delights of sense;
You, in conceptions lofty and ethereal,
I, in conceptions rather more material.

ARMANDE

Sister, the person whom one emulates
Ought to be followed for her finer traits.
If someone's worthy to be copied, it's
Not for the way in which she coughs and spits.

HENRIETTE

You and your intellect would not be here
If Mother's traits had all been fine, my dear,
And it's most fortunate for you that she
Was not wed solely to philosophy.
Relent, and tolerate in me, I pray,
That urge through which you saw the light of day,
And do not bid me be like you, and scorn
The hopes of some small scholar to be born.

ARMANDE

Your mind, I see, is stupidly contrary,
And won't give up its stubborn wish to marry.
But tell me, do, of this intended match:
Surely it's not Clitandre you aim to catch?

HENRIETTE

Why not? Of what defects could one accuse him?
Would I be vulgar if I were to choose him?

[*Act One* · *Scene One*]

ARMANDE

No. But I don't think much of your design
To lure away a devotee of mine;
Clitandre, as the world well knows, has sighed
And yearned for me, and sought me as his bride.

HENRIETTE

Yes; but such sighs, arising as they do
From base affections, are as naught to you;
Marriage is something you have risen above,
And fair philosophy has all your love.
Since, then, Clitandre isn't necessary
To your well-being, may he and I not marry?

ARMANDE

Though reason bids us shun the baits of sense,
We still may take delight in compliments;
We may refuse a man, yet be desirous
That still he pay us homage, and admire us.

HENRIETTE

I never sought to make him discontinue
His worship of the noble soul that's in you;
But once you had refused him, I felt free
To take the love which he then offered me.

ARMANDE

When a rejected suitor, full of spite,
Claims to adore you, can you trust him quite?
Do you really think he loves you? Are you persuaded
That his intense desire for me has faded?

491

HENRIETTE

Yes, Sister, I believe it; he's told me so.

ARMANDE

Sister, you're gullible; as you should know,
His talk of leaving me and loving you
Is self-deceptive bluster, and quite untrue.

HENRIETTE

Perhaps; however, Sister, if you'd care
To learn with me the facts of this affair,
I see Clitandre coming; I'm sure, my dear,
That if we ask, he'll make his feelings clear.

SCENE TWO

CLITANDRE, ARMANDE, HENRIETTE

HENRIETTE

My sister has me in uncertainties
As to your heart's affections. If you please,
Clitandre, tell us where your feelings lie,
And which of us may claim you—she or I.

ARMANDE

No, I'll not join in making you reveal
So publicly the passion which you feel;
You are, I'm sure, reluctant to confess
Your private feelings under such duress.

CLITANDRE (*to Armande*)

Madam, my heart, unused to sly pretense,
Does not reluct to state its sentiments;
I'm not at all embarrassed, and can proclaim
Wholeheartedly, without reserve or shame,
That she whom I most honor, hold most dear,
And whose devoted slave I am . . .
            (*Gesturing toward Henriette*)
                            is here.
Take no offense; you've nothing to resent:
You've made your choice, and so should be content.
Your charms enthralled me once, as many a sigh

493

And warm profession served to testify;
I offered you a love which could not fade,
Yet you disdained the conquest you had made.
Beneath your tyrant gaze, my soul has borne
A hundred bitter slights, and every scorn,
Till, wearying at last of whip and chain,
It hungered for a bondage more humane.
Such have I found, *Madame*, in these fair eyes,
      (*Gesturing once more toward Henriette*)
Whose kindness I shall ever love and prize:
They have not spurned the man you cast aside,
And, warmed by their regard, my tears have dried.
Now nothing could persuade me to be free
Of this most amiable captivity,
And I entreat you, Madam, do not strive
To cause my former feelings to revive,
Or sway my heart as once you did, for I
Propose to love this lady till I die.

ARMANDE

Well, Sir! What makes you fancy that one might
Regard you with a jealous appetite?
You're fatuous indeed to harbor such
A thought, and very brash to say as much.

HENRIETTE

Steady now, Sister. Where's that discipline
Of soul which reins one's lower nature in,
And keeps one's temper under firm command?

ARMANDE

And you, dear: are your passions well in hand
When you propose to wed a man without
The leave of those who brought your life about?

494

[*Act One* · *Scene Two*]

You owe your parents a complete submission,
And may not love except by their permission;
Your heart is theirs, and you may not bestow it;
To do so would be wicked, and you know it.

HENRIETTE

I'm very grateful to be thus instructed
In how these matters ought to be conducted.
And just to prove to you that I've imbibed
Your teachings, I shall do as you've prescribed:
Clitandre, I should thank you if you went
And gained from my dear parents their consent,
So that, without the risk of wickedness,
I could return the love which you profess.

CLITANDRE

Now that I have your gracious leave, I'll bend
My every effort towards that happy end.

ARMANDE

You look triumphant, Sister, and appear
To think me vexed by what has happened here.

HENRIETTE

By no means, Sister. I well know how you've checked
Your senses with the reins of intellect,
And how no foolish weakness could disturb
A heart so disciplined by wisdom's curb.
I'm far from thinking you upset; indeed,
I know you'll give me the support I need,
Help win my parents to Clitandre's side,
And speed the day when I may be his bride.
Do lend your influence, Sister, to promote—

ARMANDE

What childish teasing, Sister! And how you gloat
At having made a cast-off heart your prize!

HENRIETTE

Cast-off or not, it's one you don't despise.
Had you the chance to get it back from me,
You'd gladly pick it up on bended knee.

ARMANDE

I shall not stoop to answer that. I deem
This whole discussion silly in the extreme.

HENRIETTE

It is indeed, and you do well to end it.
Your self-control is great, and I commend it.

SCENE THREE

HENRIETTE

Your frank avowal left her quite unnerved.

CLITANDRE

Such frankness was no less than she deserved;
Given her haughty airs and foolish pride,
My blunt words were entirely justified.
But now, since you have given me leave, I'll seek
Your father—

HENRIETTE

      It's to Mother you should speak.
My gentle father would say yes, of course,
But his decrees, alas, have little force;
Heaven blessed him with a mild, concessive soul
Which yields in all things to his wife's control.
It's she who rules the house, requiring him
To treat as law her every royal whim.
I wish that you were more disposed to please
My mother, and indulge my Aunt Bélise,
By humoring their fancies, and thereby
Making them view you with a kindly eye.

497

[*Act One* · *Scene Three*]

My heart's too frank for that; I could not praise,
Even in your sister, such outlandish ways,
And female sages aren't my cup of tea.
A woman should know something, I agree,
Of every subject, but this proud desire
To pose as erudite I can't admire.
I like a woman who, though she may know
The answers, does not always let it show;
Who keeps her studies secret and, in fine,
Though she's enlightened, feels no need to shine
By means of pompous word and rare quotation
And brilliance on the slightest provocation.
I much respect your mother; nonetheless,
I can't encourage her in foolishness,
Agree with everything she says, and laud
Her intellectual hero—who's a fraud.
I loathe her Monsieur Trissotin; how can
She so esteem so ludicrous a man,
And class with men of genius and of vision
A dunce whose works meet always with derision,
A bore whose dreadful books end, one and all,
As wrapping paper in some market stall?

HENRIETTE

All that he writes or speaks I find a bore;
I could agree with all you say, and more;
But since the creature has my mother's ear,
He's someone you should cultivate, I fear.
A lover seeks the good opinion of
All who surround the object of his love,
And, so that no one will oppose his passion,
Treats even the house-dog in a courtly fashion.

498

CLITANDRE

You're right; yet Trissotin, I must admit,
So irks me that there's no controlling it.
I can't, to gain his advocacy, stoop
To praise the works of such a nincompoop.
It was those works which introduced me to him;
Before I ever saw the man, I knew him;
From the vile way he wrote, I saw with ease
What, in the flesh, must be his qualities:
The absolute presumption, the complete
And dauntless nature of his self-conceit,
The calm assurance of superior worth
Which renders him the smuggest man on earth,
So that he stands in awe and hugs himself
Before his volumes ranged upon the shelf,
And would not trade his baseless reputation
For that of any general in the nation.

HENRIETTE

If you could see all that, you've got good eyes.

CLITANDRE

I saw still more; for I could visualize,
By studying his dreadful poetry,
Just what the poet's lineaments must be;
I pictured him so truly that, one day,
Seeing a foppish man in the Palais,
I said, "That's Trissotin, by God!"—and found,
Upon enquiry, that my hunch was sound.

HENRIETTE

What a wild story!

CLITANDRE

Not at all; it's true.
But here's your aunt. If you'll permit me to,
I'll tell her of our hopes, in hopes that she
Will urge your mother to approve of me.

SCENE FOUR

CLITANDRE, BÉLISE

CLITANDRE

Madam, permit a lover's heart to seize
This happy opportunity, if you please,
To tell you of his passion, and reveal—

BÉLISE

Hold, Sir! Don't say too baldly what you feel.
If you belong, Sir, to the ranks of those
Who love me, let your eyes alone disclose
Your sentiments, and do not tell me bluntly
Of coarse desires which only could affront me.
Adore me if you will, but do not show it
In such a way that I'll be forced to know it;
Worship me inwardly, and I shall brook it
If, through your silence, I can overlook it;
But should you dare to speak of it outright,
I'll banish you forever from my sight.

CLITANDRE

My passions, Madam, need cause you no alarms;
It's Henriette who's won me by her charms,
And I entreat your generous soul to aid me
In my design to wed that charming lady.

[*Act One* · *Scene Four*]

BÉLISE

Ah, what a subtle dodge; you should be proud;
You're very artful, it must be allowed;
In all the novels that I've read, I've never
Encountered any subterfuge so clever.

CLITANDRE

Madam, I meant no witty indirection;
I've spoken truly of my heart's affection.
By Heaven's will, by ties that cannot part,
I'm bound to Henriette with all my heart;
It's Henriette I cherish, as I've said,
And Henriette whom I aspire to wed.
All that I ask of you is that you lend
Your influence to help me gain that end.

BÉLISE

I well divine the hopes which you have stated,
And how the name you've used should be translated.
A clever substitution, Sir; and I
Shall use the selfsame code in my reply:
"Henriette" disdains to wed, and those who burn
For her must hope for nothing in return.

CLITANDRE

Madam, why make things difficult? Why insist
Upon supposing what does not exist?

BÉLISE

Good heavens, Sir, don't stand on ceremony,
Denying what your looks have often shown me.

Let it suffice, Sir, that I am contented
With this oblique approach you have invented,
And that, beneath such decorous disguise,
Your homage is acceptable in my eyes,
Provided that you make no overture
Which is not noble, rarefied, and pure.

CLITANDRE

But—

BÉLISE

  Hush. Farewell. It's time our talk was ended.
I've said, already, more than I intended.

CLITANDRE

You're quite mistaken—

BÉLISE

     I'm blushing, can't you see?
All this has overtaxed my modesty.

CLITANDRE

I'm hanged if I love you, Madam! This is absurd.

BÉLISE

No, no, I mustn't hear another word.
    (*She exits.*)

[*Act One* · *Scene Four*]

CLITANDRE

The devil take her and her addled brain!
What stubborn fancies she can entertain!
Well, I'll turn elsewhere, and shall hope to find
Support from someone with a balanced mind.

SCENE ONE

ARISTE

ARISTE (*to Clitandre, who is making his exit*)

Yes, yes, I'll urge and plead as best I can, Sir,
Then hasten back to you and bring his answer.
Lovers! How very much they have to say,
And what extreme impatience they display!
Never—

SCENE TWO

CHRYSALE, ARISTE

ARISTE

Ah! God be with you, Brother dear.

CHRYSALE

And you, dear Brother.

ARISTE

D'you know what brings me here?

CHRYSALE

No, but I'll gladly learn of it; do tell.

ARISTE

I think you know Clitandre rather well?

CHRYSALE

Indeed; he calls here almost every day.

ARISTE

And what is your opinion of him, pray?

[*Act Two* · *Scene Two*]

CHRYSALE

He's a man of honor, breeding, wit, and spirit;
I know few lads of comparable merit.

ARISTE

Well, I am here at his request; I'm glad
To learn that you think highly of the lad.

CHRYSALE

I knew his father well, during my stay
In Rome.

ARISTE

Ah, good.

CHRYSALE

A fine man.

ARISTE

So they say.

CHRYSALE

We were both young then, twenty-eight or so,
And a pair of dashing gallants, I'll have you know.

ARISTE

I'm sure of it.

[*Act Two* · *Scene Two*]

CHRYSALE

Oh, those dark-eyed Roman maids!
The whole town talked about our escapades,
And weren't the husbands jealous!

ARISTE

Ho! No doubt!
But let me broach the matter I came about.

SCENE THREE

BÉLISE (*entering quietly and listening*),
CHRYSALE, ARISTE

ARISTE

I'm here to speak for young Clitandre, and let
You know of his deep love for Henriette.

CHRYSALE

He loves my daughter?

ARISTE

      Yes. Upon my honor,
I've never seen such passion; he dotes upon her.

BÉLISE (*to Ariste*)

No, no; I see what's happened. You're unaware
Of the true character of this affair.

ARISTE

What, Sister?

BÉLISE

    Clitandre has misled you, Brother:
The passion which he feels is for another.

[*Act Two* · *Scene Three*]

ARISTE

Oh, come. He doesn't love Henriette? Then how—

BÉLISE

I'm certain of it.

ARISTE

He said he did, just now.

BÉLISE

Of course.

ARISTE

He sent me here, please understand,
To ask her father for the lady's hand.

BÉLISE

Splendid.

ARISTE

What's more, his ardor is so great
That I'm to urge an early wedding date.

BÉLISE

Oh, how delightful; what obliquity!
We use the name of "Henriette," you see,
As a code word and camouflage concealing
The actual object of his tender feeling.
But I'll consent, now, to enlighten you.

[*Act Two* · *Scene Three*]

ARISTE

Well, Sister, since you know so much, please do
Tell us with whom his true affections lie.

BÉLISE

You wish to know?

ARISTE

I do.

BÉLISE

It's I.

ARISTE

You?

BÉLISE

I.

ARISTE

Well, Sister!

BÉLISE

What do you mean by *well?* My word,
Why should you look surprised at what you've heard?
My charms are evident, in my frank opinion,
And more than one heart's under their dominion.
Dorante, Damis, Cléonte, Valère—all these
Are proof of my attractive qualities.

[*Act Two · Scene Three*]

ARISTE

These men all love you?

BÉLISE

Yes, with all their might.

ARISTE

They've said so?

BÉLISE

None has been so impolite:
They've worshipped me as one from Heaven above,
And not presumed to breathe a word of love.
Mute signs, however, have managed to impart
The keen devotion of each humble heart.

ARISTE

Damis is almost never seen here. Why?

BÉLISE

His reverence for me has made him shy.

ARISTE

Dorante reviles you in the harshest fashion.

BÉLISE

He's seized, at times, by fits of jealous passion.

[*Act Two · Scene Three*]

ARISTE

Cléonte has lately married; so has Valère.

BÉLISE

That was because I drove them to despair.

ARISTE

Sister, you're prone to fantasies, I fear.

CHRYSALE (*to Bélise*)

Get rid of these chimeras, Sister dear.

BÉLISE

Chimeras! Well! Chimeras, did you say?
I have chimeras! Well, how very gay!
May all your thoughts, dear Brothers, be as clear as
Those which you dared, just now, to call *chimeras!*

SCENE FOUR

CHRYSALE, ARISTE

CHRYSALE

Our sister's mad.

ARISTE

   And growing madder daily.
But, once more, let's discuss our business, may we?
Clitandre longs to marry Henriette,
And asks your blessing. What answer shall he get?

CHRYSALE

No need to ask. I readily agree.
His wish does honor to my family.

ARISTE

He has, as you well know, no great amount
Of worldly goods—

CHRYSALE

   Ah, gold's of no account:
He's rich in virtue, that most precious ore;
His father and I were bosom friends, what's more.

ARISTE

Let's go make certain that your wife concurs.

CHRYSALE

I've given my consent; no need for hers.

ARISTE

True, Brother; still, 'twould do no harm if your
Decision had her strong support, I'm sure.
Let's both go—

CHRYSALE

               Nonsense, that's a needless move;
I'll answer for my wife. She will approve.

ARISTE

But—

CHRYSALE

    No. Enough. I'll deal with her. Don't worry.
The business will be settled in a hurry.

ARISTE

So be it. I'll go consult with Henriette,
And then—

CHRYSALE

           The thing's as good as done; don't fret.
I'll tell my wife about it, without delay.

SCENE FIVE

MARTINE, CHRYSALE

MARTINE

Ain't that my luck! It's right, what people say—
When you hang a dog, first give him a bad name.
Domestic service! It's a losing game.

CHRYSALE

Well, well, Martine! What's up?

MARTINE

You want to know?

CHRYSALE

Why, yes.

MARTINE

What's up is, Madam's let me go.

CHRYSALE

She's let you go?

[*Act Two · Scene Five*]

MARTINE

Yes, given me the sack.

CHRYSALE

But why? Whatever for?

MARTINE

              She says she'll whack
Me black and blue if I don't clear out of here.

CHRYSALE

No, you shall stay; you've served me well, my dear.
My wife's a bit short-tempered at times, and fussy:
But this won't do. I'll—

SCENE SIX

PHILAMINTE, BÉLISE, CHRYSALE, MARTINE

PHILAMINTE (*seeing Martine*)
What! Still here, you hussy!
Be off, you trollop; leave my house this minute,
And mind you never again set foot within it!

CHRYSALE

Gently, now.

PHILAMINTE

No, it's settled.

CHRYSALE

But—

PHILAMINTE

Off with her!

CHRYSALE

What crime has she committed, to incur—

PHILAMINTE

So! You defend the girl!

520

[Act Two · Scene Six]

CHRYSALE

No, that's not so.

PHILAMINTE

Are you taking her side against me?

CHRYSALE

Heavens, no;
I merely asked the nature of her offense.

PHILAMINTE

Would I, without good reason, send her hence?

CHRYSALE

Of course not; but employers should be just—

PHILAMINTE

Enough! I bade her leave, and leave she must.

CHRYSALE

Quite so, quite so. Has anyone denied it?

PHILAMINTE

I won't be contradicted. I can't abide it.

CHRYSALE

Agreed.

[*Act Two* · *Scene Six*]

PHILAMINTE

If you were a proper husband, you
Would take my side, and share my outrage, too.

CHRYSALE

I do, dear.
(Turning towards Martine)
Wench! My wife is right to rid
This house of one who's done the thing you did.

MARTINE

What did I do?

CHRYSALE (*aside*)

Alas, you have me there.

PHILAMINTE

She takes a light view, still, of this affair.

CHRYSALE

What caused your anger? How did all this begin?
Did she break some mirror, or piece of porcelain?

PHILAMINTE

Do you suppose that I'd be angry at her,
And bid her leave, for such a trifling matter?

CHRYSALE (*to Martine*)

What can this mean? (*To Philaminte*) Is the crime, then,
very great?

[*Act Two* · *Scene Six*]

PHILAMINTE

Of course it is. Would I exaggerate?

CHRYSALE

Did she, perhaps, by inadvertence, let
Some vase be stolen, or some china set?

PHILAMINTE

That would be nothing.

CHRYSALE (*to Martine*)

       Blast, girl, what can this be?
      (*To Philaminte*)
Have you caught the chit in some dishonesty?

PHILAMINTE

Far worse than that.

CHRYSALE

      Far worse than that?

PHILAMINTE

                Far worse.

CHRYSALE (*to Martine*)

For shame, you strumpet! (*To Philaminte*) Has she been so
  perverse—

PHILAMINTE

This creature, who for insolence has no peer,
Has, after thirty lessons, shocked my ear
By uttering a low, plebeian word
Which Vaugelas deems unworthy to be heard.

CHRYSALE

Is *that*—?

PHILAMINTE

        And she persists in her defiance
Of that which is the basis of all science—
Grammar! which even the mightiest must obey,
And whose pure laws hold princes in their sway.

CHRYSALE

I was sure she'd done the worst thing under the sun.

PHILAMINTE

What! You don't find it monstrous, what she's done?

CHRYSALE

Oh, yes.

PHILAMINTE

I'd love to hear you plead her case!

CHRYSALE

Not I!

[*Act Two* · *Scene Six*]

BÉLISE

It's true, her speech is a disgrace.
How long we've taught her language and its laws!
Yet still she butchers every phrase or clause.

MARTINE

I'm sure your preachings is all well and good,
But I wouldn't talk your jargon if I could.

PHILAMINTE

She dares describe as jargon a speech that's based
On reason, and good usage, and good taste!

MARTINE

If people get the point, that's speech to me;
Fine words don't have no use that I can see.

PHILAMINTE

Hark! There's a sample of her style again!
"Don't have no!"

BÉLISE

O ineducable brain!
How futile have our efforts been to teach
Your stubborn mind the rules of proper speech!
You've coupled *don't* with *no*. I can't forgive
That pleonasm, that double negative.

MARTINE

Good Lord, Ma'am, I ain't studious like you;
I just talk plain, the way my people do.

525

[*Act Two* · *Scene Six*]

PHILAMINTE

What ghastly solecisms!

BÉLISE

I could faint!

PHILAMINTE

How the ear shudders at the sound of "ain't"!

BÉLISE (*to Martine*)

With ignorance like yours, one struggles vainly.
"Plain" is an adjective; the adverb's "plainly."
Shall grammar be abused by you forever?

MARTINE

Me abuse Gramma? Or Grampa either? Never!

PHILAMINTE

Dear God!

BÉLISE

What I said was "grammar." You misheard.
I've told you about the origin of the word.

MARTINE

Let it come from Passy, Pontoise, or Chaillot;
It's Greek to me.

[*Act Two · Scene Six*]

BÉLISE

Alas, what *do* you know,
You peasant? It is grammar which lays down
The laws which govern adjective and noun,
And verb, and subject.

MARTINE

Madam, I'd just be lying
If I said I knew those people.

PHILAMINTE

Oh, how trying!

BÉLISE

Girl, those are parts of speech, and we must be
At pains to make those parts of speech agree.

MARTINE

Let them agree or squabble, what does it matter?

PHILAMINTE (*to her sister-in-law*)

Ah, mercy, let's be done with all this chatter!
(*To her husband*)
Sir! Will you bid her go and leave me in peace?

CHRYSALE

Yes, yes. (*Aside*) I must give in to her caprice.
(*To Martine*)
Martine, don't vex her further; you'd best depart.

[*Act Two · Scene Six*]

PHILAMINTE

So, you're afraid to wound her little heart!
The hussy! Must you be so sweet and mild?

CHRYSALE

Of course not. (*Loudly*) Wench, be off!
         (*Softly, to Martine*)
                         Go, go, poor child.

SCENE SEVEN

PHILAMINTE, CHRYSALE, BÉLISE

CHRYSALE

Well, you have had your way, and she is gone;
But I don't think much of the way you've carried on.
The girl is good at what she does, and you've
Dismissed her for a trifle. I don't approve.

PHILAMINTE

Would you have me keep her in my service here
To give incessant anguish to my ear
By constant barbarisms, and the breach
Of every law of reason and good speech,
Patching the mangled discourse which she utters
With coarse expressions from the city's gutters?

BÉLISE

It's true, her talk can drive one out of one's wits.
Each day, she tears dear Vaugelas to bits,
And the least failings of this pet of yours
Are vile cacophonies and non sequiturs.

CHRYSALE

Who cares if she offends some grammar book,
So long as she doesn't offend us as a cook?

If she makes a tasty salad, it seems to me
Her subjects and her verbs need not agree.
Let all her talk be barbarous, if she'll not
Burn up my beef or oversalt the pot.
It's food, not language, that I'm nourished by.
Vaugelas can't teach you how to bake a pie;
Malherbe, Balzac, for all their learnèd rules,
Might, in a kitchen, have been utter fools.

PHILAMINTE

I'm stunned by what you've said, and shocked at seeing
How you, who claim the rank of human being,
Rather than rise on spiritual wings,
Give all your care to base, material things.
This rag, the body—does it matter so?
Should its desires detain us here below?
Should we not soar aloft, and scorn to heed it?

CHRYSALE

My body is myself, and I aim to feed it.
It's a rag, perhaps, but one of which I'm fond.

BÉLISE

Brother, 'twixt flesh and spirit there's a bond;
Yet, as the best minds of the age have stated,
The claims of flesh must be subordinated,
And it must be our chief delight and care
To feast the soul on philosophic fare.

CHRYSALE

I don't know what your soul's been eating of late,
But it's not a balanced diet, at any rate;

You show no womanly solicitude
For—

PHILAMINTE

"Womanly"! That word is old and crude.
It reeks, in fact, of its antiquity.

BÉLISE

It sounds old-fashioned and absurd to me.

CHRYSALE

See here; I can't contain myself; I mean
To drop the mask for once, and vent my spleen.
The whole world thinks you mad, and I am through—

PHILAMINTE

How's that, Sir?

CHRYSALE (*to Bélise*)

Sister, I am addressing *you*.
The least mistake in speech you can't forgive,
But how mistakenly you choose to live!
I'm sick of those eternal books you've got;
In my opinion, you should burn the lot,
Save for that Plutarch where I press my collars,
And leave the studious life to clerks and scholars;
And do throw out, if I may be emphatic,
That great long frightful spyglass in the attic,
And all these other gadgets, and do it soon.
Stop trying to see what's happening in the moon
And look what's happening in your household here,
Where everything is upside down and queer.

[*Act Two* · *Scene Seven*]

For a hundred reasons, it's neither meet nor right
That a woman study and be erudite.
To teach her children manners, overlook
The household, train the servants and the cook,
And keep a thrifty budget—these should be
Her only study and philosophy.
Our fathers had a saying which made good sense:
A woman's polished her intelligence
Enough, they said, if she can pass the test
Of telling a pair of breeches from a vest.
Their wives read nothing, yet their lives were good;
Domestic lore was all they understood,
And all their books were needle and thread, with which
They made their daughters' trousseaus, stitch by stitch.
But women scorn such modest arts of late;
They want to scribble and to cogitate;
No mystery is too deep for them to plumb.
Is there a stranger house in Christendom
Than mine, where women are as mad as hatters,
And everything is known except what matters?
They know how Mars, the moon, and Venus turn,
And Saturn, too, that's none of my concern,
And what with all this vain and far-fetched learning,
They don't know if my roast of beef is burning.
My servants, who now aspire to culture, too,
Do anything but what they're paid to do;
Thinking is all this household thinks about,
And reasoning has driven reason out.
One spoils a sauce, while reading the dictionary;
One mumbles verses when I ask for sherry;
Because they ape the follies they've observed
In you, I keep six servants and am not served.
Just one poor wench remained who hadn't caught
The prevalent disease of lofty thought,
And now, since Vaugelas might find her lacking
In grammar, you've blown up and sent her packing.
Sister (I'm speaking to you, as I said before),

532

[*Act Two* · *Scene Seven*]

These goings-on I censure and deplore.
I'm tired of visits from these pedants versed
In Latin, and that ass Trissotin's the worst.
He's flattered you in many a wretched sonnet;
There's a great swarm of queer bees in his bonnet;
Each time he speaks, one wonders what he's said;
I think, myself, that he's crazy in the head.

PHILAMINTE

Dear God, what brutishness of speech and mind!

BÉLISE

Could particles more grossly be combined,
Or atoms form an aggregate more crass?
And can we be of the same blood? Alas,
I hate myself because we two are kin,
And leave this scene in horror and chagrin.

SCENE EIGHT

PHILAMINTE, CHRYSALE

PHILAMINTE

Have you other shots to fire, or are you through?

CHRYSALE

I? No, no. No more quarreling. That will do.
Let's talk of something else. As we've heard her state,
Your eldest daughter scorns to take a mate.
She's a philosopher—mind you, I'm not complaining;
She's had the finest of maternal training.
But her younger sister's otherwise inclined,
And I've a notion that it's time to find
A match for Henriette—

PHILAMINTE

Exactly, and
I'll now inform you of the match I've planned.
That Trissotin whose visits you begrudge,
And whom you so contemptuously judge,
Is, I've decided, the appropriate man.
If you can't recognize his worth, I can.
Let's not discuss it; it's quite unnecessary;
I've thought things through; it's he whom she should marry.

[*Act Two · Scene Eight*]

Don't tell her of my choice, however; I choose
To be the first to let her know the news.
That she will listen to reason I have no doubt,
And if you seek to meddle, I'll soon find out.

SCENE NINE

ARISTE, CHRYSALE

ARISTE

Ah, Brother; your wife's just leaving, and it's clear
That you and she have had a conference here.

CHRYSALE

Yes.

ARISTE

Well, shall Clitandre have his Henriette?
Is your wife willing? Can the date be set?

CHRYSALE

Not altogether.

ARISTE

What, she refuses?

CHRYSALE

No.

ARISTE

Is she wavering, then?

CHRYSALE

I wouldn't describe her so.

ARISTE

What, then?

CHRYSALE

There's someone else whom she prefers.

ARISTE

For a son-in-law?

CHRYSALE

Yes.

ARISTE

Who is this choice of hers?

CHRYSALE

Well . . . Trissotin.

ARISTE

What! That ass, that figure of fun—

537

CHRYSALE

Who babbles verse and Latin? Yes, that's the one.

ARISTE

Did you agree to him?

CHRYSALE

I? No; God forbid!

ARISTE

What did you say, then?

CHRYSALE

Nothing; and what I did
Was wise, I think, for it left me uncommitted.

ARISTE

I see! What strategy! How nimble-witted!
Did you, at least, suggest Clitandre, Brother?

CHRYSALE

No. When I found her partial toward another,
It seemed best not to push things then and there.

ARISTE

Your prudence, truly, is beyond compare!
Aren't you ashamed to be so soft and meek?
How can a man be so absurdly weak

538

As to yield his wife an absolute dominion
And never dare contest her least opinion?

CHRYSALE

Ah, Brother, that's easy enough for you to say.
You've no idea how noisy quarrels weigh
Upon my heart, which loves tranquillity,
And how my wife's bad temper frightens me.
Her nature's philosophic—or that's her claim,
But her tongue's sharp and savage all the same;
All this uplifting thought has not decreased
Her rancorous behavior in the least.
If I cross her even slightly, she will loose
An eight-day howling tempest of abuse.
There's no escape from her consuming ire;
She's like some frightful dragon spitting fire;
And yet, despite her devilish ways, my fear
Obliges me to call her "pet" and "dear."

ARISTE

For shame. That's nonsense. It's your cowardice
Which lets your wife rule over you like this.
What power she has, your weakness has created;
She only rules because you've abdicated;
She couldn't bully you unless you chose,
Like an ass, to let her lead you by the nose.
Come now: despite your timid nature, can
You not resolve for once to be a man,
And, saying "This is how it's going to be,"
Lay down the law, and make your wife agree?
Shall you sacrifice your Henriette to these
Besotted women and their fantasies,
And take for son-in-law, and *heir*, a fool
Who's turned your house into a Latin school,
A pedant whom your dazzled wife extols

As best of wits, most erudite of souls
And peerless fashioner of galiant verse,
And who, in all respects, could not be worse?
Once more I say, for shame: it's ludicrous
To see a husband cringe and cower thus.

CHRYSALE

Yes, you're quite right; I see that I've been wrong.
It's high time, Brother, to be firm and strong,
To take a stand.

ARISTE

Well said.

CHRYSALE

It's base, I know,
To let a woman dominate one so.

ARISTE

Quite right.

CHRYSALE

She's taken advantage of my patience.

ARISTE

She has.

CHRYSALE

And of my peaceful inclinations.

540

[*Act Two · Scene Nine*]

ARISTE

That's true.

CHRYSALE

But, as she'll learn this very day,
My daughter's mine, and I shall have my way
And wed her to a man who pleases me.

ARISTE

Now you're the master, as I'd have you be.

CHRYSALE

Brother, as young Clitandre's spokesman, you
Know where to find him. Send him to me, do.

ARISTE

I'll go this instant.

CHRYSALE

Too long my will's been crossed;
Henceforth I'll be a man, whatever the cost.

ACT 3

SCENE ONE

PHILAMINTE, ARMANDE, BÉLISE,
TRISSOTIN, LÉPINE

PHILAMINTE

Let's all sit down and savor, thought by thought,
The verses which our learnèd guest has brought.

ARMANDE

I burn to see them.

BÉLISE

Yes; our souls are panting.

PHILAMINTE (*to Trissotin*)

All that your mind brings forth, I find enchanting.

ARMANDE

For me, your compositions have no peer.

BÉLISE

Their music is a banquet to my ear.

545

[*Act Three* · *Scene One*]

PHILAMINTE

Don't tantalize your breathless audience.

ARMANDE

Do hurry—

BÉLISE

And relieve this sweet suspense.

PHILAMINTE

Yield to our urging; give us your epigram.

TRISSOTIN (*to Philaminte*)

Madam, 'tis but an infant; still, I am
In hopes that you may condescend to love it,
Since on your doorstep I was delivered of it.

PHILAMINTE

Knowing its father, I can do no other.

TRISSOTIN

Your kind approval, then, shall be its mother.

BÉLISE

What wit he has!

546

SCENE TWO

HENRIETTE, PHILAMINTE, ARMANDE,
BÉLISE, TRISSOTIN, LÉPINE

PHILAMINTE *(to Henriette, who has
entered and has turned at once to go)*
Ho! Don't rush off like that.

HENRIETTE

I feared I might disrupt your pleasant chat.

PHILAMINTE

Come here, and pay attention, and you shall share
The joy of hearing something rich and rare.

HENRIETTE

I'm no fit judge of elegance in letters;
I leave such heady pastimes to my betters.

PHILAMINTE

That doesn't matter. Stay, and when we're through
I shall reveal a sweet surprise to you.

TRISSOTIN *(to Henriette)*

What need you know of learning and the arts,
Who know so well the way to charm men's hearts?

547

HENRIETTE

Sir, I know neither; nor is it my ambition—

BÉLISE

Oh, please! Let's hear the infant composition.

PHILAMINTE (*to Lépine*)

Quick, boy, some chairs.
(*Lépine falls down in bringing a chair.*)
Dear God, how loutish! Ought you
To fall like that, considering what we've taught you
Regarding equilibrium and its laws?

BÉLISE

Look what you've done, fool. Surely you see the cause?
It was by wrongly shifting what we call
The center of gravity, that you came to fall.

LÉPINE

I saw that when I hit the floor, alas.

PHILAMINTE (*to Lépine, as he leaves*)

Dolt!

TRISSOTIN

It's a blessing he's not made of glass.

ARMANDE

What wit! It never falters!

BÉLISE

Not in the least.
(*All sit down.*)

PHILAMINTE

Now then, do serve us your poetic feast.

TRISSOTIN

For such great hunger as confronts me here,
An eight-line dish would not suffice, I fear.
My epigram's too slight. It would be wiser,
I think, to give you first, as appetizer,
A sonnet which a certain princess found
Subtle in sense, delectable in sound.
I've seasoned it with Attic salt throughout,
And you will find it tasty, I have no doubt.

ARMANDE

How could we not?

PHILAMINTE

Let's listen, with concentration.

BÉLISE (*interrupting Trissotin each time
he starts to read*)

My heart is leaping with anticipation.
I'm mad for poetry, and I love it best
When pregnant thoughts are gallantly expressed.

549

PHILAMINTE

So long as we talk, our guest can't say a word.

TRISSOTIN

SON–

BÉLISE (*to Henriette*)

Niece, be silent.

ARMANDE

Please! Let the poem be heard.

TRISSOTIN

SONNET TO THE PRINCESS URANIE,
REGARDING HER FEVER

Your prudence, Madam, must have drowsed
When you took in so hot a foe
And let him be so nobly housed,
And feasted and regaled him so.

BÉLISE

A fine first quatrain!

ARMANDE

And the style! How gallant!

PHILAMINTE

For metric flow he has a matchless talent.

[*Act Three* · *Scene Two*]

ARMANDE

"Your *prudence* must have *drowsed*": a charming touch.

BÉLISE

"So hot a foe" delights me quite as much.

PHILAMINTE

I think that "feasted and regaled" conveys
A sense of richness in so many ways.

BÉLISE

Let's listen to the rest.

TRISSOTIN

Your prudence, Madam, must have drowsed
When you took in so hot a foe
And let him be so nobly housed,
And feasted and regaled him so.

ARMANDE

"Your prudence must have drowsed"!

BÉLISE

"So hot a foe"!

PHILAMINTE

"Feasted and regaled"!

TRISSOTIN

Say what they may, the wretch must go!
From your rich lodging drive away
This ingrate who, as well you know,
Would make your precious life his prey.

BÉLISE

Oh! Pause a moment, I beg you; one is breathless.

ARMANDE

Let us digest those verses, which are deathless.

PHILAMINTE

There's a rare something in those lines which captures
One's inmost heart, and stirs the soul to raptures.

ARMANDE

"Say what they may, the wretch must go!
From your rich lodging drive away . . ."

How apt that is—"rich lodging." I adore
The wit and freshness of that metaphor!

PHILAMINTE

"Say what they may, the wretch must go!"

That "Say what they may" is greatly to my liking.
I've never encountered any words more striking.

ARMANDE

Nor I. That "Say what they may" bewitches me.

[*Act Three* · *Scene Two*]

BÉLISE

"Say what they may" is brilliant, I agree.

ARMANDE

Oh, to have said it.

BÉLISE

It's a whole poem in a phrase.

PHILAMINTE

But have you fully grasped what it conveys,
As I have?

ARMANDE and BÉLISE

Oh! Oh!

PHILAMINTE

"Say what they may, the wretch must go"!

That means, if people take the fever's side,
Their pleadings should be scornfully denied.

"Say what they may, the wretch must go,
Say what they may, say what they may"!

There's more in that "Say what they may" than first appears.
Perhaps I am alone in this, my dears,
But I see no limit to what that phrase implies.

BÉLISE

It's true, it means a great deal for its size.

553

PHILAMINTE (*to Trissotin*)

Sir, when you wrote this charming "Say what they may,"
Did you know your own great genius? Can you say
That you were conscious, then, of all the wit
And wealth of meaning we have found in it?

TRISSOTIN

Ah! Well!

ARMANDE

I'm very fond of "ingrate," too.
It well describes that villain fever, who
Repays his hosts by causing them distress.

PHILAMINTE

In short, the quatrains are a great success.
Do let us have the tercets now, I pray.

ARMANDE

Oh, please, let's once more hear "Say what they may."

TRISSOTIN

Say what they may, the wretch must go!

PHILAMINTE, ARMANDE, and BÉLISE

"Say what they may"!

TRISSOTIN

From your rich lodging drive away . . .

[*Act Three* · *Scene Two*]

PHILAMINTE, ARMANDE, and BÉLISE

"Rich lodging"!

TRISSOTIN

This ingrate who, as well you know . . .

PHILAMINTE, ARMANDE, and BÉLISE

That "ingrate" of a fever!

TRISSOTIN

Would make your precious life his prey.

PHILAMINTE

"Your precious life"!

ARMANDE and BÉLISE

Ah!

TRISSOTIN

What! Shall he mock your rank, and pay
No deference to the blood of kings?

PHILAMINTE, ARMANDE, and BÉLISE

Ah!

TRISSOTIN

Shall he afflict you night and day,
And shall you tolerate such things?

555

No! To the baths you must repair,
And with your own hands drown him there.

PHILAMINTE

I'm overcome.

BÉLISE

I'm faint.

ARMANDE

I'm ravished, quite.

PHILAMINTE

One feels a thousand tremors of delight.

ARMANDE

"And shall you tolerate such things?"

BÉLISE

"No! To the baths you must repair . . ."

PHILAMINTE

"And with your own hands drown him there."
Drown him, that is to say, in the bath-water.

ARMANDE

Your verse, at each step, gives some glad surprise.

[*Act Three · Scene Two*]

BÉLISE

Wherever one turns, fresh wonders greet the eyes.

PHILAMINTE

One treads on beauty, wandering through your lines.

ARMANDE

They're little paths all strewn with eglantines.

TRISSOTIN

You find the poem, then—

PHILAMINTE

                           Perfect, and, what's more,
Novel: the like was never done before.

BÉLISE (*to Henriette*)

What, Niece, did not this reading stir your heart?
By saying nothing, you've played a dreary part.

HENRIETTE

We play what parts we're given, here below;
Wishing to be a wit won't make one so.

TRISSOTIN

Perhaps my verses bored her.

HENRIETTE

No indeed;
I didn't listen.

PHILAMINTE

The epigram! Please proceed.

TRISSOTIN

CONCERNING A VERMILION COACH, GIVEN
TO A LADY OF HIS ACQUAINTANCE . . .

PHILAMINTE

There's always something striking about his titles.

ARMANDE

They ready us for the wit of his recitals.

TRISSOTIN

Love sells his bonds to me at such a rate . . .

PHILAMINTE, ARMANDE, and BÉLISE

Ah!

TRISSOTIN

I've long since spent the half of my estate;
And when you see this coach, embossed
With heavy gold at such a cost

That all the dazzled countryside
Gapes as my Laïs passes in her pride . . .

PHILAMINTE

Listen to that. "My Laïs." How erudite!

BÉLISE

A stunning reference. So exactly right.

TRISSOTIN

And when you see this coach, embossed
With heavy gold at such a cost
That all the dazzled countryside
Gapes as my Laïs passes in her pride,
Know by that vision of vermilion
That what was mine is now *her* million.

ARMANDE

Oh! Oh! I didn't foresee that final twist.

PHILAMINTE

We have no subtler epigrammatist.

BÉLISE

"Know by that vision of vermilion
That what was mine is now *her* million."

The rhyme is clever, and yet not forced: "*ver*milion, *her*
million."

PHILAMINTE

Since first we met, Sir, I have had the highest
Opinion of you; it may be that I'm biased;
But all you write, to my mind, stands alone.

TRISSOTIN (*to Philaminte*)

If you'd but read us something of your own,
One might reciprocate your admiration.

PHILAMINTE

I've no new poems, but it's my expectation
That soon, in some eight chapters, you may see
The plans I've made for our Academy.
Plato, in his *Republic*, did not go
Beyond an abstract outline, as you know,
But what I've shaped in words, I shall not fail
To realize, in most concrete detail.
I'm much offended by the disrespect
Which men display for women's intellect,
And I intend to avenge us, every one,
For all the slighting things which men have done—
Assigning us to cares which stunt our souls,
And banning our pursuit of studious goals.

ARMANDE

It's too insulting to forbid our sex
To ponder any questions more complex
Than whether some lace is pretty, or some brocade,
And whether a skirt or cloak is nicely made.

BÉLISE

It's time we broke our mental chains, and stated
Our high intent to be emancipated.

TRISSOTIN

My deep respect for women none can deny;
Though I may praise a lady's lustrous eye,
I honor, too, the lustre of her mind.

PHILAMINTE

For that, you have the thanks of womankind;
But there are some proud scholars I could mention
To whom we'll prove, despite their condescension,
That women may be learnèd if they please,
And found, like men, their own academies.
Ours, furthermore, shall be more wisely run
Than theirs: we'll roll all disciplines into one,
Uniting letters, in a rich alliance,
With all the tools and theories of science,
And in our thought refusing to be thrall
To any school, but making use of all.

TRISSOTIN

For method, Aristotle suits me well.

PHILAMINTE

But in abstractions, Plato *does* excel.

ARMANDE

The thought of Epicurus is very keen.

BÉLISE

I rather like his atoms, but as between
A vacuum and a field of subtle matter
I find it easier to accept the latter.

TRISSOTIN

On magnetism, Descartes supports my notions.

ARMANDE

I love his falling worlds . . .

PHILAMINTE

        And whirling motions!

ARMANDE

I can't wait for our conclaves. We shall proclaim
Discoveries, and they shall bring us fame.

TRISSOTIN

Yes, to your keen minds Nature can but yield,
And let her rarest secrets be revealed.

PHILAMINTE

I can already offer one such rarity:
I have seen men in the moon, with perfect clarity.

BÉLISE

I'm not sure I've seen men, but I can say
That I've seen steeples there, as plain as day.

ARMANDE

To master grammar and physics is our intent,
And history, ethics, verse, and government.

[*Act Three* · *Scene Two*]

PHILAMINTE

Ethics, which thrills me in so many respects,
Was once the passion of great intellects;
But it's the Stoics to whom I'd give the prize;
They knew that only the virtuous can be wise.

ARMANDE

Regarding language, we aim to renovate
Our tongue through laws which soon we'll promulgate.
Each of us has conceived a hatred, based
On outraged reason or offended taste,
For certain nouns and verbs. We've gathered these
Into a list of shared antipathies,
And shall proceed to doom and banish them.
At each of our learned gatherings, we'll condemn
In mordant terms those words which we propose
To purge from usage, whether in verse or prose.

PHILAMINTE

But our academy's noblest plan of action,
A scheme in which I take deep satisfaction,
A glorious project which will earn the praise
Of all discerning minds of future days,
Is to suppress those *syllables* which, though found
In blameless words, may have a shocking sound,
Which naughty punsters utter with a smirk,
Which, age on age, coarse jesters overwork,
And which, by filthy double meanings, vex
The finer feelings of the female sex.

TRISSOTIN

You have most wondrous plans, beyond a doubt!

563

[*Act Three · Scene Two*]

BÉLISE

You'll see our by-laws, once we've worked them out.

TRISSOTIN

They can't fail to be beautiful and wise.

ARMANDE

By our high standards we shall criticize
Whatever's written, and be severe with it.
We'll show that only we and our friends have wit.
We'll search out faults in everything, while citing
Ourselves alone for pure and flawless writing.

SCENE THREE

LÉPINE, TRISSOTIN, PHILAMINTE, BÉLISE,
ARMANDE, HENRIETTE, VADIUS

LÉPINE (*to Trissotin*)

There's a man outside to see you, Sir; he's wearing
Black, and he has a gentle voice and bearing.

(*All rise.*)

TRISSOTIN

It's that learnèd friend of mine, who's begged me to
Procure for him the honor of meeting you.

PHILAMINTE

Please have him enter; you have our full consent.
     (*Trissotin goes to admit Vadius; Philaminte
     speaks to Armande and Bélise.*)
We must be gracious, and *most* intelligent.
     (*To Henriette, who seeks to leave*)
Whoa, there! I told you plainly, didn't I,
That I wished you to remain with us?

HENRIETTE

                      But why?

PHILAMINTE

Come back, and you shall shortly understand.

TRISSOTIN (*returning with Vadius*)

Behold a man who yearns to kiss your hand.
And in presenting him, I have no fear
That he'll profane this cultured atmosphere:
Among our choicest wits, he quite stands out.

PHILAMINTE

Since you present him, his worth's beyond a doubt.

TRISSOTIN

In classics, he's the greatest of savants,
And knows more Greek than any man in France.

PHILAMINTE (*to Bélise*)

Greek! Sister, our guest knows Greek! How marvelous!

BÉLISE (*to Armande*)

Greek, Niece! Do you hear?

ARMANDE

Yes, Greek! What joy for *us!*

PHILAMINTE

Think of it! Greek! Oh, Sir, for the love of Greek,
Permit us each to kiss you on the cheek.
(*Vadius kisses them all save Henriette, who refuses.*)

566

[*Act Three* · *Scene Three*]

HENRIETTE

I don't know Greek, Sir; permit me to decline.

PHILAMINTE

I think Greek books are utterly divine.

VADIUS

In my eagerness to meet you, I fear I've come
Intruding on some grave symposium.
Forgive me, Madam, if I've caused confusion.

PHILAMINTE

Ah, Sir, to bring us Greek is no intrusion.

TRISSOTIN

My friend does wonders, too, in verse and prose,
And might well show us something, if he chose.

VADIUS

The fault of authors is their inclination
To dwell upon their works in conversation,
And whether in parks, or parlors, or at table,
To spout their poems as often as they're able.
How sad to see a writer play the extorter,
Demanding oh's and ah's from every quarter,
And forcing any gathering whatever
To tell him that his labored verse is clever.
I've never embraced the folly of which I speak,
And hold the doctrine of a certain Greek
That men of sense, however well endowed,

Should shun the urge to read their works aloud.
Still, here are some lines, concerning youthful love,
Which I'd be pleased to hear your judgments of.

TRISSOTIN

For verve and beauty, your verses stand alone.

VADIUS

Venus and all the Graces grace your own.

TRISSOTIN

Your choice of words is splendid, and your phrasing.

VADIUS

Your *ethos* and your *pathos* are amazing.

TRISSOTIN

The polished eclogues which you've given us
Surpass both Virgil and Theocritus.

VADIUS

Your odes are noble, gallant, and refined,
And leave your master Horace far behind.

TRISSOTIN

Ah, but your little love songs: what could be sweeter?

VADIUS

As for your well-turned sonnets, none are neater.

TRISSOTIN

Your deft *rondeaux;* are any poems more charming?

VADIUS

Your madrigals—are any more disarming?

TRISSOTIN

Above all, you're a wizard at *ballades.*

VADIUS

At *bouts-rimés*, you always have the odds.

TRISSOTIN

If France would only recognize your merits—

VADIUS

If the age did justice to its finer spirits—

TRISSOTIN

You'd have a gilded coach in which to ride.

VADIUS

Statues of you would rise on every side.
                    (*To Trissotin*)
Hem! Now for my *ballade.* Please comment on it
In the frankest—

[*Act Three* · *Scene Three*]

TRISSOTIN

        Have you seen a certain sonnet
About the fever of Princess Uranie?

VADIUS

Yes. It was read to me yesterday, at tea.

TRISSOTIN

Do you know who wrote it?

VADIUS

             No, but of this I'm sure:
The sonnet, frankly, is very, very poor.

TRISSOTIN

Oh? Many people have praised it, nonetheless.

VADIUS

That doesn't prevent its being a sorry mess,
And if you've read it, I know you share my view.

TRISSOTIN

Why no, I don't in the least agree with you;
Not many sonnets boast so fine a style.

VADIUS

God grant I never write a thing so vile!

570

TRISSOTIN

It couldn't be better written, I contend;
And I should know, because I wrote it, friend.

VADIUS

You?

TRISSOTIN

I.

VADIUS

Well, how this happened I can't explain.

TRISSOTIN

What happened was that you found my poem inane.

VADIUS

When I heard the sonnet, I must have been distrait;
Or perhaps 'twas read in an unconvincing way.
But let's forget it; this *ballade* of mine—

TRISSOTIN

Ballades, I think, are rather asinine.
The form's old-hat; it has a musty smell.

VADIUS

Still, many people like it very well.

TRISSOTIN

That doesn't prevent my finding it dull and flat.

VADIUS

No, but the form is none the worse for that.

TRISSOTIN

The *ballade* is dear to pedants; they adore it.

VADIUS

How curious, then, that you should not be for it.

TRISSOTIN

You see in others your own drab qualities.

(*All rise.*)

VADIUS

Don't see your own in me, Sir, if you please.

TRISSOTIN

Be off, you jingling dunce! Let's end this session.

VADIUS

You scribbler! You disgrace to the profession!

TRISSOTIN

You poetaster! You shameless plagiarist!

[*Act Three* · *Scene Three*]

VADIUS

You ink-stained thief!

PHILAMINTE

Oh, gentlemen! Please desist!

TRISSOTIN (*to Vadius*)

Go to the Greeks and Romans, and pay back
The thousand things you've filched from them, you hack.

VADIUS

Go to Parnassus and confess your guilt
For turning Horace into a crazy-quilt.

TRISSOTIN

Think of your book, which caused so little stir.

VADIUS

And you, Sir, think of your bankrupt publisher.

TRISSOTIN

My fame's established; in vain you mock me so.

VADIUS

Do tell. Go look at the *Satires* of Boileau.

TRISSOTIN

Go look at them yourself.

VADIUS

As between us two,
I'm treated there more honorably than you.
He gives me a passing thrust, and links my name
With several authors of no little fame;
But nowhere do his verses leave you in peace;
His witty attacks upon you never cease.

TRISSOTIN

It's therefore I whom he respects the more.
To him, you're one of the crowd, a minor bore;
You're given a single sword-thrust, and are reckoned
Too insignificant to deserve a second.
But me he singles out as a noble foe
Against whom he must strive with blow on blow,
Betraying, by those many strokes, that he
Is never certain of the victory.

VADIUS

My pen will teach you that I'm no poetaster.

TRISSOTIN

And mine will show you, fool, that I'm your master.

VADIUS

I challenge you in verse, prose, Latin, and Greek.

TRISSOTIN

We'll meet at Barbin's bookshop, in a week.

SCENE FOUR

TRISSOTIN, PHILAMINTE, ARMANDE,
BÉLISE, HENRIETTE

TRISSOTIN (*to Philaminte*)

Forgive me if my wrath grew uncontrolled;
I felt an obligation to uphold
Your judgment of that sonnet he maligned.

PHILAMINTE

I'll try to mend your quarrel; never mind.
Let's change the subject. Henriette, come here.
I've long been troubled because you don't appear
At all endowed with wit or intellect;
But I've a remedy, now, for that defect.

HENRIETTE

Don't trouble, Mother; I wish no remedy.
Learnèd discourse is not my cup of tea.
I like to take life easy, and I balk
At trying to be a fount of clever talk.
I've no ambition to be a parlor wit,
And if I'm stupid, I don't mind a bit.
I'd rather speak in a plain and common way
Than rack my brains for brilliant things to say.

PHILAMINTE

I know your shameful tastes, which I decline
To countenance in any child of mine.
Beauty of face is but a transient flower,
A brief adornment, the glory of an hour,
And goes no deeper than the outer skin;
But beauty of mind endures, and lies within.
I've long sought means to cultivate in you
A beauty such as time could not undo,
And plant within your breast a noble yearning
For higher knowledge and the fruits of learning;
And now, at last, I've settled on a plan,
Which is to mate you with a learnèd man—
(*Gesturing toward Trissotin*)
This gentleman, in short, whom I decree
That you acknowledge as your spouse-to-be.

HENRIETTE

I, Mother?

PHILAMINTE

Yes, you. Stop playing innocent.

BÉLISE (*to Trissotin*)

I understand. Your eyes ask my consent
Before you pledge to her a heart that's mine.
Do so. All claims I willingly resign:
This match will bring you wealth and happiness.

TRISSOTIN (*to Henriette*)

My rapture, Madam, is more than I can express:
The honor which this marriage will confer
Upon me—

HENRIETTE

Hold! It's not yet settled, Sir;
Don't rush things.

PHILAMINTE

What a reply! How overweening!
Girl, if you dare . . . Enough, you take my meaning.
        (*To Trissotin*)
Just let her be. Her mind will soon be changed.

SCENE FIVE

ARMANDE

What a brilliant match our mother has arranged!
She's found for you a spouse both great and wise.

HENRIETTE

Why don't you take him, if he's such a prize?

ARMANDE

It's you, not I, who are to be his bride.

HENRIETTE

For my elder sister, I'll gladly step aside.

ARMANDE

If I, like you, yearned for the wedded state,
I'd take your offer of so fine a mate.

HENRIETTE

If I, like you, were charmed by pedantry,
I'd think the man a perfect choice for me.

578

[*Act Three* · *Scene Five*]

ARMANDE

Our tastes may differ, Sister, but we still
Owe strict obedience to our parents' will;
Whether or not you're fractious and contrary,
You'll wed the man our mother bids you marry. . . .

SCENE SIX

CHRYSALE, ARISTE, CLITANDRE,
HENRIETTE, ARMANDE

CHRYSALE (*to Henriette, presenting
Clitandre*)

Now, Daughter, you shall do as I command.
Take off that glove, and give this man your hand,
And think of him henceforward as the one
I've chosen as your husband and my son.

ARMANDE

In this case, Sister, you're easy to persuade.

HENRIETTE

Sister, our parents' will must be obeyed;
I'll wed the man my father bids me marry.

ARMANDE

Your mother's blessing, too, is necessary.

CHRYSALE

Just what do you mean?

[*Act Three · Scene Six*]

ARMANDE

I much regret to state
That Mother has a rival candidate
For the hand of Henri—

CHRYSALE

Hush, you chatterer!
Go prate about philosophy with her,
And cease to meddle in what is my affair.
Tell her it's settled, and bid her to beware
Of angering me by making any fuss.
Go on, now.

ARISTE

Bràvo! This is miraculous.

CLITANDRE

How fortunate I am! What bliss! What joy!

CHRYSALE (*to Clitandre*)

Come, take her hand, now. After you, my boy;
Conduct her to her room. (*To Ariste*) Ah, Brother, this is
A tonic to me; think of those hugs, those kisses!
It warms my old heart, and reminds me of
My youthful days of gallantry and love.

SCENE ONE

ARMANDE, PHILAMINTE

ARMANDE

Oh, no, she didn't waver or delay,
But, with a flourish, hastened to obey.
Almost before he spoke, she had agreed
To do his bidding, and she appeared, indeed,
Moved by defiance toward her mother, rather
Than deference to the wishes of her father.

PHILAMINTE

I soon shall show her to whose government
The laws of reason oblige her to consent,
And whether it's matter or form, body or soul,
Father or mother, who is in control.

ARMANDE

The least they could have done was to consult you;
It's graceless of that young man to insult you
By trying to wed your child without your blessing.

PHILAMINTE

He's not yet won. His looks are prepossessing,
And I approved his paying court to you;

But I never liked his manners. He well knew
That writing poetry is a gift of mine,
And yet he never asked to hear a line.

SCENE TWO

CLITANDRE (*entering quietly and listening unseen*), ARMANDE, PHILAMINTE

ARMANDE

Mother, if I were you, I shouldn't let
That gentleman espouse our Henriette.
Not that I care, of course; I do not speak
As someone moved by prejudice or pique,
Or by a heart which, having been forsaken,
Asks vengeance for the wounds which it has taken.
For what I've suffered, philosophy can give
Full consolation, helping one to live
On a high plane, and treat such things with scorn;
But what he's done to you cannot be borne.
Honor requires that you oppose his suit;
Besides, you'd never come to like the brute.
In all our talks, I cannot recollect
His speaking of you with the least respect.

PHILAMINTE

Young whelp!

ARMANDE

Despite your work's great reputation,
He icily withheld his approbation.

[*Act Four* · *Scene Two*]

PHILAMINTE

The churl!

ARMANDE

    A score of times, I read to him
Your latest poems. He tore them limb from limb.

PHILAMINTE

The beast!

ARMANDE

       We quarreled often about your writing.
And you would not believe how harsh, how biting—

CLITANDRE (*to Armande*)

Ah, Madam, a little charity, I pray,
Or a little truthful speaking, anyway.
How have I wronged you? What was the offense
Which makes you seek, by slanderous eloquence,
To rouse against me the distaste and ire
Of those whose good opinion I require?
Speak, Madam, and justify your vicious grudge.
I'll gladly let your mother be our judge.

ARMANDE

Had I the grudge of which I stand accused,
I could defend it, for I've been ill-used.
First love, Sir, is a pure and holy flame
Which makes upon us an eternal claim;

'Twere better to renounce this world, and die,
Than be untrue to such a sacred tie.
Fickleness is a monstrous crime, and in
The moral scale there is no heavier sin.

CLITANDRE

Do you call it fickleness, *Madame*, to do
What your heart's cold disdain has driven me to?
If, by submitting to its cruel laws,
I've wounded you, your own proud heart's the cause.
My love for you was fervent and entire;
For two whole years it burned with constant fire;
My duty, care, and worship did not falter;
I laid my heart's devotion on your altar.
But all my love and service were in vain;
You dashed the hopes I dared to entertain.
If, thus rejected, I made overtures
To someone else, was that my fault, or yours?
Was I inconstant, or was I forced to be?
Did I forsake you, or did you banish me?

ARMANDE

Sir, can you say that I've refused your love
When all I've sought has been to purge it of
Vulgarity, and teach you that refined
And perfect passion which is of the mind?
Can you not learn an ardor which dispenses
Entirely with the commerce of the senses,
Or see how sweetly spirits may be blended
When bodily desires have been transcended?
Alas, your love is carnal, and cannot rise
Above the plane of gross material ties;
The flame of your devotion can't be fed
Except by marriage, and the marriage bed.

[*Act Four · Scene Two*]

How strange is such a love! And oh, how far
Above such earthliness true lovers are!
In their delights, the body plays no part,
And their clear flames but marry heart to heart,
Rejecting all the rest as low and bestial.
Their fire is pure, unsullied, and celestial.
The sighs they breathe are blameless, and express
No filthy hankerings, no fleshliness.
There's no ulterior goal they hunger for.
They love for love's sake, and for nothing more,
And since the spirit is their only care,
Bodies are things of which they're unaware.

CLITANDRE

Well, *I'm* aware, though you may blush to hear it,
That I have both a body and a spirit;
Nor can I part them to my satisfaction;
I fear I lack the power of abstraction
Whereby such philosophic feats are done,
And so my body and soul must live as one.
There's nothing finer, as you say, than these
Entirely spiritual ecstasies,
These marriages of souls, these sentiments
So purified of any taint of sense;
But such love is, for my taste, too ethereal;
I am, as you've complained, a bit material;
I love with all my being, and I confess
That a whole woman is what I would possess.
Need I be damned for feelings of the kind?
With all respect for your high views, I find
That men in general feel my sort of passion,
That marriage still is pretty much in fashion,
And that it's deemed an honorable estate;
So that my asking you to be my mate,
And share with me that good and sweet condition,
Was scarcely an indecent proposition.

[*Act Four* · *Scene Two*]

ARMANDE

Ah well, Sir: since you thrust my views aside,
Since your brute instincts must be satisfied,
And since your feelings, to be faithful, must
Be bound by ties of flesh and chains of lust,
I'll force myself, if Mother will consent,
To grant the thing on which you're so intent.

CLITANDRE

It's too late, Madam: another's occupied
Your place; if I now took you as my bride,
I'd wrong a heart which sheltered and consoled me
When, in your pride, you'd treated me so coldly.

PHILAMINTE

Sir, do you dream of my consenting to
This other marriage which you have in view?
Does it not penetrate your mind as yet
That I have other plans for Henriette?

CLITANDRE

Ah, Madam, reconsider, if you please,
And don't expose me thus to mockeries;
Don't put me in the ludicrous position
Of having Trissotin for competition.
What a shabby rival! You couldn't have selected
A wit less honored, a pedant less respected.
We've many pseudo-wits and polished frauds
Whose cleverness the time's bad taste applauds,
But Trissotin fools no one, and indeed
His writings are abhorred by all who read.
Save in this house, his work is never praised,
And I have been repeatedly amazed

591

[*Act Four* · *Scene Two*]

To hear you laud some piece of foolishness
Which, had you written it, you would suppress.

PHILAMINTE

That's how you judge him. We feel otherwise
Because we look at him with different eyes.

SCENE THREE

TRISSOTIN, ARMANDE, PHILAMINTE,
CLITANDRE

TRISSOTIN (*to Philaminte*)

I bring you, Madam, some startling news I've heard.
Last night, a near-catastrophe occurred:
While we were all asleep, a comet crossed
Our vortex, and the Earth was all but lost;
Had it collided with our world, alas,
We'd have been shattered into bits, like glass.

PHILAMINTE

Let's leave that subject for another time;
This gentleman, I fear, would see no rhyme
Or reason in it; it's ignorance he prizes;
Learning and wit are things which he despises.

CLITANDRE

Kindly permit me, Madam, to restate
Your summary of my views: I only hate
Such wit and learning as twist men's brains awry.
Those things are excellent in themselves, but I
Had rather be an ignorant man, by far,
Than learnèd in the way some people are.

TRISSOTIN

Well, as for me, I hold that learning never
Could twist a man in any way whatever.

CLITANDRE

And I assert that learning often breeds
Men who are foolish both in words and deeds.

TRISSOTIN

What a striking paradox!

CLITANDRE

          Though I'm no **wit**,
I'd have no trouble, I think, in proving it.
If arguments should fail, I'm sure I'd find
That living proofs came readily to mind.

TRISSOTIN

The living proofs you gave might not persuade.

CLITANDRE

I'd not look far before my point was made.

TRISSOTIN

I cannot think, myself, of such a case.

CLITANDRE

I can; indeed, it stares me in the face.

594

TRISSOTIN

I thought it was by ignorance, and not
By learning, Sir, that great fools were begot.

CLITANDRE

Well, you thought wrongly. It's a well-known rule
That no fool's greater than a learnèd fool.

TRISSOTIN

Our common usage contradicts that claim,
Since "fool" and "ignoramus" mean the same.

CLITANDRE

You think those words synonymous? Oh no, Sir!
You'll find that "fool" and "pedant" are much closer.

TRISSOTIN

"Fool" denotes plain and simple foolishness.

CLITANDRE

"Pedant" denotes the same, in fancy dress.

TRISSOTIN

The quest for knowledge is noble and august.

CLITANDRE

But knowledge, in a pedant, turns to dust.

TRISSOTIN

It's clear that ignorance has great charms for you,
Or else you wouldn't defend it as you do.

CLITANDRE

I came to see the charms of ignorance when
I made the acquaintance of certain learnèd men.

TRISSOTIN

Those certain learnèd men, it may turn out,
Are better than certain folk who strut about.

CLITANDRE

The learnèd men would say so, certainly;
But then, those certain folk might not agree.

PHILAMINTE (*to Clitandre*)

I think, Sir—

CLITANDRE

          Madam, spare me, please. This rough
Assailant is already fierce enough.
Don't join him, pray, in giving me a beating.
I shall preserve myself, now, by retreating.

ARMANDE

You, with your brutal taunts, were the offender;
'Twas you—

596

[*Act Four* · *Scene Three*]

CLITANDRE

More reinforcements! I surrender.

PHILAMINTE

Sir, witty repartee is quite all right,
But personal attacks are impolite.

CLITANDRE

Good Lord, he's quite unhurt, as one can tell.
No one in France takes ridicule so well.
For years he's heard men gibe at him, and scoff,
And in his smugness merely laughed it off.

TRISSOTIN

I'm not surprised to hear this gentleman say
The things he's said in this unpleasant fray.
He's much at court, and as one might expect,
He shares the court's mistrust of intellect,
And, as a courtier, defends with zest
The ignorance that's in its interest.

CLITANDRE

You're very hard indeed on the poor court,
Which hears each day how people of your sort,
Who deal in intellectual wares, decry it,
Complain that their careers are blighted by it,
Deplore its wretched taste, and blame their own
Unhappy failures on that cause alone.
Permit me, Mister Trissotin, with due
Respect for your great name, to say that you
And all your kind would do well to discuss

The court in tones less harsh and querulous;
That the court is not so short of wit and brain
As you and all your scribbling friends maintain;
That all things, there, are viewed with common sense,
That good taste, too, is much in evidence,
And that its knowledge of the world surpasses
The fusty learning of pedantic asses.

TRISSOTIN

It has good taste, you say? If only it had!

CLITANDRE

What makes you say, Sir, that its taste is bad?

TRISSOTIN

What makes me say so? Rasiùs and Baldùs
Do France great honor by what their pens produce,
Yet the court pays these scholars no attention,
And neither of them has received a pension.

CLITANDRE

I now perceive your grievance, and I see
That you've left your own name out, from modesty.
Well, let's not drag it into our debate.
Just tell me: how have your heroes served the State?
What are their writings worth, that they expect
Rewards, and charge the nation with neglect?
Why should they whine, these learnèd friends of yours,
At not receiving gifts and sinecures?
A precious lot they've done for France, indeed!
Their tomes are just what court and country need!
The vanity of such beggars makes me laugh:

[*Act Four* · *Scene Three*]

Because they're set in type and bound in calf,
They think that they're illustrious citizens;
That the fate of nations hangs upon their pens;
That the least mention of their work should bring
The pensions flocking in on eager wing;
That the whole universe, with one wide stare,
Admires them; that their fame is everywhere,
And that they're wondrous wise because they know
What others said before them, long ago—
Because they've given thirty years of toil
And eyestrain to acquire, by midnight oil,
Some jumbled Latin and some garbled Greek,
And overload their brains with the antique
Obscurities which lie about in books.
These bookworms, with their smug, myopic looks,
Are full of pompous talk and windy unction;
They have no common sense, no useful function,
And could, in short, persuade the human race
To think all wit and learning a disgrace.

PHILAMINTE

You speak most heatedly, and it is clear
What feelings prompt you to be so severe;
Your rival's presence, which seems to irk you greatly—

SCENE FOUR

JULIEN, TRISSOTIN, PHILAMINTE,
CLITANDRE, ARMANDE

JULIEN

The learnèd man who visited you lately,
And whose valet I have the honor to be,
Sends you this note, *Madame*, by way of me.

PHILAMINTE

Whatever the import of this note you bring,
Do learn, my friend, that it's a graceless thing
To interrupt a conversation so,
And that a rightly trained valet would go
To the servants first, and ask them for admission.

JULIEN

Madam, I'll bear in mind your admonition.

PHILAMINTE (*reading*)

"Trissotin boasts, Madam, that he is going to marry your daughter. Let me warn you that that great thinker is thinking only of your wealth, and that you would do well to put off the marriage until you have seen the poem which I am now composing against him. It is to be a portrait in verse, and I propose to depict him for you in his true colors. Meanwhile,

[*Act Four · Scene Four*]

I am sending herewith the works of Horace, Virgil, Terence,
and Catullus, in the margins of which I have marked, for
your benefit, all the passages which he has plundered."

Well, well! To thwart the match which I desire,
A troop of enemies has opened fire
Upon this worthy man; but I'll requite
By one swift action their dishonest spite,
And show them all that their combined assault
Has only hastened what they strove to halt.
(To Julien)
Take back those volumes to your master, and
Inform him, so that he'll clearly understand
Precisely how much value I have set
Upon his sage advice, that Henriette
(Pointing to Trissotin)
Shall wed this gentleman, this very night.
(To Clitandre)
Sir, you're a friend of the family. I invite
You most sincerely to remain and see
The contract signed, as shortly it shall be.
Armande, you'll send for the notary, and prepare
Your sister for her part in this affair.

ARMANDE

No need for me to let my sister know;
This gentleman, I'm sure, will quickly go
To tell her all the news, and seek as well
To prompt her saucy spirit to rebel.

PHILAMINTE

We'll see by whom her spirit will be swayed;
It doesn't suit me to be disobeyed.

SCENE FIVE

ARMANDE

I'm very sorry for you, Sir; it seems
Things haven't gone according to your schemes.

CLITANDRE

Madam, I mean to do my very best
To lift that weight of sorrow from your breast.

ARMANDE

I fear, Sir, that your hopes are not well-grounded.

CLITANDRE

It may be that your fear will prove ill-founded.

ARMANDE

I hope so.

CLITANDRE

I believe you; nor do I doubt
That you'll do all you can to help me out.

ARMANDE

To serve your cause shall be my sole endeavor.

CLITANDRE

For that, you'll have my gratitude forever.

SCENE SIX

CHRYSALE, ARISTE, HENRIETTE, CLITANDRE

CLITANDRE

I shall be lost unless you help me, Sir:
Your wife's rejected my appeals to her,
And chosen Trissotin for her son-in-law.

CHRYSALE

Damn it, what ails the woman? I never saw
What in this Trissotin could so attract her.

ARISTE

He versifies in Latin, and that's a factor
Which makes him, in her view, the better man.

CLITANDRE

To marry them tonight, Sir, is her plan.

CHRYSALE

Tonight?

CLITANDRE

Tonight.

CHRYSALE

Her plan, then, will miscarry.
I promise that, tonight, you two shall marry.

CLITANDRE

She's having a contract drawn by the notary.

CHRYSALE

Well, he shall draw another one for me.

CLITANDRE (*indicating Henriette*)

Armande has orders to inform this lady
Of the wedding match for which she's to be ready.

CHRYSALE

And I inform her that, by my command,
It's you on whom she shall bestow her hand.
This is my house, and I shall make it clear
That I'm the one and only master here.
(*To Henriette*)
Wait, Daughter; we'll join you when our errand's done.
Come, Brother, follow me; you too, my son.

HENRIETTE (*to Ariste*)

Please keep him in this mood, whatever you do.

ARISTE

I'll do my utmost for your love and you.

SCENE SEVEN

HENRIETTE, CLITANDRE

CLITANDRE

Whatever aid our kind allies may lend,
It's your true heart on which my hopes depend.

HENRIETTE

As to my heart, of that you may be sure.

CLITANDRE

If so, my own is happy and secure.

HENRIETTE

I must be strong, so as not to be coerced.

CLITANDRE

Cling to our love, and let them do their worst.

HENRIETTE

I'll do my best to make our cause prevail;
But if my hope of being yours should fail,
And if it seems I'm to be forced to marry,
A convent cell shall be my sanctuary.

[*Act Four* · *Scene Seven*]

CLITANDRE

Heaven grant that you need never give to me
Such painful proof of your fidelity.

ACT 5

SCENE ONE

HENRIETTE, TRISSOTIN

HENRIETTE

It seems to me that we two should confer
About this contemplated marriage, Sir,
Since it's reduced our household to dissension.
Do give my arguments your kind attention.
I know that you expect to realize,
By wedding me, a dowry of some size;
Yet money, which so many men pursue,
Should bore a true philosopher like you,
And your contempt for riches should be shown
In your behavior, not in words alone.

TRISSOTIN

It's not in wealth that your attraction lies:
Your sparkling charms, your soft yet flashing eyes,
Your airs, your graces—it is these in which
My ravished heart perceives you to be rich,
These treasures only which I would possess.

HENRIETTE

I'm honored by the love which you profess,
Although I can't see what I've done to earn it,
And much regret, Sir, that I can't return it.
I have the highest estimation of you,

But there's one reason why I cannot love you.
A heart's devotion cannot be divided,
And it's Clitandre on whom my heart's decided.
I know he lacks your merits, which are great,
That I'm obtuse to choose him for my mate,
That you should please me by your gifts and wit;
I know I'm wrong, but there's no help for it;
Though reason chides me for my want of sense,
My heart clings blindly to its preference.

TRISSOTIN

When I am given your hand and marriage vow,
I'll claim the heart Clitandre possesses now,
And I dare hope that I can then incline
That heart, by sweet persuasions, to be mine.

HENRIETTE

No, no: first love, Sir, is too strong a feeling.
All your persuasions could not prove appealing.
Let me, upon this point, be blunt and plain,
Since nothing I shall say could cause you pain.
The fires of love, which set our hearts aglow,
Aren't kindled by men's merits, as you know.
They're most capricious; when someone takes our eye,
We're often quite unable to say why.
If, Sir, our loves were based on wise selection,
You would have all my heart, all my affection;
But love quite clearly doesn't work that way.
Indulge me in my blindness, then, I pray,
And do not show me, Sir, so little mercy
As to desire that others should coerce me.
What man of honor would care to profit by
A parent's power to make a child comply?
To win a lady's hand by such compulsion,
And not by love, would fill him with revulsion.

Don't, then, I beg you, urge my mother to make
Me bow to her authority for your sake.
Take back the love you offer, and reserve it
For some fine woman who will more deserve it.

TRISSOTIN

Alas, what you command I cannot do.
I'm powerless to retract my love for you.
How shall I cease to worship you, unless
You cease to dazzle me with loveliness,
To stun my heart with beauty, to enthrall—

HENRIETTE

Oh, come, Sir; no more nonsense. You have all
These Irises and Phyllises whose great
Attractiveness your verses celebrate,
And whom you so adore with so much art—

TRISSOTIN

My mind speaks in those verses, not my heart.
I love those ladies in my poems merely,
While Henriette, alone, I love sincerely.

HENRIETTE

Please, Sir—

TRISSOTIN

　　　　　If by so speaking I offend,
I fear that my offense will never end.
My ardor, which I've hidden hitherto,
Belongs for all eternity to you;

I'll love you till this beating heart has stopped;
And, though you scorn the tactics I adopt,
I can't refuse your mother's aid in gaining
The joy I'm so desirous of obtaining.
If the sweet prize I long for can be won,
And you be mine, I care not how it's done.

HENRIETTE

But don't you see that it's a risky course
To take possession of a heart by force;
That things, quite frankly, can go very ill
When a woman's made to wed against her will,
And that, in her resentment, she won't lack
For means to vex her spouse, and pay him back?

TRISSOTIN

I've no anxiety about such things.
The wise man takes whatever fortune brings.
Transcending vulgar weaknesses, his mind
Looks down unmoved on mishaps of the kind,
Nor does he feel the least distress of soul
Regarding matters not in his control.

HENRIETTE

You fascinate me, Sir; I'm much impressed.
I didn't know philosophy possessed
Such powers, and could teach men to endure
Such tricks of fate without discomfiture.
Your lofty patience ought, Sir, to be tested,
So that its greatness could be manifested;
It calls, Sir, for a wife who'd take delight
In making you display it, day and night;
But since I'm ill-equipped, by temperament,

To prove your virtue to its full extent,
I'll leave that joy to one more qualified,
And let some other woman be your bride.

TRISSOTIN

Well, we shall see. The notary for whom
Your mother sent is in the neighboring room.

SCENE TWO

CHRYSALE, CLITANDRE,
MARTINE, HENRIETTE

CHRYSALE

Ah, Daughter, I'm pleased indeed to find you here.
Prepare to show obedience now, my dear,
By doing as your father bids you do.
I'm going to teach your mother a thing or two;
And, first of all, as you can see, I mean
To thwart her will and reinstate Martine.

HENRIETTE

I much admire the stands which you have taken.
Hold to them, Father; don't let yourself be shaken.
Be careful lest your kindly disposition
Induce you to abandon your position;
Cling to your resolutions, I entreat you,
And don't let Mother's stubbornness defeat you.

CHRYSALE

What! So you take me for a booby, eh?

HENRIETTE

Heavens, no!

CHRYSALE

Am I a milksop, would you say?

HENRIETTE

I'd not say that.

CHRYSALE

Do you think I lack the sense
To stand up firmly for my sentiments?

HENRIETTE

No, Father.

CHRYSALE

Have I too little brain and spirit
To run my own house? If so, let me hear it.

HENRIETTE

No, no.

CHRYSALE

Am I the sort, do you suppose,
Who'd let a woman lead him by the nose?

HENRIETTE

Of course not.

CHRYSALE

Well then, what were you implying?
Your doubts of me were scarcely gratifying.

HENRIETTE

I didn't mean to offend you, Heaven knows.

CHRYSALE

Under this roof, my girl, what I say goes.

HENRIETTE

True, Father.

CHRYSALE

No one but me has any right
To govern in this house.

HENRIETTE

Yes, Father; quite.

CHRYSALE

This is my family, and I'm sole head.

HENRIETTE

That's so.

CHRYSALE

I'll name the man my child shall wed.

[*Act Five* · *Scene Two*]

HENRIETTE

Agreed!

CHRYSALE

By Heaven's laws, I rule your fate.

HENRIETTE

Who questions that?

CHRYSALE

                And I'll soon demonstrate
That, in your marriage, your mother has no voice,
And that you must accept your father's choice.

HENRIETTE

Ah, Father, that's my dearest wish. I pray you,
Crown my desires by making me obey you.

CHRYSALE

If my contentious wife should dare to take—

CLITANDRE

She's coming, with the notary in her wake.

CHRYSALE

Stand by me, all of you.

[*Act Five · Scene Two*]

MARTINE

Trust me, Sir. I'm here
To back you up, if need be. Never fear.

SCENE THREE

PHILAMINTE, BÉLISE, ARMANDE, TRISSOTIN,
THE NOTARY, CHRYSALE, CLITANDRE,
HENRIETTE, MARTINE

PHILAMINTE (*to the Notary*)

Can't you dispense with jargon, Sir, and write
Our contract in a style that's more polite?

THE NOTARY

Our style is excellent, Madam; I'd be absurd
Were I to modify a single word.

PHILAMINTE

Such barbarism, in the heart of France!
Can't you at least, for learning's sake, enhance
The document by putting the dowry down
In talent and drachma, rather than franc and crown?
And do use ides and calends for the date.

THE NOTARY

If I did, Madam, what you advocate,
I should invite professional ostracism.

PHILAMINTE

It's useless to contend with barbarism.
Come on, Sir; there's a writing table here.

[*Act Five* · *Scene Three*]

(Noticing Martine)
Ah! Impudent girl, how dare you reappear?
Why have you brought her back, Sir? Tell me why.

CHRYSALE

I'll tell you that at leisure, by and by.
First, there's another matter to decide.

THE NOTARY

Let us proceed with the contract. Where's the bride?

PHILAMINTE

I'm giving away my younger daughter.

THE NOTARY

I see.

CHRYSALE

Yes. Henriette's her name, Sir. This is she.

THE NOTARY

Good. And the bridegroom?

PHILAMINTE *(indicating Trissotin)*

This is the man I choose.

CHRYSALE *(indicating Clitandre)*

And I, for my part, have a bit of news:
This is the man she'll marry.

622

[*Act Five · Scene Three*]

THE NOTARY

Two grooms? The law
Regards that as excessive.

PHILAMINTE

Don't hem and haw;
Just write down Trissotin, and your task is done.

CHRYSALE

Write down Clitandre; he's to be my son.

THE NOTARY

Kindly consult together, and agree
On a single person as the groom-to-be.

PHILAMINTE

No, no, Sir, do as I have indicated.

CHRYSALE

Come, come, put down the name that I have stated.

THE NOTARY

First tell me by whose orders I should abide.

PHILAMINTE (*to Chrysale*)
What's this, Sir? Shall my wishes be defied?

623

[*Act Five* · *Scene Three*]

CHRYSALE

I won't stand by and let this fellow take
My daughter's hand just for my money's sake.

PHILAMINTE

A lot your money matters to him! Indeed!
How dare you charge a learnèd man with greed?

CHRYSALE

Clitandre shall marry her, as I said before.

PHILAMINTE (*pointing to Trissotin*)

This is the man I've chosen. I'll hear no more.
The matter's settled, do you understand?

CHRYSALE

My! For a woman, you have a heavy hand.

MARTINE

It just ain't right for the wife to run the shop.
The man, I say, should always be on top.

CHRYSALE

Well said.

MARTINE

Though I'm sacked ten times for saying so,
It's cocks, not hens, should be the ones to crow.

624

[*Act Five · Scene Three*]

CHRYSALE

Correct.

MARTINE

      When a man's wife wears the breeches, folks
Snicker about him, and make nasty jokes.

CHRYSALE

That's true.

MARTINE

      If I had a husband, I wouldn't wish
For him to be all meek and womanish;
No, no, he'd be the captain of the ship,
And if I happened to give him any lip,
Or crossed him, he'd be right to slap my face
A time or two, to put me in my place.

CHRYSALE

Sound thinking.

MARTINE

      The master's heart is rightly set
On finding a proper man for Henriette.

CHRYSALE

Yes.

MARTINE

Well then, here's Clitandre. Why deny
The girl a fine young chap like him? And why
Give her a learnèd fool who prates and drones?
She needs a husband, not some bag of bones
Who'll teach her Greek, and be her Latin tutor.
This Trissotin, I tell you, just don't suit her.

CHRYSALE

Right.

PHILAMINTE

We must let her chatter until she's through.

MARTINE

Talk, talk, is all these pedants know how to do.
If I ever took a husband, I've always said,
It wouldn't be no learnèd man I'd wed.
Wit's not the thing you need around the house,
And it's no joy to have a bookish spouse.
When I get married, you can bet your life
My man will study nothing but his wife;
He'll have no other book to read but me,
And won't—so please you, Ma'am—know A from B.

PHILAMINTE

Has your spokesman finished? And have I not politely
Listened to all her speeches?

CHRYSALE

The girl spoke rightly.

[*Act Five · Scene Three*]

PHILAMINTE

Well then, to end all squabbling and delay,
Things now shall go exactly as I say.
                    (*Indicating Trissotin*)
Henriette shall wed this man at once, d'you hear?
Don't answer back; don't dare to interfere;
And if you've told Clitandre that he may wed
One of your daughters, give him Armande instead.

CHRYSALE

Well! . . . There's one way to settle this argument.
                    (*To Henriette and Clitandre*)
What do you think of that? Will you consent?

HENRIETTE

Oh, Father!

CLITANDRE

        Oh, Sir!

BÉLISE

                    There's yet another bride
By whom he might be yet more satisfied;
But that can't be; the love we share is far
Higher and purer than the morning star;
Our bonds are solely of the intellect,
And all extended substance we reject.

ARISTE, CHRYSALE, PHILAMINTE, BÉLISE,
HENRIETTE, ARMANDE, TRISSOTIN,
THE NOTARY, CLITANDRE, MARTINE

ARISTE

I hate to interrupt this happy affair
By bringing you the tidings which I bear.
You can't imagine what distress I feel
At the shocking news these letters will reveal.
                    (*To Philaminte*)
This one's from your attorney.
                    (*To Chrysale*)
                              And the other
Is yours; it's from Lyons.

CHRYSALE

                    What news, dear Brother,
Could be so pressing, and distress you so?

ARISTE

There is your letter; read it, and you'll know.

PHILAMINTE (*reading*)

"Madam, I have asked your brother to convey to you this
message, advising you of something which I dared not come

628

and tell you in person. Owing to your great neglect of your affairs, the magistrate's clerk did not notify me of the preliminary hearing, and you have irrevocably lost your lawsuit, which you should in fact have won."

CHRYSALE (*to Philaminte*)

You've lost your case!

PHILAMINTE

My! Don't be shaken so!
I'm not disheartened by this trivial blow.
Do teach your heart to take a nobler stance
And brave, like me, the buffetings of chance.

"This negligence of yours has cost you forty thousand crowns, for it is that amount, together with the legal expenses, which the court has condemned you to pay."

Condemned! What shocking language! That's a word
Reserved for criminals.

ARISTE

True; your lawyer erred,
And you're entirely right to be offended.
He should say that the court has *recommended*
That you comply with its decree, and pay
Forty thousand and costs without delay.

PHILAMINTE

What's in this other letter?

CHRYSALE (*reading*)

"Sir, my friendship with your brother leads me to take an interest in all that concerns you. I know that you have

629

put your money in the hands of Argante and Damon, and
I regret to inform you that they have both, on the same day,
gone into bankruptcy."

Lost! All my money! Every penny of it!

PHILAMINTE

What a shameful outburst, Sir. Come, rise above it!
The wise man doesn't mourn the loss of pelf;
His wealth lies not in things, but in himself.
Let's finish this affair, with no more fuss:
                    (*Pointing to Trissotin*)
His fortune will suffice for all of us.

TRISSOTIN

No, Madam, urge my cause no further. I see
That everyone's against this match and me,
And where I am not wanted, I shan't intrude.

PHILAMINTE

Well! That's a sudden change of attitude.
It follows close on our misfortunes, Sir.

TRISSOTIN

Weary of opposition, I prefer
To bow out gracefully, and to decline
A heart which will not freely yield to mine.

PHILAMINTE

I see now what you are, Sir. I perceive
What, till this moment, I would not believe.

[*Act Five* · *Scene Four*]

TRISSOTIN

See what you like; I do not care one whit
What you perceive, or what you think of it.
I've too much self-respect to tolerate
The rude rebuffs I've suffered here of late:
Men of my worth should not be treated so:
Thus slighted, I shall make my bow, and go.
                    (*He leaves.*)

PHILAMINTE

What a low-natured, mercenary beast!
He isn't philosophic in the least!

CLITANDRE

Madam, I'm no philosopher; but still
I beg to share your fortunes, good or ill,
And dare to offer, together with my hand,
The little wealth I happen to command.

PHILAMINTE

This generous gesture, Sir, I much admire,
And you deserve to have your heart's desire.
I grant your suit, Sir. Henriette and you—

HENRIETTE

No, Mother, I've changed my mind. Forgive me, do,
If once more I oppose your plans for me.

CLITANDRE

What! Will you cheat me of felicity,
Now that the rest have yielded, one and all?

HENRIETTE

I know, Clitandre, that your wealth is small.
I wished to marry you so long as I
Might realize my sweetest hopes thereby,
And at the same time mend your circumstances.
But after this great blow to our finances,
I love you far too deeply to impose
On you the burden of our present woes.

CLITANDRE

I welcome any fate which you will share,
And any fate, without you, I couldn't bear.

HENRIETTE

So speaks the reckless heart of love; but let's
Be prudent, Sir, and thus avoid regrets.
Nothing so strains the bond of man and wife
As lacking the necessities of life,
And in the end, such dull and mean vexations
Can lead to quarrels and recriminations.

ARISTE (*to Henriette*)

Is there any reason, save the one you've cited,
Why you and Clitandre shouldn't be united?

HENRIETTE

But for that cause, I never would say no;
I must refuse because I love him so.

ARISTE

Then let the bells ring out for him and you.
The bad news which I brought was all untrue.

632

[*Act Five* · *Scene Four*]

'Twas but a stratagem which I devised
In hopes to see your wishes realized
And undeceive my sister, showing her
The baseness of her pet philosopher.

CHRYSALE

Now, Heaven be praised for that!

PHILAMINTE

                    I'm overjoyed
To think how that false wretch will be annoyed,
And how the rich festivities of this
Glad marriage will torment his avarice.

CHRYSALE (*to Clitandre*)

Well, Son, our firmness has achieved success.

ARMANDE (*to Philaminte*)
Shall you sacrifice me to their happiness?

PHILAMINTE

Daughter, your sacrifice will not be hard.
Philosophy will help you to regard
Their wedded joys with equanimity.

BÉLISE

Let him be careful lest his love for me
Drive him, in desperation, to consent
To a rash marriage of which he will repent.

633

CHRYSALE (*to the Notary*)

Come, come, Sir, it is time your task was through;
Draw up the contract just as I told you to.